W9-BCC-133

CONGRESS: THE SAPLESS BRANCH

CONGRESS:

The Sapless Branch

JOSEPH S. CLARK

United States Senator from Pennsylvania

HARPER & ROW, PUBLISHERS

New York, Evanston, and London

 For information address Harper & Row, Publishers, Incorporated, 49 East 33rd Street, New York 16, N. Y.

First Edition

Library of Congress Catalog Number: 64-12669

D-O

To my wife

CONTENTS

INTRODUCTION

It is a special pleasure to write an introduction for an important book written by an old friend who is such a distinguished public servant as Senator Joseph Clark of Pennsylvania. The topic he has chosen to treat, the diagnoses he makes and the remedies he suggests are of interest to the whole free world. For I think it can be said that the Congress of the United States is the last really important legislative body. It is not merely a matter of the power of the government of the United States, or the power of the American people. That power would make the American legislature important in any event. But there is more to be said than merely to call attention to the power of the American government and consequently of its legislative branch.

It can be said, I think with justice, that this is an age of legislative decline. Even the House of Commons, "the Mother of Parliaments," is now almost completely under the control of the executive branch. France, "Mother of Revolutions," has chosen to give herself a government very heavily weighted on the executive side. Germany is emerging, if she is emerging, from a long period of extremely forceful executive leadership. The future of parliamentary government is uncertain in countries as diverse as Italy, India and Japan. But, negatively at any rate, the Congress of the United States possesses in fact the powers given to it in form by the Constitution. Congress can and does hold up the program of even the most forceful and popular president, Congress can and does thwart with impunity the wishes of the American electors. An American election cannot be a mandate to the temporary detainers of the national sovereignty as it is in Great Britain. It can only give a broad hint or a polite suggestion to the men who, in fact, keep in their custody the legislative power of the United States.

I have deliberately chosen the word "temporary" for an ironical reason, because the power of the Congress of the United States is not temporarily in the hands of certain groups of Senators and Representatives. It is permanently in their hands. By the working of the committee system and of the seniority rule in the committee system, effective power, at any rate effective negative power, is in the hands of a group of elder statesmen who may be very unrepresentative of the general trend of public opinion. Necessarily since power goes by seniority, it is much better to represent one of the safe districts of the United States or one of the safe states than to represent either a district or a state where public opinion is lively and changeable. This accounts in practice for the curious discrepancy between the formal and the real party structure. A party may have adopted a generally popular platform and may have a popular and generally respected leader in the President and yet the voter can have no confidence that the platform will be enacted or the leader effectually followed. This state of affairs has produced increasing frustration over the last twenty-five years, as Senator Clark makes plain. It is probable that one of the reasons for the comparatively low voting record of the American people, in such marked contrast to the high voting record of the people of Britain or France, is the sense of frustration which this system breeds in the average voter, who has often, in fact, no way of giving effective expression to his views.

There are many reasons why the American party cannot be as formally symmetrical as it is in Britain. There are reasons arising out of the size and diversity of the country, but there are also institutional reasons for the blurring of party lines in the last generation. But the obvious agreement between the leaders of both parties in both houses to prevent anything very drastic from being done, on the home front at any rate, has made party organization and party discipline far less meaningful than they should be. The first of the serious faults to which Senator Clark directs himself is the emasculation of the party platform and the destruction of any responsible party system. It is not a question of arguing for blind party discipline (Senator Clark himself has not always displayed regard for blind party discipline!). It is a case of arguing for a high degree of party responsibility, which it is almost impossible to expect or get under the present system.

The consequences of this state of affairs are very serious and they are, paradoxically, very serious for Congress itself. Because Congress seems for a great part of the time to be thwarting party leadership and public opinion with success, it is possible to regard Congress as an extremely potent body. It is an extremely potent body, but potent mainly for negative purposes. It is a commonplace of American history that effective leadership in a positive direction must come from the White House. But no one that I know of is arguing or has argued that Congress should become a "rubber stamp," to use one of the favorite phrases of Congressional "naysayers." Because of its success in thwarting the executive, Congress has tended to overlook that it is also thwarting itself. If, as is true, Congress is inadequately reported in the press or on TV, if the great Congressional figures are often unknown to the general public, and if known disliked, the fault is very largely that of Congress itself.

Until Congress reforms its own procedure and changes its state of mind, it will continue to suffer increasing public discredit or public indifference—and this would be a disastrous trend for the United States. For it should be noted that Congress, for all its power to hold up real politics, has not gotten or has lost whatever power it had of legislative initiative. It is intrinsically improbable that in an age so full of rapid and dangerous change as ours the United States can go on with the ideas and practices of a horse-and-buggy era. Yet a great part of the business of both houses is conducted, mechanically and spiritually, in the fashion of the horse-and-buggy era. This means that power, which abhors a vacuum, necessarily slips away on the one hand to the President and on the other to the courts. It is not accidental that all the most important innovations in domestic politics in the United States, whether dealing with school segregation or with manifestly unjust election systems in seats in state legislatures and in the national legislature, should have been the work not of Congress, but of the courts. Indeed, as I write, Congress has not yet got around effectually to adopting, much less enacting, adequate civil rights legislation to keep in touch with the new jurisprudence of the Supreme Court. It may be that the decision of the courts to force state legislatures into a more just system of apportionment of seats may transform the character both of the state legislatures and of Congress itself. There are signs of this, notably in the South, and with the disappearance of some of the more outrageous "rotten boroughs," North and South alike, the spirit as well as the personnel of American politics may well be changed. Like Senator Clark, I certainly hope so.

But this transformation of the political personnel and this redistribution of political power, while they will no doubt make the role of the Congressional leadership of the two so-called national parties more difficult, will not make it impossible. This leadership can be reformed or overthrown only by the action of Congress itself, and until that is done the American voters will be frustrated and will, for quite good reasons, tend to stay away from the polls. It cannot be a healthy state of affairs that the only political election in which the mass of the people takes a living interest is the election of a President, and if the voter begins to feel that the only important office for which he has to cast his vote is the Presidency, the decline in Congressional prestige and, in the not very long run, in its power will continue.

Senator Clark is quite well aware that his criticisms both of the existing methods of doing Congressional business and of electing Representatives and Senators will be highly unpopular on the Hill. The present system suits a good many elder statesmen perfectly. Any change in the mechanics or spirit of Congressional government would endanger power situations acquired often by industry as well as by longevity. For it must not be thought that Congressional leaders do not require, as a rule, some positive talents as well as those of staying alive and getting re-elected. There have been notorious instances of chairmen of important committees visibly unfit for their jobs and yet being re-elected to those jobs by their complaisant colleagues in Congress. But of course most committee chairmen have both ability and industry; otherwise the machine would grind to a halt, as in some areas of legislation it does. But industry and honesty and a reasonable degree of intelligence are not a substitute for political responsibility, and both houses are organized today not only to perpetuate this state of affairs, but in effect to make it harder for the common voter to know what is going on. Debating in the Senate and still more in the House attracts little public attention since it is suspected by millions of voters that the real business is done elsewhere—in the committee rooms. Thus one of the most important functions of any legislative body—that of being an educational forum—is lost.

But being an educational forum, a place where differing points of view and different interests are publicly represented, is not the only or possibly even the main function of a legislature. The most important function is to make laws. It is convenient and commonplace to say that the United States does not need any new laws; it is possible to hold that all is for the best in the best of possible political worlds. It is also possible to hold that the earth is flat. But neither the defenders of a hands-off policy in Congress nor the defenders of a flat earth are really helpful in this day and age. The Congress of the United States must take notice of the fact that the world is in a state of chaos and in a state of acute danger. The most reassuring platitudes of the Founding Fathers are not really very helpful except as soporifics, and there is no visible necessity for Congress to be aided to go to sleep more than it does naturally. As Senator Clark points out, it is inevitable that power should, as I have suggested above, shift. We used to be told in old-fashioned textbooks of physics that "Work is done when the point of application of a force moves." Application of the force necessarily comes from the President, but the movement in many instances necessarily comes from Congress. If it does not come, frustration, irritation and danger result. There is, I think, in both houses of Congress a sense of irritation and frustration which is sometimes reflected in foolish words and foolish actions. A Senator or a Representative may well feel that his genuine services are disregarded by his countrymen, that the white light of publicity plays only on the White House, and that the general public regards Congress as at best something to laugh about and sometimes something to swear about.

I am, in fact, perfectly prepared to believe that Congress is underestimated by the average voter, and certainly many Representatives and Senators I know work much harder, more efficiently and more honestly than most voters realize. But as long as Congressional business is done or not done under the elaborate and confusing rules described by Senator Clark, as long as power is so dissipated as to be invisible, public indifference or even public contempt is inevitable. It is not a question of whether there are Congressional equivalents today of Webster, Clay or Calhoun. It is a question of whether Congress today, organized as it is in terms of yesterday, can do its job and can be seen to do its job. It may be doing its job (although I doubt this), but it is certainly not seen to be doing it. Until Congress casts a cold eye on itself and takes seriously the bold proposals to reform itself which Senator Clark and others advocate, its national image and its effectiveness will not improve. It is not only a matter of improving the internal discipline of each house by avoiding scandals and of abating the high degree of toleration of what it would be polite to call its eccentricities; it is a matter of making the legislative department of the government of the the United States adequate for the age of the H-bomb. This involves a willingness to scrap some sanctified practices and conventions and to consider some very bold reforms indeed. Senator Clark both examines the present system and proposes reforms with no regard for the sacred cows of the Congress. His book will not endear him to the present ruling class on "the Hill," but it is not intended to. It is intended to stimulate the average responsible voter, and to awaken the average responsible member of Congress, to the needs of this age, and to the only means whereby the Congress of the United States can restore some of its pristine glory.

DENIS BROGAN

January 25, 1964

AUTHOR'S NOTE

This book was suggested to me in May of 1963 by Donald MacCampbell, whose encouragement overcame my reluctance to undertake so arduous a task in so short a time. Its title was plagiarized, with his consent, from a column in *Newsweek* written by Kenneth Crawford. It could not have been written without the effective research by Professors Richard F. Schier and Sidney Wise of Franklin and Marshall College and Assistant Professor Alan Rosenthal of Hunter College. It would never have been finished had not the thrice-revised text been taken out of my hands and cleared with the publisher during the hectic closing days of the first session of the Eighty-eighth Congress by my administrative assistant, Bernard Norwitch. The manuscript would not have reached the publisher by the agreed deadline of January 1, 1964, had not Mrs. Marie Littman and her devoted slaves in my Washington office burned many hours of midnight oil (not at taxpayers' expense) deciphering my longhand scribblings and turning out mimeographed copy after revised mimeographed copy of constantly rewritten text.

I am particularly grateful to Mrs. Margaret Butterfield of Harper & Row for her suggestions. Congressman Henry Reuss of Wisconsin was kind enough to read the manuscript and give me the benefit of his deep understanding of the workings of the House of Representatives. And I raise my hat to the publisher, Cass Canfield, for his understanding handling of his temperamental author, the senior United States Senator from Pennsylvania.

CONGRESS:
THE SAPLESS BRANCH

I

THE MAKING OF A MAVERICK

I was elected to the United States Senate as a Democrat from Pennsylvania in November, 1956, by a plurality of 17,900 votes over Senator James H. Duff, Republican. In the same election Dwight D. Eisenhower was re-elected President of the United States. He carried Pennsylvania by a majority of 615,000 votes. The total vote that year in our Commonwealth was in excess of 4,500,000. My margin of victory represented less than one percent of the total vote cast.

In December, 1956, Senator Hubert Humphrey of Minnesota, an old friend, who was then serving as a delegate to the General Assembly of the United Nations, had lunch with me at the Harvard Club of New York.

"Tell me how to behave when I get to the Senate," I asked him around half-past twelve.

He did—for an hour and a half. I left the luncheon I hope a wiser man, as well briefed as a neophyte seeking admission to a new order can be.

In essence he said, "Keep your mouth shut and your eyes open. It's a friendly, courteous place. You will have no trouble getting along. Paul Douglas and I will help you. Lyndon Johnson runs the Senate and will treat you well.

"You will clash on the filibuster rule with Dick Russell and the Southerners as soon as you take the oath of office. Don't let your ideology embitter your personal relationships. It won't if you behave with maturity.

"Try to get on committees where your past experience gives you some competence.

"And above all keep your mouth shut for a while."

About the same time, when it was learned that the Democrats had retained a slim majority in the Senate, six Democratic Senators, Douglas, Humphrey, James Murray of Montana, Patrick McNamara of Michigan, Richard Neuberger of Oregon and Wayne Morse of Oregon, had written to all Democratic Senators urging them to support a program in the Eighty-fifth Congress which would carry out the promises of the 1956 national platform of the Democratic party. Among the subjects stressed were majority rule in the Senate, civil rights, immigration, aid for depressed areas, housing and aid for education. The hope was to carry into the Senate the political philosophy of the Democratic Advisory Committee, which had kept the ideology of the national party before the public during President Eisenhower's first term. Since the House would also be Democratic, it was hoped that this statement would provide a standard around which those who believed in the principles of the party could rally.

I found myself in complete agreement with this statement and attended a meeting in the office of Senator Clinton Anderson of New Mexico shortly after coming to Washington at which Adlai Stevenson met with a group of liberal Democratic Senators in an effort to obtain adequate Senatorial representation on the Democratic Advisory Committee. Unfortunately the Congressional* leadership in both houses was unwilling to cooperate and the effort was stillborn. This was the first evidence I had noted of a

* Throughout this book "Congressional" and "Congressman" are used to include both Senators and Representatives.

Congressional group within our party which was not in sympathy with the philosophy so articulately advanced by our Presidential nominee in both 1952 and 1956. I was soon to see the rift grow wider.

On January 3, 1957, the Democratic Senate Conference met in the Old Senate Office Building. The Senate then consisted of forty-seven Republicans and forty-nine Democrats. One of the forty-nine was Frank Lausche, former Governor of Ohio, just elected to the Senate as a conservative Democrat. He did not show up at our conference. Nobody knew where he was or what he was up to. There were rumors he was going to vote with the Republicans to organize the Senate.

We elected Senator Lyndon Johnson of Texas our Democratic leader. In his speech of thanks he said he did not know whether he was going to be Majority or Minority Leader. For if Lausche voted with the Republicans, the resulting tie of 48-48 would be broken by Vice President Richard Nixon, and William F. Knowland of California would be Majority Leader.

There was no discussion of party policy or program at the conference. We chose unanimously and without discussion Mike Mansfield of Montana as Majority Whip; Thomas Hennings of Missouri, Secretary; and Carl Hayden of Arizona, President Pro Tempore.

I thought the absence of discussion on a party program odd. But since the conference met only one hour before the Senate convened, I assumed there would be meetings later to discuss legislation and party strategy.

I was wrong. The conference never met again in 1957. At noon we went to the floor. A motion was made to elect Lyndon B. Johnson Majority Leader. Senator Knowland moved to substitute himself. The "ayes and nays" were ordered by a show of hands; an aye vote was for Knowland and a nay vote for Johnson. There was no debate. The clerk began to call the roll in alphabetical order.

Frank Lausche was in the seat temporarily assigned to him.

When his name was called there was a dramatic pause. Finally he voted "no." There was a sudden buzz of conversation on the floor and in the galleries. The doubt which had persisted all morning and the tension which went with it were dissolved. The Democrats had organized the Senate by the skin of their teeth.

The next day, January 4, Senator Clinton Anderson of New Mexico moved to proceed immediately to consider the adoption of Senate rules. If successful, the next move would be to change Rule XXII governing cloture of debate. The Majority Leader announced he would move to table the Anderson motion. I had attended several meetings called by Senator Douglas to rally support for Anderson's move. A unanimous consent agreement was entered into providing for a vote at six P.M. The debate was spirited on the part of the proponents, led by Senators Anderson, Douglas and Humphrey. Heeding Humphrey's advice, I kept quiet. The motion to table carried 55 to 38. Rules reform was dead for the session.

It was a good deal later that I learned the ways of the Southern Senators and their conservative Republican colleagues. They knew from a "nose count," conducted for them by Bobby Baker, majority secretary, and Mark Trice, his Republican opposite number, that they could table the Anderson motion. It was therefore unnecessary for them to filibuster as they did in 1959, 1961 and 1963. At the time I was surprised to discover how many Senators I had thought were proponents of civil rights nonetheless voted to table Senator Anderson's motion to consider new rules. It was some little time before I learned how the Establishment (i.e., those who really run the Senate) operated.

On January 8 I got my committee assignments to the Banking and Currency, Post Office and Civil Service and District of Columbia Committees. I was pleased because of my long-standing interest in housing (handled somewhat surprisingly by Banking and Currency), Civil Service reform and municipal government. For the next two years, I was to be a busy freshman Senator sticking to my knitting and not worrying my head about matters of high political strategy.

On January 15, 1957, the Majority Leader gave a lunch for the newly elected freshman Democratic Senators. Only six of us had successfully breasted the Eisenhower tidal wave of the preceding November—Frank Church of Idaho, John Carroll of Colorado, Frank Lausche of Ohio, Herman Talmadge of Georgia, Strom Thurmond of South Carolina, who had served briefly in the Senate before, and I. As we sat down to our steaks at the long table in the office of Felton M. (Skeeter) Johnston, Secretary of the Senate, an urbane and popular Mississippian, we found at our places copies of *Citadel: The Story of the U.S. Senate*,[1*] autographed "with all good wishes" not only by its author William S. White, Pulitzer Prize winning biographer of Robert A. Taft, but by the Majority Leader as well.

During the course of the lunch, which was attended by the other recently re-elected leaders, Senator Johnson encouraged us to consider Mr. White's book as a sort of McGuffey's *Reader* from which we could learn much about the "greatest deliberative body in the world" and how to mold ourselves into its way of life.

In his book Mr. White eulogized the post World War II Senate much as Allen Drury did later in *Advise and Consent*.[2] He wrote with affection of its "tone and timelessness," the concept of the Senate as a "club," its ability to divorce itself almost completely from the outside world, to a part of which, nonetheless, a third of its members must return every six years to seek re-election. With tender sympathy he sketched an atmosphere redolent of mint juleps and Confederate gentlemen.

I was impressed. It was not until some time later that I came to believe that Donald R. Matthews was closer to the truth when he referred to Mr. White's infatuation with the Senate of the mid-fifties and earlier as "an almost embarrassing love affair." Matthews, in *U.S. Senators and Their World*,[3] spoke of the Senate

* Superior numbers refer to a section of notes beginning on page 253.

as "a legislative chamber of imposing power which sometimes finds it impossible to act; an institution heavy with tradition whose members occasionally act like schoolboys on a spree." I was to learn the validity of this comment as time went on.

As the sessions of the Eighty-fifth Congress rolled by it became obvious to me that there was no real Democratic Senatorial legislative program; and none in the House either. It was not fashionable to refer to the national party platform. President Eisenhower had no particular Republican program he wished enacted. Within both parties there were conservative and liberal elements; but they were not clearly defined and neither had a constructive legislative program to offer the Congress. And even if there had been some agreed-upon party program, the close division made carrying it out practically impossible.

Life in the Senate during the Eighty-fifth Congress was, nevertheless, a delightful personal experience. Colleagues were uniformly kind and some became warm friends. John Carroll, Frank Church and I sat side by side in the back row on the Democratic side, voting almost always together, and flanked on our right by Albert Gore, a wise counselor who usually saw issues the way we did despite his Southern constituency. A few seats to Gore's right was Senator John Fitzgerald Kennedy of Massachusetts, still in his first term.

Each of us had a Victorian desk the flat top of which opened to reveal inside a copy of *Senate Procedure*, compiled by the Parliamentarians, Charles Watkins and Floyd Riddick; the *Rules and Manual, United States Senate*, which also included Jefferson's Manual, the Declaration of Independence, the Constitution of the United States and a number of other documents of interest; and the *Congressional Directory for the First Session of the 85th Congress* with our names in gold letters on the cover. This volume gave us, in addition to a great deal of other information, the brief authorized biographies, state by state, of all Senators and Representatives. Some were full of offices held, organizations joined and honorary degrees received. Significant, perhaps, was the shortest of the lot, that of the senior Senator from Georgia: "Richard Brevard Russell, Democrat, of Winder, Georgia." He could, with all modesty, have written a great deal more.

The center aisle separated the two parties. The desks were moved around the chamber from time to time as the number of Republicans and Democrats changed with each election. (By the end of 1963 four new desks had been added for the Senators from Hawaii and Alaska, three on the Democratic, one on the Republican, side of the aisle. And fifteen Republican desks had been moved over to the Democratic side, leaving more elbow-room for the minority party and putting the majority members cheek by jowl.)

A custom had developed of writing one's name in the bottom of the lower drawer. My first desk had served a good many Senators before it caught up with me, crossing the center aisle several times during its life. Here were my predecessors: Martin of Pennsylvania, Gore of Oklahoma, Sheppard of Texas, King of Utah, O'Mahoney of Wyoming, Andrews of Florida, Bone of Washington, Downey of California, Murdock of Utah, Kem of Missouri, Withers of Kentucky, Nixon of California, Case of New Jersey, Goldwater of Arizona and Allott of Colorado.

The days were busy but not nerve-racking for a freshman Senator. The nights, if one had the inclination—and my wife and I did—were full of a fascinating social life. We practically never went to cocktail parties, the bane of civilized conversation. I held to a minimum the political and lobbying sessions I attended. But we dined out a lot and entertained small groups at home frequently. Life was gay and hopes ran high in '57 and '58.

I was happier than I had ever been since I first entered public life.

The legislative record of the Eighty-fifth Congress was pretty meager. The usual appropriations bills, including foreign aid, were passed. The National Defense Education Act was enacted. A Space Agency and the atoms for peace programs were initiated. Alaska was admitted to statehood. Social Security and unemployment compensation were tinkered with in minor ways. So was the military organization at the Pentagon. And that was about all.

To be sure, the first civil rights bill in eighty-two years was enacted. But it was a pallid little measure which has been ineffective in assisting the Negro to secure that due process and equal protection of the laws to which he is entitled under the Fourteenth and Fifteenth Amendments to the Constitution. And the method of its passage was unworthy of a great legislative body.

The bill as finally enacted was a modified version of a proposal by President Eisenhower. The House passed the Eisenhower bill virtually intact on June 18, 1957. The Senate, during the next two months, proceeded to hack it to pieces. In the end, the measure merely created a Civil Rights Commission, expanded the Civil Rights Division in the Attorney General's office and empowered the Attorney General to seek an injunction to protect an individual's right to vote. Much of the debate and some of the sections of the bill dealt with civil and criminal contempt and the right to a jury trial of those cited for contempt. The tender solicitude for those, presumably white, charged by a judge with violating an order protecting the constitutional rights of those, presumably black, who desired to exercise their right to vote seemed sardonic to many of us.

Technically there was no filibuster—only "prolonged discussion" at the end of the session when everybody wanted to go home. Actually we legislated under the threat of a filibuster which could defeat the bill.

It took from June 20 to July 16 even to agree to a motion to consider the House bill. The truncated bill finally passed the Senate August 7. Twenty more days were consumed in conference.

The Senate conferees knew that if they yielded in any important particular to the House the conference report would be filibustered indefinitely when it returned to the Senate. In the end the House conferees gave in and took the Senate bill with a face-saving minor amendment on jury trials in contempt cases. On August 29 the conference report was approved by the Senate. The next day we adjourned and went home.

As the 1958 election drew near liberal Democrats held high hopes for substantial Congressional gains which would make it possible to send to the White House, for signature or veto, bills embodying the Democratic platform pledges made at the 1956 convention.

In anticipation of electoral success, Douglas, Humphrey, Pat McNamara, John Carroll and I met in Paul Douglas' office on July 24, 1958, on the assumption that we would add a substantial number of liberal Democratic Senators in November. Our problem was how this augmented band of liberals could make its weight proportionately felt in party action in the Senate. It seemed clear the way to do it was to get control of the key legislative committees away from the Southern bloc. But this would require a shake-up in the composition of the Policy and Steering Committees of the party, of which more hereafter. For the present it is enough to say that these important committees were in the control of a group of conservative Southern Senators who had no interest in the platform of the national Democratic party.

We determined to make an effort after the election to organize the liberals to press for a substantially larger voice in determining and carrying out party legislative policy.

The election results of November, 1958, exceeded our fondest hopes. Not only were fifteen new Democratic Senators, most of them liberal, elected, but the thin ranks of the liberal Republicans were augmented while a number of right-wing Republican conservatives retired voluntarily or were defeated by Democrats.

The newly elected Democratic Senators joined the back row and soon began to mutter their discontent with the established order. The augmented liberal group had great hopes that the leadership would see things our way. On November 18 I wrote the Majority Leader in Texas congratulating him on his very substantial contribution to the Democratic Senatorial victory and passing on to him some thoughts and suggestions regarding organization of the Eighty-sixth Congress, which would meet in January, 1959.

I stressed the need for our party to make an appeal to the big urban and industrial states in order to capture the White House in 1960 and expressed my fear that liberal Republicans such as Senators Clifford Case, Jacob Javits and Thomas Kuchel might take these states away from us. I urged strengthening the position of Northern and Midwestern Senators in the institutional structure of the Democratic party in the Senate by giving proportional representation on the Steering and Policy Committees to these Senators through enlarging both committees.

Copies of my letter went to several of the liberal Senators and to the Majority Whip, Senator Mansfield of Montana. I did not release the letter to the press, but, most unfortunately as matters turned out, a copy leaked. Senator Johnson was put on the spot and the matter was played up as though I, and perhaps other liberal Senators, were seeking to undermine his leadership. In fact, we were not.

I received no direct reply from the Majority Leader, but on December 9 Mike Mansfield, who was then serving as a delegate to the General Assembly of the United Nations in New York, wrote me. It was a very friendly letter, but it expressed opposition to any changes in the composition of either the Steering or Policy Committees on the ground that there was no need to make the changes I recommended.

The Democratic Conference met on Wednesday, January 7, 1959, to re-elect our officers and to hear an interesting talk by Hubert Humphrey about his eight-hour marathon visit with Khrushchev a few weeks earlier. It did not meet again during that year. No changes were made in the composition of the Policy or Steering Committees, nor was the question raised at the conference. A little later Senator Proxmire of Wisconsin, who had come to the Senate in the summer of 1957, made a series of speeches on the floor suggesting the need for more Democratic conferences to keep all Senators advised of the plans of the leadership and to develop a stronger sense of participation and unity among the Democrats. But nothing happened that year. None of us felt in a position as yet to make a fight. We all hoped that with our very much larger majority we would make a strong legislative record in support of the national Democratic party platform as laid down at the convention in 1956.

But the record of the first session of the Eighty-sixth Congress was a sorry one. Another effort to change the cloture rule, led by Senators Anderson, Douglas and Humphrey and opposed by both the Democratic and Republican leadership, was defeated. The temporary unemployment compensation bill was mangled in the Finance Committee, only partially restored on the floor, and the Senate improvements were murdered in conference. The conferees for the Senate, chosen with one exception by seniority, jettisoned in twenty minutes the Senate amendment sponsored by Eugene McCarthy of Minnesota which would have substantially improved the House bill. As a result hundreds of thousands of the unemployed in industrial states, thrown out of work by the second Eisenhower recession, lost their unemployment compensation and went on the relief rolls.

The Landrum-Griffin Act, going a good deal further in its antilabor provisions than the Taft-Hartley Act, was passed. No significant liberal legislation was passed by either the Senate or the House.

I was getting more restless and frustrated week by week, feeling, with a good many others, that we were given no real chance to be heard on questions of party policy. We felt that the leadership was "sitting on the lid" of this discontent, supporting the chairmen of the standing committees, who were selected by seniority and many of whom were not in sympathy with the principles and platform of the modern Democratic party.

Shortly before the annual Democratic Conference met on January 7, 1960, Senators Gore, Humphrey, McNamara, Douglas,

Proxmire and I determined to speak out. I offered a resolution that the conference should meet at least every two weeks on the request of fifteen Senators, to attempt to find common ground on the recommendations of the State of the Union message, the interest ceiling on government bonds, the economic message, wage-hour and school construction legislation. There was a long debate, some Senators supporting the suggestion, the more senior members generally speaking in opposition.

The Majority Leader ended the matter by announcing he would call a conference any time at the request of any Senator. The next day our group requested in writing a further conference to discuss the school construction bill and, if time permitted, the methods of selecting the Policy Committee.

The latter subject was raised by Albert Gore at a conference called by the Majority Leader on January 12, but no action was taken on his motion although there was spirited discussion. The former matter was fully discussed at a conference on January 20.

Another conference was held on January 15 at the request of Senator Ed Muskie and others at which the Majority Leader read his "State of the Union" message, and there was a general and, I thought, useful discussion of party policy. On January 18 the conference met to discuss tax legislation.

But that was the end. The conference did not meet again in 1960, largely because those of us who wanted regular meetings became convinced that without leadership support, which was not forthcoming, we could not turn out enough members to make the conferences worthwhile. Attendance dwindled from a full complement of nearly sixty Senators on January 7 to twenty-six on the 15th, and twenty-four on the 18th. The conference on the 20th brought out thirty-eight, but that was because the education bill was then close to floor action. Had future conferences been called by the leadership prior to action on other important legislation, I believe they would have been more fully attended and would have been useful.

The principal achievement of the second session of the Eighty-sixth Congress was passage of the Civil Rights Act of 1960. Again the final legislation was rather innocuous; again the House passed a bill not essentially different from that recommended by President Eisenhower; again the Senate chewed it up. But this time there was a full-blown filibuster before the Southerners would agree to let the final watered-down bill come to a vote. Debate in the Senate occupied thirty-seven days, during which there were forty-five roll call votes on motions, amendments and final passage.

A filibuster has to be seen to be believed. During its progress the floor is practically empty. One of the eighteen Solid South Senators holds the floor. He will speak for approximately two hours, almost always "to the point," in Jefferson's phrase. As one Senator comes to the end of his speech a companion in arms arrives on the scene. The retiring Senator suggests the absence of a quorum. It is always a "live quorum," requiring fifty-one Senators to come to the floor to answer to their names. This often takes as long as an hour. When a quorum is present, the next Southerner takes the floor and a new act of the farce begins.

We went "around the clock" in 1960 from February 29 through March 8. That meant the Senate stayed in continuous session for nine days. Those of us who wanted to break the filibuster, somewhat more than a majority but never as many as the two-thirds required for cloture, slept on cots or sofas in our offices or in the rest rooms in the Senate baths. The quorum call bell would ring. We would awaken, rub our eyes, pull on our pants and head for the floor. Having answered our names, we would go back to restless sleep—if we could—for another two hours.

Meanwhile, every two hours a well-rested Southerner would turn up on the floor, fresh from a good night's sleep. His schedule had been well planned. He did not have to answer the quorum calls. He would have been pleased had a quorum not shown up. Since there were eighteen participants in the filibuster, it could have gone on indefinitely, making the Senate even more the laughingstock of the country and, indeed, of the civilized world.

In the end, the leadership on both sides of the aisle capitulated to the Southern generalissimo, Richard B. Russell of Georgia. He did not demand unconditional surrender. Indeed, he was a gracious victor. A few crumbs were thrown to the frustrated civil rights advocates. The bill as passed (1) provided penalties for interfering with federal court orders; (2) provided penalties for interstate activities in connection with bombing: (3) implemented the right given the Attorney General under the '57 Act to intervene in litigation to protect and secure voting rights; and (4) continued the life of the Civil Rights Commission and gave it the right to administer oaths.

After the final vote, I spoke briefly, directing my remarks at Senator Russell.

"Dick, here is my sword. I hope you will give it back to me so that I can beat it into a plowshare for the spring planting.

"Surely in this battle on the Senate floor the roles of Grant and Lee at Appomattox have been reversed.

"The eighteen implacable defenders of the way of life of the Old South are entitled to congratulations from those of us they have so disastrously defeated. To be sure, at critical moments they had the assistance of the President of the United States, the Attorney General, the Minority Leader and the Majority Leader. But they nevertheless carried the brunt of the battle.

"I regret that, in my judgment, the people of the United States of America, indeed, the people of the whole free world, are the losers in this fight.

"I, for one, believe we are approaching the end of an era; that the national mood will change; that new and vigorous leadership will arise and that the day will come again, and come soon, when the Senate and the Congress and another President will reverse the action they took on civil rights this long hard winter, and will rally again to its earlier ideals. . . ."

I then proceeded, with what in retrospect seems undue dramatic emphasis, to read "The Battle Hymn of the Republic."

By the summer of 1960 I had concluded that basic changes in

the organization of the Senate itself were required. On July 1, therefore, I introduced a series of resolutions to change the Senate rules. Here is the argument I made:

"The great difficulty which the Congress is having in passing needed legislation before adjournment calls attention once again to the archaic and undemocratic rules and procedures under which we on Capitol Hill attempt to legislate.

"The harsh fact is that the present rules and methods of operation of the Senate and of the House are stacked against the people of the United States. They penalize those who seek action in the national interest in a time of world crisis. They reward those who cling to an outmoded status quo which threatens our very survival.

"We in Congress have been critical of the Eisenhower administration for not running a tight ship. Our willingness to extract the mote from the President's eye has, however, not been accompanied by any desire to remove the beam from our own.

"Actually, we have organized ourselves so sloppily that we may well be unable to meet the critical challenge to pass effective legislation in the national interest which will confront us next January. It is bad enough to have dilly-dallied through the eight years of the Eisenhower administration. We will be playing Russian roulette with our national survival if we do not set our house in order before the next President presents his State of the Union message.

"We must leave to the other body the task of solving its own procedural problems in a way which will no longer permit a small group of ultraconservatives to block the will of a large majority of the House. We will have enough trouble modernizing our own Senate rules. In my judgment, there is no other legislative body in the free world as incapable of action, when action is desired by a large majority but strongly resisted by a minority, as the Senate of the United States."

We recessed in July for the two national conventions, returning in August for a futile effort to enact some of the measures endorsed in the Democratic platform of 1960, including civil rights legislation. I returned to the subject of Congressional reform on August 31, calling not only for rules reform but for a reorganization of the Democratic Senatorial majority in anticipation of the election of President Kennedy in November.

Nothing happened. In fact, I did not expect it to. I was given a polite hearing before a subcommittee on Standing Rules of the Senate chaired by Senator Hayden. With all deliberate speed the subcommittee rejected all of my proposed rules changes save one.

With the elevation of Senator Johnson to the Vice Presidency, Mike Mansfield became Majority Leader and Hubert Humphrey Whip. The story of the minor victories and major defeats of those of us seeking comprehensive Congressional reform in the years from 1961 to 1964 is in large part the story of this book. We have started down the road, but there is still a long, long way to go before the Congress can be so organized that it can adequately perform its constitutional responsibilities.

When that day comes, and come it will, this maverick will consent to be branded.

II

A LOOK AT THE LEGISLATIVE BRANCH

There is nothing wrong today with the Declaration of Independence. These truths are self-evident. All men are created equal. They are all entitled to life, liberty and the pursuit of happiness. And to secure these rights governments are instituted among men, deriving their just powers from the consent of the governed. What is wrong is the way the Declaration is soft-pedaled by those who wish to limit its application by a strict and literal interpretation of the Constitution of the United States.

And those who wish to do so, who venerate what they nowadays call constitutional government, are in control of Congress. The trouble with Congress today is that it exercises negative and unjust powers to which the governed, the people of the United States, have never consented. And it exercises this negative power at a time when it should be doing just the opposite: acting positively to solve the complex and difficult problems of our time. The heart of the trouble is that the power is exercised by minority, not majority, rule.

The role of government in securing our rights has continually increased since Jefferson wrote the Declaration in his lodgings in Philadelphia in 1776. But this expansion of government—particularly in the twentieth century—has been the inevitable result of revolutionary economic, social and political forces which so threaten life, liberty and the pursuit of happiness that the government of the United States has had to act in areas and concern itself with problems never thought of by Jefferson.

It can be argued, of course, that this increasing role of government is undesirable. But I would defend the proposition that this expansion is good, not bad. Surely we have reached the point where we can say, for our time at least, that in one aspect of his thinking Jefferson was wrong: that government is *not* best which governs least, as he demonstrated himself when he became a forceful and energetic President. The philosophy of the eighteenth-century Americans who hated the tyranny of George III is the same as that of twentieth-century America's antitotalitarian liberals. In fact, the tyrannies of the left and right which we Americans face in our time are far more challenging and deadly. But we are hampered in our fight against the totalitarian evils of the twentieth century by our obsessive concern with the specific and different problems of the eighteenth century. We are reacting too much to the past and not enough to the present. In today's world a national government must be capable of prompt action, taken under strong popular leadership. Otherwise, democracy cannot survive.

The fallacy in Jefferson's argument is the assumption that the expansion of government leads to the curtailment of individual freedoms. This is just not true. Government may infringe on liberty or nurture it. Which it will do is not just a question of size or strength, but also of intention, tradition and the response of elected representatives to the desires and needs of the governed. Despite the moans of those who thought Lincoln a tyrant, Franklin Roosevelt a dictator and the Kennedys a dynasty, the history of personal freedom in this country is one of which we can be proud.

There are, to be sure, blots on our escutcheon from the days of the Alien and Sedition Acts to the reign of Joe McCarthy. But on the whole, the force of government has been on the side of the

Bill of Rights and of a free individualistic society. Where the civil liberties of our people have not been adequately protected, as in the case of Negro Americans, the failure is one of government inaction, not government action.

The question, then, is not concerned with the power of the government itself, but whether that power is invoked and used to promote justice and national well-being or is exercised by an irresponsible oligarchy without the consent of a majority of the governed.

The influence in our economy of the private power of the officers of the corporation and the labor union—responsible to their own stockholders and their own members—requires the countervailing public power of a forceful, democratic government accountable to the electorate and responsible for social justice. It is in this sense that strong government, representing the public interest at home and abroad, is required to protect both freedom and democracy. It is accordingly as salutary as it is inevitable.

A strong government is as necessary in foreign as it is in domestic affairs. The totalitarian state is able to act at a moment's notice, without any of the delays inherent in the democratic process. If we are to compete on even terms, we too must be able to act promptly where action is required, whether that action is peaceful or militant, to trade or to land troops. If further cooperative international action to prevent political, social and economic chaos is our goal, and is to be successful, this is especially important. Sensible, intelligent men from all countries are gradually learning to work together for international advancement. Creative control over world problems is an actual possibility. The basic lawlessness of past international doctrines, including, alas, the recent past, is increasingly discredited. World opinion now requires government to hold to the minimum standards of decency long imposed by law in civilized societies on the individual. It would be sad, indeed, if our democratic governmental institutions could not meet the challenge of these responsibilities in the new world of the nuclear age.

The problem thus becomes whether our federal structure can meet these new challenges on both the domestic and international fronts.

We have inherited a governmental system which divides, separates, and fragments our capacity to solve problems. On the national level, the members of our two-house legislature represent different territorial units and are elected for different terms. The Congress is filled with the plea that "What's best for Podunk is best for America," while the Executive looks at his constituency and replies that "What's best for the nation helps Podunk."

Within each of the states are governments which are themselves of separated powers, while on the local level the cities, counties, school districts, townships, boroughs and villages and the hundreds of special districts and authorities each speak for particular interests. The whole, then, is frequently quite different from the sum of its parts—at least in government.

Local, state and national governments, moreover, have interlacing responsibilities in specific areas: in housing and urban renewal, in the use of water, in transportation, labor-management relations, education, law enforcement, health and hygiene, land-planning and use, and employment.

Under these circumstances, it is extraordinary how much we accomplish and perhaps amazing that we accomplish anything at all. Our forms of government are heavily weighted against any kind of action, and especially any that might alter significantly the status quo. It takes too many units of government to consent before anything can get done.

Of course, inaction is what the Founding Fathers intended—inaction until such time as an overwhelming consensus, at all governmental levels and among all factions, had been reached that action of some sort was necessary—usually a compromise. They were right in their day. But they would be wrong in ours.

It is tempting to suggest that our Founding Fathers embraced the doctrine of separated powers because a distinguished French philosopher misunderstood English government—Montesquieu's

Spirit of the Laws was an obsolete analysis of the British system by the time it was published.* But it is more likely that the Fathers embraced Montesquieu because he offered a sophisticated rationale for conclusions already held. He outlined a system which would "bring about a state of repose or inaction." The Fathers agreed —on both counts.

The idea of a legislature selected from small election districts, but thought to be representative of a whole nation, comes to us from England. But George III's ascendancy over the Parliament, temporary and unfortunate though it was, resulted in a form of government in the United States quite different from that of the mother country. The division of power both horizontally and vertically, thought the framers of the Constitution, would check interest with interest, ambition with ambition, and class with class; it would, in Edmund Randolph's candid phrase, "restrain, if possible, the fury of Democracy."

None of this is, after all, very surprising when one considers the time, the place and the condition of the world in the eighteenth century. Alexis de Tocqueville was warning the crowned heads of Europe of the fury of this new thing democracy fifty years later, and John Stuart Mill and Matthew Arnold were still worrying about the mob in the halcyon days of Victoria Regina. We might even recall how late in the day it was when Senators were elected by the people and women were allowed to vote in the United States of America. And there is good reason to assert we do not have true universal suffrage in this country yet.

The structure of our federal government and that magnificent document incorporating it, the Constitution of the United States,

* Montesquieu in 1748 wrote that "When the legislative and executive powers are united in the same person or in the same body of magistrates, there can be no liberty." But six years earlier and thirty-five years before our Constitutional Convention Sir Robert Walpole, in 1742, had established the supremacy of the legislature over the Crown by forcing the King to choose a Prime Minister acceptable to the House of Commons. For some time thereafter, with a brief interlude under George III, Parliament—the legislature—ruled supreme. Now, today, a new executive, the Prime Minister and his Cabinet, has usurped most of the traditional power of Parliament.

are sufficiently familiar to need no recitation here. The fifty-five men who met in Philadelphia and created the world's longest and most successful democratic experiment under a written Constitution devised a scheme of government compounded of rebellion, tradition, genius, compromise, fear, hope and humanity. It was a design based on the premise that for every political action there is an equal and opposite political reaction (à la Newton), and on the assumption that government must somehow be responsible to the people, but not to too many people, not too quickly and not too directly.

The state of both the Union and the world today cannot fail to heighten our concern for the present adequacy of our ancient form of government. Yet, though we are stuck with the doctrine of the separation of powers under our Constitution, our many different governments actually manage in the modern world better than we have any right to expect.

Municipal government has revived since the war under the leadership of dynamic mayors. State government is the weakest link in the chain, but our governors, many of them struggling under obsolete state constitutions, are for the most part increasingly aware of the need for their states to play a more effective part in the growth of their regional economies. Respect for the office of President of the United States, whatever one's politics, has been justifiably high among serious students of government in the years since the death of Warren G. Harding. The courts, state and federal, have usually played a wise and statesmanlike role in adjusting ancient jurisprudence to modern needs while protecting essential civil liberties.

It is the third branch of government, the legislative, where things have gone awry. Whether we look at city councils, the state legislatures or the Congress of the United States, we react to what we see with scarcely concealed contempt. This is the area where democratic government is breaking down. This is where the vested-interest lobbies tend to run riot, where conflict of interest is concealed from the public, where demagoguery, sophisticated or primitive, knows few bounds, where political lag keeps needed action often a generation behind the times, where the nineteenth century sometimes reigns supreme in committees, where ignorance can be at a premium and wisdom at a discount, where the evil influence of arrogant and corrupt political machines, at the local and state level, ignores most successfully the general welfare, where the lust for patronage and favors for the faithful do the greatest damage to the public interest.

As a former chief executive of a large American city, as a member of the United States Senate, as a public servant who, in both capacities, has been obliged to know a good deal about the workings of state government, I have no hesitation in stating my deep conviction that the legislatures of America, local, state and national, are presently the greatest menace in our country to the successful operation of the democratic process.

This book is concerned with only one legislative body, the Congress of the United States. It has had a varied history since its first session met in Philadelphia in 1789. But there can be little doubt that, at least since the end of the first Wilson administration in 1916, it has declined both in terms of its power of positive action and in public esteem.

Congress has lost much of its capacity for prompt effective action and hence its ability to join the executive and the judiciary in meeting the challenges of the modern world. Its capacity for obstruction has, however, increased. In frighteningly Freudian fashion, Congress compensates for its inability to act creatively by exercising its negative power to the hilt.

It is rare for Congress to initiate an important piece of legislation which survives a Presidential veto. Usually, the President tries with varying degrees of success—often not much—to persuade a balky and recalcitrant Congress to pass measures he and his party committed themselves to during the preceding Presidential campaign. One can count on the fingers of one hand measures of importance initiated and passed to enactment by

Congress in the last fifty years without Presidential prodding. It delves into military contracts like the TFX, labor racketeering, even—when forced to—internal scandal. It can start widely publicized inquiries into the affairs of Billy Sol Estes or Jimmy Hoffa or Bobby Baker. But it often reflects a distinct lack of interest in the program of either major political party or of the President of the United States.

This is no new problem. Since the foundation of the Republic, Congress has rarely initiated anything, rarely faced up to current problems, even more rarely resolved them. Customarily, it has reacted, frequently adversely, to executive initiative. On many an occasion its procedures have made it impossible to bring the President's recommendations to a vote. Consider throughout American history the important activities and legislation for which Congress must take primary responsibility, where there was no active participation of the executive in the initial recommendation:

The Alien and Sedition Laws in John Adams' administration
The War of 1812 in Madison's term.
The effort to renew the Charter of the Bank of the United States in Jackson's day
The Missouri Compromise of 1819 and the Compromise of 1850
Reconstruction legislation after the Civil War; the impeachment of Andrew Johnson
The War against Spain in 1898
Pension laws after the Civil War. The various bonus bills after World Wars I and II
The Neutrality Acts of the late 1930s
The Buy American Act
The McCarran-Walter Immigration Act
The Taft-Hartley Act
The Landrum-Griffin Act

Some of this legislation was passed in response to strong and all too frequently whipped-up public demand. Some of it may have been desirable. But, on the whole, the record is a negative and undistinguished one. It is not, in fact, unreasonable to postulate that the country would have been better off without any (or at least most) of it.

Consider how often the failure of Congress to act has resulted in grave damage to the state of the Union and the continuation of years of abuses which should have been terminated much earlier.

Shouldn't the slavery question have been solved by Congress about the same time the slave trade was outlawed in 1808—or any time between then and the Civil War over fifty years later?

Shouldn't the growth of monopoly and the concentration of wealth in the Robber Baron era have been dealt with before the pallid Sherman Antitrust Act was passed in 1890 and the Clayton Act a generation later?

Wasn't the Pendleton Civil Service Act of 1883 decades overdue? Was it really necessary to have a President assassinated to put a curb on the spoils system?

Did equal justice under the law, proclaimed under the Fourteenth and Fifteenth Amendments, have to wait almost a hundred years before the Congress authorized effective implementing legislation?

Why couldn't an effective full employment act have been passed in 1946? And why are we still unable to deal effectively with massive unemployment in 1964?

Consider the major problems which confront the country and the world today. And consider how the Congress is reacting to them.

Nothing is more important than the search for a just and lasting peace now that we have the capability of destroying whole civilizations in a matter of hours. Nothing is more obvious to me—and I am not alone—than that disarmament and the establishment of a rule of enforceable law in the world are our best and perhaps our last hopes in that search. And yet the indifference in

Congress to the real problems involved in this issue is staggering. Of stump-speech patriotism, and just plain demagoguery, there is plenty. But of adequate understanding, even serious attention to the problem, there is precious little. We can pass a $50 billion Defense bill in the Senate in a few hours, but we will cut the budget of the Arms Control and Disarmament Agency from $15 million to less than half that amount without even discussing the matter on the floor.

The Disarmament Subcommittee of the Senate hangs by a thread, and would in all likelihood have been cut off by now were it not attached to the web of the ubiquitous Hubert Humphrey. But the Senate Preparedness Subcommittee, a forum for military, scientific and industrial opinion, generally opposed to the international policies of the Secretaries of Defense and State and the President of the United States on disarmament, is a fortress of the ruling clique in the Senate.

To be sure, the Senate ratified the partial Nuclear Test Ban Treaty over the opposition of the Preparedness Subcommittee, none of whose members were enthusiastic for the treaty but some of whom did not in the end vote against it. But the Senate would not, in my view, have ratified a really comprehensive treaty. A small step was taken because of the overwhelming public demand for it. But instead of offering the public leadership in this life-and-death matter, instead of encouraging the administration to take another and perhaps larger step, the Senate crouches sullenly in a corner refusing to look over the walls of its Alamo. The House, which did not have to consent to the treaty, probably suffers from even greater lag behind the President and the public on the road to peace. The depressing evidence, for those who want it, is in the daily pages of the *Congressional Record.*

There is another vital issue about which you could find, until recently, nothing at all in the pages of the *Congressional Record* —the population explosion. The measure of Congressional failure to face up to this problem is best taken by the fact that, much less than do anything about it, Congress won't even talk about it.

The Roman Catholic Church, other governments, the executive branch, public and private groups, the head of the World Bank, the United Nations—every well-informed person who has confronted the facts about the world birth rate—are all concerned that we have no feasible way to bring about population control. Over half the people on earth are underfed. Many tens of millions go to bed hungry every night. In most countries of Asia, Africa and Latin America—the poverty-stricken nations of the world—population is growing at a rate of between 2 and 4 percent annually. The world population will, if present trends continue, *double again* by the year 2000. And that includes the United States, where the population is expected to be 360 million in thirty-five years.

How effective, in the face of these figures, is foreign aid, the Alliance for Progress, the efforts of the international lending institutions—all the programs, public and private, to industrialize, democratize and develop the deprived nations of the world? And what of our unemployment, our economic growth rate, our social and welfare services at home? We are not solving these problems at home or abroad under present conditions and with our present efforts. How can we possibly make any real headway until we do something about population control?

Yet in Congress the subject is virtually taboo, and, save for a few of us willing to speak out, to make recommendations, to press for money for research, study, education and modest action, the population problem is unsung and unmet.*

Assuming we have the wit to save ourselves from a nuclear holocaust and the courage to do something constructive about the population problem, what of the state of our own society? How are we faring with the multifarious dilemmas brought about by a

* To be sure, Senator Fulbright quietly added to the Foreign Aid Authorization Bill of 1963 a provision (Sec. 105) authorizing the expenditure of money for research in methods of population control and for technical assistance to countries requesting it; but the House in conference insisted on striking the second half of the authorization. Senator Ernest Gruening of Alaska and I were the only members of either House or Senate who spoke on the floor in support of the Fulbright proposal and protested the House action.

technological and manpower revolution, disparate affluence, the growth of megalopolis and the Negro question? Having held eight months of hearings in the Senate Employment and Manpower Subcommittee on the problems of manpower utilization (which I like to call "Staffing Freedom"), cybernation and the economics of unemployment, I can report that Congress has much more to do than it has so far realized if we are to deal seriously and in depth with the fundamentals of human resource allocation.

We have had an average of 5 percent unemployment in this country for about five years. We have had even longer an economic growth rate hovering around 3 percent—which reduces to little more than one percent on a per capita basis. The labor force is increasing by over a million would-be workers a year as a result of the bumper baby crop after World War II. We must *create* ten thousand new jobs a week just to permit the unemployment rate to stand still, but automation and cybernation—the marriage of the computor to the machine—are *eliminating*, one witness told our committee, forty thousand jobs each week. Our large middle class grows larger and thrives, while millions of Americans—about one-fifth of our population—sink deeper and deeper in permanent poverty, misery and deprivation. There is, indeed, a cleavage nowadays in America between the haves and the have-nots which is different and more difficult to heal than that of the Great Depression.

Is this too bleak a picture? Perhaps it is. Certainly it is not the picture that stares out at us from the mass media—from the four-color ads in the slick magazines and the multicolor dazzle of our happy TV screens. It is not, certainly, the picture that the Congress sees. But from where I sit as a United States Senator from Pennsylvania this is the picture I see, and know, and have to face when I go home.

The Area Redevelopment Act, the Accelerated Public Works Act, the Manpower Development and Training Act—all of which I had a part in enacting—are inadequate, though necessary, measures which have had only mild success. They do not strike at the root of our economic woes. Yet it took a good deal of popular support, many years of work, executive insistence and all manner of legislative compromise to get them through the Congress.

The recent history of the effort to get Congressional action on a major tax reform program and a tax cut to spur economic growth speaks for itself. President Kennedy made his recommendations early in 1962. Months of delay and a propaganda barrage of primitive economic thinking not worthy of Adam Smith followed in Congress. It was the spring of 1964 before a pallid version of the President's original recommendations could be enacted into law.

When reason and persuasion can be brought to bear in the Congress on our presently haphazard and obsolete philosophy of employment, training, education and the allocation of human and physical resources, I shrink from suggesting. No man wants to be a prophet of gloom and doom; but the time will not arrive until drastic Congressional reform is achieved.

Lewis Mumford makes a similar point in another area of public responsibility. He says with reference to that new physical community we call the metropolitan area, or megalopolis:

> Those who believe that there are no alternatives to the present proliferation of metropolitan tissue perhaps overlook too easily the historic outcome of such a concentration of urban power: they forget that this has repeatedly marked the last stage in the classic cycle of civilization, before its complete disruption and downfall.[1]

These are strong words, and I hope too pessimistic. But it is a fact that the Congress refused to create a Department of Urban Affairs to represent at the Cabinet table the overwhelming majority of Americans who live in urban areas, despite the fact that the Department of Agriculture, created over a hundred years ago and now employing 85,000 people, represents only that shrinking 7.1 percent of our population required to raise food for the rest of us.

The housing legislation of recent years, particularly the Housing Act of 1961, has recognized and dealt wisely with some urban problems. But the approach is piecemeal and uncoordinated, and the Congress legislates for the city in highway bills, the accelerated works program, water and air pollution programs, mass transit and even education bills without over-all plan or program. The Congress has so far proved unwilling to accept the reality of our urban mode of life and to deal with it logically, sensibly and —if Lewis Mumford is right—in time.

Look at civil rights. On the major social issue of our time, the Supreme Court has ruled wisely and well. Beginning with the monumental school desegregation case of 1954, the Court has awakened the American Negro, startled the nation, finally moved the executive branch to action. But the Congress is just beginning to move away from the *status quo ante*. *Ante* the decision, and even—I am not being humorous—*ante* bellum, 1860.

The record of the Congress on equal rights for all Americans is the classic example of unjust delay. The Senate is in many ways, as one of its stoutest defenders put it, the South's revenge on the North for having lost the Civil War. The price has been paid over and over and over again. It has been paid for nearly two centuries, every minute of the day, every day in the week, by every Negro American. Not just as a Senator, but as a man and an American, I am ashamed of this record.

The fact that we have at last taken some remedial action does not mean that we have faced up to our job. There is vastly more to be done. And getting it done means going far beyond the specific question of civil rights legislation. It means doing something about the Congress itself.

All of these problems require doing something about the Congress. If, that is, we are dedicated to the purpose of keeping Western civilization alive. If we want to save ourselves from nuclear destruction, help the world feed its children and protect their lands from totalitarian Communism, put our people to work and make our cities habitable, and realize the fact as well as the name of equality.

If, that is, we still hold with the Declaration of Independence that certain truths are self-evident. . . .

III

THE ROAD TO CONGRESS

There are a number of different roads to Capitol Hill. For a few it is a nonstop highway stretching from their birthplace to Washington. The Longs of Louisiana, Bankheads of Alabama, Byrds of Virginia, Roosevelts of New York and Kennedys of Massachusetts have taken this path. For more, those in one-party states or districts where there is no "boss" control, it is customarily a rocky road through a rough primary campaign—perhaps against a dozen opponents—a safe and easy ride through the general election, and then smooth re-election for as long as one cares to run. For those in the increasingly one-party cities and in boss-controlled rural areas, too, it is frequently a combination of party service, luck, nationality group and time that rewards the faithful with the gift of a machine-backed nomination and a free ride to re-election thereafter as long as the "organization" is not defied.

For some, in the doubtful states and districts, it requires getting the nomination by hard intensive work within the party power structure, sometimes winning a contested primary and then riding in with the ticket or on one's own in a hard-fought general election. For these unfortunates each effort at re-election means the same rat race all over again.

But whether the Senator or Representative obtains his seat as a matter of birthright, or by fighting his way up via the state legislature or a county office, or at the price of subservience to an organization boss, or whether he is hand-picked by the political leaders because of union connections or business relationships—whatever the initial impetus or ambition that makes him a candidate and gets him on the road—he is in the end elected by the people of his individual district or state for largely local reasons. And the road that takes him to Washington leads right back to that home district if he wants to hold his seat. This is something no member of Congress dares ever to forget. Those who remain in Congress are on the whole those who have it most firmly in mind and regulate their behavior accordingly.

Whether he is elected by a mere 20,000 voters, as in the case of Judge Smith of Virginia, the overlord of the House Rules Committee, or 250,000, as in the case of Alphonzo Bell, a second-term Congressman from California, they are the people to whom he considers himself chiefly responsible and worries most about. Representative Adam Clayton Powell put it succinctly in a recent article on the "Duties and Responsibilities of a Congressman of the United States." "The primary and overriding duty and responsibility of each member of the House of Representatives and the Senate is to get re-elected."[1] Congressman Powell has his detractors, largely outside his district, but none of them has suggested that he is not a shrewd and successful politician.

The point is that the member of Congress is elected and re-elected because a majority of the electors who come to the polls vote for him, and Congressmen are convinced that their voters are primarily influenced by local, not national, issues. His power base is, therefore, his district or state: the party organization, the people, the parochialism, the local problems. The trend of governmental power has been increasingly national, but the trend of political power remains local. This localism has always characterized American politics and continues to do so, even as the world and the districts shrink. "The basic political fact of federalism," Professor David Truman has written, "is that it creates separate, self-sustaining centers of power, privilege and profit."[2]

Members of Congress are the product of this party power structure. And it should be noted that a long history during which so many of our domestic problems were sectional or regional, and foreign affairs were of little interest to most Americans, contributed heavily to placing a distinctively local stamp on Congress. The result is that even today our legislator tends to think of himself first as a Senator from Georgia or a Representative from the Sixth Congressional District of Missouri and only secondly as a member of a *national* legislative body.

The persistent localism of Congressional election politics is largely responsible for the doctrinal untidiness of the parties. "Any man who can carry a Republican primary is a Republican," said Senator William E. Borah. "He might believe in . . . every policy that the Democratic Party ever advocated; yet if he carried his Republican primary, he would be a Republican. He might go to the other extreme and believe in the communistic state . . . yet, if he carried his Republican primary, he would still be a Republican."[3]

Senator Borah was a maverick; an old regular might disagree. Yet today most practical politicians would go along with Borah. Political party leaders think of the party as a big tent with room in it for everyone who votes the party ticket no matter how divergent his views. The thought of party discipline in the Congress, of voting the party position or risking expulsion from the party—as in the British Parliament—is repugnant to most Congressmen. Yet this very lack of discipline is one major reason for the ineffectiveness of Congress.

The great wealth of the nation and our isolation from the rest of the world, the diversity of American society and the heterogeneity of the economy for most of our history made a loose party structure both attractive and feasible. It is a party structure geared to the attainment of office rather than the execution of policy. This party system solidly based on localism rather than a national interest worked well enough in the past when effective government was not imperative. It serves us badly today.

One result is that the national party leadership sometimes receives its strongest support from the areas where the party at the local level is weakest. In these areas, party leaders will feel that their only hope of personal success lies in a national success of sufficient magnitude to tilt favorably the usually unfavorable local balance. Areas where the local party is strong enough to elect its own candidates, on the other hand, are not infrequently indifferent to the national fortunes. Since the ideological and philosophical ties within the party are weak or nonexistent, and since loyalty to the state and national platforms is just about irrelevant, the basic organizational strength of the party remains fixed at the local level.

In this structure, the Congressional election becomes more of a by-product than an end product of the party process. Concern for the Presidency in national elections and concern with state and local offices, particularly executive offices with their attendant patronage and fund-raising perquisites, come close to exhausting the attention of the regular party organization. The Representatives and the Senators are secondary considerations. In most cases they have too little patronage to build a party organization of their own, and they are too far away from the local scene to exercise control of the party machinery. The exceptions are those few Congressmen who are also party bosses in their own districts.

The candidate for Congress is thus placed in a rather unusual position vis-à-vis his party. In the mid-Presidential term election he is almost on his own as far as the national party is concerned. In Presidential years he is more or less important according to the help or harm he can be—or wishes to be—to the Presidential candidate. At the same time the regular party organization is not necessarily disposed to consider the race for Congress of weighty importance in a Presidential year. In the odd-numbered years of purely county and city elections the Congressman is often ignored.

When I sought re-election to the Senate in 1962, for example, the office of Governor of Pennsylvania was also to be filled in the same election. Both parties and all candidates for major office agreed that unemployment and the economic condition of the state were the principal issues of the campaign. The pollsters and the press verified this view. It was well known and generally accepted that the Kennedy administration was more popular than the Democratic state administration.

My identification with Washington and President Kennedy and the role I had played in passage of federal legislation dealing with economic problems, such as the Area Redevelopment Act, the Manpower Development and Training Act and the Accelerated Public Works Program, were considerable assets both to the ticket and to me personally. Additionally, I was the only incumbent among the four major candidates—with the attendant advantages of having been elected before, given six years of service to constituents, and being well known—and my name came first on the ballot. (This minor piece of luck is worth a good deal more in the primary than in the general election, but is an advantage in November as well.) Most important of all, the power to really do something about the economically depressed condition of Pennsylvania—to put a lot of people back to work—lies largely with the federal and not the state government.

On top of all this the press, pollsters and professional politicians generally agreed that the Republican gubernatorial candidate was stronger than my Senatorial opponent.

It seemed obvious to me, therefore, that our best chance of carrying the entire ticket of my party to victory in Pennsylvania in 1962 was to put the Senatorial race front and center, focus attention on it as the "top of the ticket," and make the most of the popularity of our national government.

I was bold and, perhaps, immodest enough to suggest this to the party leaders. My campaign assistants pressed this idea somewhat more aggressively. But my suggestion fell on deaf ears. I was accused of egotism and my loyal staff was felt to be disinterested in the fate of the rest of the ticket.

The political powers wielded by the Governor—any Governor—of Pennsylvania over the years and the scandalously large number of patronage appointments available to him had conditioned the party organization to regard the gubernatorial office as the real and only prize. As one party stalwart put it, "Never mind all that stuff that goes on in Washington. What about jobs in the Highway Department?" The political organization's attitude over the years has so fixed the political traditions of the state that the press, the interest groups and most of the public shared the same outlook.

State issues and the candidates for state offices dominated the campaign. My candidacy seemed, at times, to serve only the purpose of providing a drawing card for political rallies and a speaker for county fund-raising dinners. The toastmaster on these occasions would often introduce me with some such phrase as: "Let us not forget we are also choosing a United States Senator in this election. . . ." The enthusiasm, effort and money mobilized by the Democratic party were utilized primarily in an unsuccessful effort to elect a governor.

Under such circumstances a candidate for Congress from a doubtful district or state must seek direct contact with his electorate over the head of his local or state party organization. This lesson, which Senators and Representatives learn early, is the price of survival.

Nevertheless, the party organization is very important to the quest for nomination or renomination in almost all states and districts. Successful mavericks in primary elections are few and far between; and the organization in general elections performs the indispensable function of securing the solid vote of the faithful. But in a doubtful state or district this is not enough. The Congressional candidate finds, as I did, that his election is of no special importance to the regulars even though they support him.

Of course if he runs in a one-party constituency, this nominal support is indeed enough to secure his election. But in a close two-party constituency the candidate must supplement that assistance by developing popular support that is uniquely his own.

Such interest as is shown by the party organization in the Congressional or Senatorial contest usually derives from estimates of the impact a candidate will have on the rest of the ticket. Nobody wanted to deny me the nomination in 1962. Most Democrats agreed I would help the ticket. But strong candidates are sought less because of the importance of the office they seek than as part of the philosophy of putting together a ticket that will contribute to victory in the offices deemed most valuable to the party hierarchy. So long as the candidates for local or state offices have wide popular appeal this works to the benefit of the Congressional candidate. When, as sometimes happen, they don't, he must strike out for himself.

The results of the 1962 election in Pennsylvania are a case in point. I was re-elected, while our gubernatorial and other statewide candidates, with the exception of Genevieve Blatt, who nosed out her opponent for Secretary of Internal Affairs in a very close race, lost. Genevieve and I won because we were able to summon the independent support of tens of thousands of voters who did not vote for the other candidates on our ticket.

The key to our success was the relatively recent and increasingly important tendency of American voters to "split their tickets"—to vote for the man or woman and not the party, to choose among the candidates of both parties those whom they prefer for reasons beyond and perhaps above the party label. In Pennsylvania this trend is particularly strong. Hugh Scott, my Republican colleague in the Senate, and I have both been elected while the opposite party was carrying the state and electing either a governor or a President.

The rise of the independent voter, the voter who is less and less attached to party labels and more influenced by the personal qualifications and/or attractiveness of the candidate, is one of the most important political developments of our time. In national elections and in most statewide elections the independent voters hold the balance of power. Neither of the two major political parties is able to elect a United States Senator or a President without winning the support of a majority of independent voters. But in the individual Congressional districts this is not necessarily the case. Though the support of the independent voter is gaining in importance in many Congressional districts, especially in the suburban areas, in a much larger number of House districts the party label and the party organization appear to be enough.

To understand what the Congress is like and what is wrong with it, it is crucial to recognize that most members of the House and many Senators are elected permanently when they are elected once.

Ordinarily the risk that an intraparty fight will jeopardize success at the general election dictates that the party renominate incumbents. This is a source of comfort to incumbents, of course, but it is subject to the sobering knowledge that it is precisely in these close two-party constituencies that party support may well be insufficient to secure re-election without independent support built by the incumbent himself. And even then he may become the victim of some national trend too great for the combined efforts of his friends and his party to withstand.

The situation is far different, however, in those very numerous areas where meaningful competition between the parties simply does not exist. Here an incumbent has advantages in retaining his position that are nearly overwhelming. With no contested general election to face, he need concern himself only with the unlikely prospect of losing his party's nomination in the primary. This prospect is, in ordinary cases, fairly remote because as a member of the dominant party he is normally assured of the support of the only effective political organization in the area. A candidate in a primary challenging an incumbent must put together his own organization. This is understandably beyond the resources of a good many prospective candidates, though the number of wealthy men (or men with wealthy friends) entering the political arena is increasing.

Democracy may be defined in various ways, but basic to its central conception is some kind of meaningful dialogue between candidates offering policy alternatives to the electorate. The absence of such meaningful dialogue in a great many of the nation's Congressional constituencies is a very serious problem in contemporary American politics.

Politicians normally use a rule of thumb that districts in which one party receives more than 55 percent of the vote are "safe." It takes a political overturn of major dimensions to convert a majority of this size into a victory for the minority party in the next election. In the 1962 Congressional elections 358 of the 435 members of the House of Representatives were returned by margins above 55 percent. Only 77 seats (17.7 percent) could be considered as marginal districts. Moreover, this situation has become more pronounced in recent years, as the table below indicates:

Doubtful House Districts, 1950-62[4]

(won by less than 55% of the total vote)

Year	*Democratic*	*Republican*	*Total*
1950	37	58	95
1952	45	40	85
1954	31	63	94
1956	52	38	90
1958	44	61	105
1960	37	48	85
1962	41	36	77

The increase in doubtful districts in 1958 coincides with the Democratic sweep of that year. The decrease in doubtful districts in the next two elections indicates in part the normal recapture of Republican seats lost temporarily to the Democrats in 1958.

This represents a very substantial change over earlier periods in America's history when a very large turnover in the composition of the House was common. The average term of House members in the mid-nineteenth century was only a few years, and in the period 1861-81 every new Congress contained a House majority made up of members serving their first terms. A century later, in 1961, the average length of service for House members was nearly ten years.[5]

In the 1962 election, which returned 364 incumbents to the House, nine newcomers won out of thirty-three Senate seats at stake. Two other Senators who had served briefly under appointment won election for the first time and two more now serve under appointment made when vacancies occurred after election. But only four incumbents, two Republicans and two Democrats, were defeated.

This situation is not only a problem of the so-called one-party South. It is fairly evenly distributed throughout the country. Nor is it a problem that need concern only liberals on the theory that it is only conservative members who stem from safe districts. The liberally oriented Americans for Democratic Action gave a 100 percent rating to eighty-nine members of the Eighty-seventh Congress on the basis of their 1961 voting record. Seventy-one of these eighty-nine (80 percent) were veterans who came from districts in which their margin of victory was greater than 55 percent.

On the other side of the coin, 100 percent ratings were given to sixteen House members of that same Congress by the conservative Americans for Constitutional Action (this lower number apparently indicates either more exacting standards or a more extreme philosophy). Eleven of the sixteen (69 percent) came for similarly safe districts—most of them, it may be added, from predominantly rural constituencies.

The significance of these statistics lies in the fact that a substantial majority of the members of the House can afford to be indifferent to all but the most major national political currents. This large majority gives to the House, as Mr. MacNeil notes, "a solidity in its rank and file" made up of members who cannot "readily be pressured to alter their political views on pending legislation."[6] Solidity is thus purchased at the expense of the party platforms and national democracy.

Nomination at a primary election, then, rather than the November general election is the really meaningful part of the electoral process for a large majority of the House because of the preponderance of one-party districts. The composition of the House is thus, to a degree not generally recognized, pretty well determined before the national campaign and Presidential election begin. The same is true in the "off-year" elections. Only a minority of Representatives from doubtful districts and Senators from doubtful states remain to be selected. On this minority, however, hangs the balance of power in Congress. Despite the folklore that the composition of the Congress depends on a vigorous debate of national issues in the campaign preceding the general election, the holders of some 358 out of 435 seats in the House were decided before the national campaign really got under way in 1962 and are likely to be again in 1964.

Ironically enough, the Senate is less affected by this tendency than the House. In fact, election to the Senate has become increasingly competitive in recent years with the diminution of one-party states both in the North and South, both Republican and Democratic. Maine and New Hampshire each now have a Democratic Senator; Texas has a Republican Senator. States which had been one-party for many years—Indiana, the Dakotas, Utah, Idaho—are one-party no longer. The South is not "safe" for the Democrats and the Midwest is not "safe" for the Republicans. Hardly more than a quarter of the Senate comes from states where re-election is assured.

The political turbulence of the thirties, the unique impact of Franklin Roosevelt, and the Second World War all contributed to this change. The extraordinary mobility of our population (nearly 5.8 million Americans move each year, many of them crossing state lines as they do) has a good deal to do with this also.[7] And as the population shifts west and south it also shifts within the state boundaries toward the urban and away from the rural areas. This is also a contributing factor.

Yet as our politics become more competitive in the Senate the number of competitive House districts is declining. This results in part from the American drive toward residential homogeneity. Our housing and income patterns stratify geographically the national income levels which produce competitive politics. Thus Democratic Congressman Robert Nix's Philadelphia district is largely low-income and Negro. Republican Congressman E. Y. Berry of South Dakota has a district which is Protestant, white, conservative and primarily interested in ranching. The venerable John McCormack of Massachusetts represents an Irish, Catholic, working-class district which is overwhelmingly Democratic, while John Lindsay's silk-stocking Manhattan district is liberal Republican. Jimmy Roosevelt's district is a California-style melting-pot with large Mexican, Japanese and Negro population.

The decline of doubtful districts also results in part from bipartisan reapportionment agreements at the state level made to keep the number of competitive districts at a minimum and to protect incumbents of both parties. In Pennsylvania's latest Congressional reapportionment two hitherto "safe" districts became one doubtful district when our state lost three Congressmen and had to consolidate two districts, one safely Democratic, the other safely Republican. Both incumbents in the new doubtful district considered themselves mistreated. The Democrat, George Rhodes of Berks County, won. In the other eliminated districts one Democrat, Mrs. Kathryn Granahan, was dropped, and subsequently appointed Treasurer of the United States by President Kennedy. One Republican, Representative James Van Zandt, ran for the Senate and lost, leaving his consolidated district to the other Republican incumbent, Representative Irving Whalley. All the other twenty-four incumbents were protected from serious challenge by the geography of reapportionment.

In many states where competition is real enough for statewide contests for governor and Senator the composition of the

House delegation provides few real contests. Of Pennsylvania's twenty-seven Congressional seats eleven are safely Democratic, thirteen safely Republican and only three are "swing" districts. Thus while statewide contests are hard fought, only a fraction of my state's voters cast a meaningful vote for their Congressman.

Under these circumstances state representation in the federal House of Representatives tends to stabilize. It is not easy to enlist enthusiasm for unseating a Congressman who two years ago carried his district by more than 55 percent of the vote. Denied much prospect of success, the minority is deprived of incentive to compete seriously.

This, in turn, produces the further irony that the House of Representatives, intended by the Founding Fathers to be the pre-eminent organ of the popular will, is less susceptible to changes by the voters than is its allegedly patrician counterpart, the Senate. Many House members are thus more secure in tenure and hence less responsive to the popular will than most Senators, despite the latters' six-year terms.

Party control of the state legislature has a decisive impact on the composition of the House of Representatives in Washington because of the state legislature's responsibility for reapportioning Congressional districts every ten years. Since it has not always fairly lived up to this constitutional responsibility, judicial action is now forcing it to do so; and the spur of judicial intervention is upsetting the familiar pattern of that deliberate gerrymandering, or scarcely less deliberate inaction, which has seriously distorted the representative character of the national House of Representatives. But while it now seems reasonably certain that fair numerical reapportionment of all Congressional districts will result from the recent Supreme Court decision,* there is no assurance that the legislatures will not find ways to favor incumbents and maintain one-party districts of approximately equal and predominantly homogeneous popula-

* Wesberry *v.* Sanders, 32 U. S. Law Week 4142, Feb. 17, 1964.

tion. The possibility of more two-party districts is accordingly remote. Much of the sluggishness of the political parties in reacting to changing events is due to the fact that the lines of political struggle are to a great extent dominated by the lines of legislative apportionment. When these lines are drawn so as to mute or silence that struggle, the political system is unable to reflect political currents because it is impervious to them.

We now accept as routine substantial Presidential participation in Congressional elections. Not only do the Presidential candidates dominate the campaign in Presidential years, with inevitable de-emphasis upon the candidates for Congress, but Presidential intervention in mid-term elections has come to be common. National leadership in the Congressional election process is increasingly projected into the nominating process as well. Party leadership is beginning to discover that if it does not concern itself with the nominating process, intervention in the general election is fruitless because too late: the party candidate is simply unattractive or unacceptable on policy grounds.

Vice President Nixon's explanation to the Cabinet for the 1954 Republican setbacks in the Congressional elections was brutally candid: "There were just too many turkeys running on the Republican ticket."[8]

Actually, there is more *sub rosa* intervention from both national and state party leadership concerning prospective Congressional nominees than is generally recognized. In the special Congressional election in Pennsylvania on July 30, 1963, to fill the vacancy resulting from the death of Representative Francis E. Walter, for example, the choice of both Republican and Democratic candidates was taken out of the hands of the local county chairmen, who under the party rules were entitled to make the nomination. In both parties the nomination was dictated by the state leaders.

So long as this intervention from above takes the affirmative form of encouraging able candidates to present themselves, it does not arouse general resentment. When, however, it takes the form of defeating incumbents ("purging" in the political lexicon), the reaction is otherwise. Then resentment at the local level is inevitable, and the candidate to be purged is apt to become a potential local martyr and thus likely to be renominated over the objection of the state or national party leaders. The national party chiefs must move with great caution in their efforts to punish for party irregularity.

Nevertheless, in 1954 Steven Mitchell took an unprecedented step as Democratic National Chairman in announcing that the National Committee would withhold help from two Democrats seeking nominations for Congress under California's cross-filing system. In 1962 the Democratic National Committee again intervened with covert assistance in support of liberal candidates in several Southern primaries. In the summer of 1963 Washington buzzed with rumors that elements of the Democratic National Committee and some White House figures, not including President Kennedy, had marked a dozen conservative Southerners for extinction. It was a group of Washington Democrats, not the party leadership in Ohio, which initiated the move to dump Senator Steve Young and support the astronaut John Glenn for nomination to the Senate.

Such intervention, covert and sporadic, will probably continue and even increase. It seems likely, however, that any formal centralization in the Congressional nominating process is a long way off. Identity of viewpoint between the Presidential and Congressional candidates is more likely to be achieved through domination of the campaign dialogue by Presidential candidates than by ignoring the traditional right of local political leaders to determine who their candidate shall be.

At mid-term elections the nationalizing influence of the Presidency is largly diminished and in many cases absent. In two-party doubtful states and districts support or opposition to the program of the President plays a part and he may be called in personally to campaign; but this is rarely as important as local and state issues and personalities.

Federalism, the historic importance of local and sectional issues, and the decentralization of American parties are thus reasserted in off-year elections and emphasize the lack of political ideology manifested by the parties in Congress.

Nearly every member of Congress and almost all Congressional candidates must make some adjustments between the position of their party on the issues and the realities of life among the constituency of their districts. Republican farm state Senators from the Midwest, for example, have deserted their party's position on agricultural legislation fairly consistently in recent years, and with obvious success. Many wheat state Republicans voted in favor of wheat sales to Russia against the views of their party leadership. It would be impossible for a Congressman from Philadelphia or Pittsburgh to refuse to support meaningful civil rights legislation. There are too many Negro voters in those cities. But more often these adjustments will mean no more than moderating or soft-pedaling some one platform plank or emphasizing more strongly some other party proposal. This is altogether defensible, and within moderate limits it gives a needed flexibility to the system. It does not, however, justify efforts to make consistent party unorthodoxy the basis of political success. It is always easy to make headlines by defying the party leadership, and there may be circumstances in which the conscience of the legislator or the nature of his constituency will require that this be done. But if our political system is to offer the voters a choice between two alternatives, constant opposition to national party policy cannot be justified by those who carry the party banner into electoral campaigns. In such circumstances the courageous action would be to follow the lead of Senator Wayne Morse of Oregon and switch party allegiance.

The existence of separate campaign committees for each house of Congress by each party is an acknowledgment by party leaders that the party's success in the Congressional elections may hinge on different factors from those of concern to the two national parties. Although these Congressional campaign committees are theoretically part of the formal party hierarchy, they are in truth entirely separate entities—wholly disowned subsidiaries, one might say. Their principal function is to raise money from lobbyists which is distributed among the candidates pretty much as the contributors indicate, thus successfully insulating the contributor from public revelation of his interest in the particular candidate.

These campaign committees are partly the result of the concern of members of Congress that, as one member put it, "The national committee spends 90 percent of its campaign funds to elect the two candidates at the head of the ticket and forgets about the candidates below the top." The committees concern themselves with maintaining and, hopefully, enlarging their parties' membership in Congress. To this end, they supply certain technical services, public relations material, research assistance and, most important of all, money. Since the resources of the committees are always less than the needs of the party's candidates, assistance must be rationed. The decision as to where resources will be committed, therefore, can frequently be an important weapon for the party leadership—and for the contributing lobbyist.

Since the four Congressional campaign committees, two in the House and two in the Senate, are to a substantial extent prisoners of the lobbies, this rationing can be used by the Congressional party leadership to support its aims—and its friends.

Thus the conservative oil and gas lobbies, which contribute so heavily to the Democratic Senatorial Campaign Committee, had not the slightest interest in the re-election of Senator Paul Douglas of Illinois in 1960, he having been a staunch advocate of cutting the depletion allowance. But they were vitally interested in the re-election of the late Senator Bob Kerr of Oklahoma, who was the most articulate spokesman for the oil interests in the Senate. Quite naturally Senator Kerr received a very much larger contribution from the Senatorial Campaign Committee than Senator Douglas. The lobbies quietly earmarked their contribution to the committee for Senator Kerr, and the committee, as an implicit condition to receiving the money, sent it to Oklahoma, where it wasn't needed, rather than to Illinois, where it was.

The quasi independence of the Congressional Campaign Committees from the National Committees serves to create intraparty divisions on policy rather than to integrate the disparate forces within each party. Other Presidents could echo the sentiments of President Eisenhower on this score: "Imagine the head of the Congressional Campaign Committee going around—and after getting four hundred thousand dollars from the National Committee—and advising Republican candidates to choose carefully what parts of the President's program they should support!"[8]

The separate committees provide a separate focus for the determination and dissemination of party policy. The Congressional Committees, in particular, are not policy-oriented and tend to conceive of politics as a game in which all members of the party, regardless of party orthodoxy, are entitled to support by techniques and services that are irrelevant to policy. During my campaign for re-election in 1962, for example, the Democratic Senatorial Campaign Committee announced that it was assigning Senators to those of us up for election who would be asked to appear in our behalf at rallies and party functions. Senators Eastland and Stennis of Mississippi were assigned to me! The three of us learned of this from a public announcement by the Senatorial Campaign Committee, which caused some raised eyebrows in both Pennsylvania and Mississippi. We promptly disengaged ourselves from a political mésalliance which was as embarrassing to my colleagues from Mississippi as it was to me.

Senator Herman Talmadge of Georgia and I were both first elected to the Senate in 1956. Despite our quite different political views we soon became good friends. It was not long before we were offering to appear publicly in Georgia and Pennsylvania *against* each other in 1962 in order to assure each other's re-election. (Commitments which neither of us kept. We both won anyway.)

Thus, though the road to Congress is traveled in many different ways by many different men and women, an obstacle course for some and a joy ride for others, it has a fundamental bearing on the nature, makeup and kind of Congress we have. Its importance is not diminished when the election is won and the candidate is a member of Congress. On the contrary, as we shall see, the road to Congress for most members becomes a path within the Congress to power, success, attainment and recognition. And it always leads right back again to the constituents at home.

The traditional American political processes—the selection of the candidate, the issues on which he runs, the way the campaign is financed, the geography of the district, the differences between Presidential and Congressional campaigns—all these combine to make the Congress what it is, and the Congressman the kind of man he is.

Is the Congress today what the Founding Fathers intended? Does it meet the requirements for a national legislative body in the second half of the twentieth century? I believe the answer to both questions is no. And the principal reason is because a Representative or Senator is elected today as a result of political processes never anticipated by the framers of the Constitution.

The House of Representatives is not a reflection or a microcosm of the national will. It is certainly not the mirror of popular passions, aggressive action or the surge of democracy, as the members of the Philadelphia Convention contemplated.

The Senate is not an aloof, aristocratic, reserved group holding in check the unreflective activities and hasty deeds of a House responsive to the turbulent emotions of the masses, which the Founding Fathers certainly expected it to be.

There is nothing in itself wrong with the fact that the Congress which has evolved over the years is not the Congress the Founding Fathers envisioned. What is wrong is that, partly because of the way the selection of Representatives and Senators has evolved, the Congress appears incapable of performing adequately the work of a legislative body in the atomic age.

There is nothing in the Constitution about political parties or political processes. There is nothing to stop us from altering our political processes to meet the needs of the times except ourselves. Until we make some changes in the character of the road to Congress we are starting out with too heavy a load to carry. Congress as an institution needs an overhaul from within—as I hope to make clear. But that is only part of the task we face. We must also make some changes in the way we select members of Congress, because the makeup of Congress is so largely determined by the selection process itself.

IV

THE WONDERFUL WORLD OF CONGRESS

The election is over and won. For hundreds of members of Congress nothing very unusual has happened. They are the incumbents and the re-elected, who will be able to continue the work they are doing, and perhaps, with increased seniority in Congress, improve their committee assignments. If there has been a relatively large change of seats, as in the Democratic sweep of the Congressional elections of 1958, the chances of getting a different committee closer to one's heart or more important to one's district are naturally improved.

For newly elected members there are the tasks of moving families to Washington and setting up offices. Some members commute—mostly those members of the House known as the Tuesday-Thursday Club, Congressmen from the area near Washington, who remain in town for three days, usually at a hotel, and spend the rest of the time back in their districts. But most Congressmen bring their families to Washington and establish homes there. In view of the length of recent Congressional sessions, eight months and frequently more, it is necessary to do this if any appreciable time is to be spent with one's family. Indeed, for a good many members of Congress Washington becomes home, their children go to school, they make friends and spend most of their time there. What used to be home becomes a retreat for weekends and holidays and headquarters for fence-mending trips around the district or state.

Whatever the arrangements, the Congressman must live in two places and travel back and forth between them a great deal. This imposes a heavy financial burden. It costs me money, quite a lot of my own money every year, to be a United States Senator. For those who have nothing in their pocket to take out, ways must be found to supplement the inadequate salary and expenses now paid members of Congress. Usually this means beating one's way along the "honorarium" trail picking up two hundred dollars here, five hundred there, to pay for the groceries and shoes for the kids.

Setting up an office, or several offices, is easier. Here the government is more generous (or the Congress is more sensible). The Congressman gets an office in Washington in one of the three House or two Senate office buildings—expensive, overadorned, inefficient buldings all of them. The two newest are, inexcusably, the most tasteless, poorly designed and expensive of them all. A Representative will get a suite of at least three rooms now that the Sam Rayburn House Office Building is completed (he used to get two). A Senator will get five or six rooms (he used to get three before the New S.O.B.—as it is known—was built several years ago). Committee chairmen and senior members of both houses get additional rooms, committee suites and hideaways in the Capitol itself.

The suites appear to be designed to impress the constituents or perhaps the member's ego; it is impossible to believe they were designed for genuine office use. The ceilings are high, the rooms deep, the woodwork massive and the furnishings Congressional (there is no other way to describe them). The member's personal office is usually lavishly enhanced by a marble fireplace in which you can't light a fire, a hidden wall safe that is rarely used, a refrigerator that is very useful indeed and private toilet facilities.

In the newer office buildings some thought has been given to built-in shelves and space for filing cabinets, but not much, And it is common to see the rather Edwardian elegance of the huge rooms in the Old Senate Office Building cut up and crisscrossed with ugly, homemade (in the carpentry shop in the basement) room dividers so that place can be found for the equipment, material and tools of work, and so that those on the staff who require it can have some semblance of privacy. It is typical that in my office the stationery must be stored in large, handsome, old-fashioned walnut bookcases with glass doors and curtains.

In addition, the Congressman may have an office or several offices right in his own district or state, usually in some federal building—a courthouse or post office, for example. These are rent-free and he gets an allowance to cover the housekeeping cost to the government of servicing them with heat, electricity, cleaning and so on. Because they are in ordinary federal buildings under the jurisdiction of the General Services Administration, these offices are a far cry from the Washington headquarters and are more likely to be shabby and underequipped.

The average House member has about six employees; it is normal to have four of them in the Washington office and two in the district. Of these, the two top aides usually do legislative and administrative staff work, and the remaining members of the staff do secretarial and clerical work. While there is an increasing tendency among Congressmen to have a high-caliber staff assistant doing full-time legislative work, many do their own legislative work or rely on committee staffs to advise them. In such cases—and they are numerous—the emphasis may be placed on an assistant whose principal forte is public relations or politics or both, since the two go hand in hand on the Hill. Almost inevitably, the other top assistant, sometimes female, is a combination office manager, government liaison worker, problem handler and greeter. These women, who swarm in the House of Representatives, are the mainstays of the offices. A freshman Congressman, if he is wise, finds or steals one to set up his office. For this is the woman who knows her way around in the complicated and illogical world of Congressional stationery offices, service departments, document rooms, who has mastered disbursing procedures and understands the importance of executive branch liaison. It is a bewildering and in some ways fantastic world, which would astonish the ordinary businessman and convulse a systems analyst.

In the district office, or offices, the Congressman may very well have a politician and secretary, though occasionally the order is reversed and most of the staff works out of the district office instead of Washington. Of the Pennsylvania delegation, only one House member chooses this latter course, though there are some who divide the personnel and the workload with equal emphasis on Washington and the district.

On the Senate side of the Hill the allowance for staff and equipment is much larger, and the Senatorial staff is therefore not only more numerous but more specialized. As a Senator from a large state I receive approximately $170,000 each year from the government for these purposes. Under a system so complicated as to be unintelligible, the larger states get more money, but not proportionately more, than the states with smaller populations.

There is an equally absurd and complicated system fixing staff salaries in arbitrary categories which must be adhered to. It was originally devised to conceal from the public the actual amount paid the employee. There is a covert quality about all this old-fashioned and illogical nonsense which makes the Congress appear petty and secretive. If there once was the excuse that these book-keeping procedures were nobody's business (neither the public's, the press's nor even the junior members of Congress's), that excuse was removed a few years ago when a diligent reporter began exposing these weird practices and brought sufficient public pressure to bear on Congress to make the facts available. The press and the public must still go to considerable trouble to obtain payroll information on Congressional salaries and positions, but for those who are interested enough to dig for it and diligent enough to study the rather obscure form in which the information is made available, it can be had.

All this might be quaint, and even amusing, were it unique—a relatively harmless example of a quill-pen tradition to remind us of the preautomated world. But it is not. The way Congress goes about its housekeeping chores is symptomatic of the deadly grip that traditions, customs and styles of the past have over the mentality of the nation's highest legislative body. For the new member of Congress, these details are his first glimpse of the special mystique and the peculiar malaise which have the Congress in thrall.

An even more important aspect of the neophyte's indoctrination into the ways of the Congressional world is the "word" he gets from those who run it. The late Sam Rayburn, Speaker of the House of Representatives longer than any man in history, gave each freshman class of Representatives the same advice for a generation: "To get along, go along." Speaker Rayburn's most illustrious protégé, President Lyndon Johnson, gave the same advice to newly elected Democratic Senators during his tenure as Majority Leader of the Senate. The Republicans heard, if not the same words, the same story. "To get along, go along" is the password to power on Capitol Hill.

Getting along and going along mean, for the first few months, being seen but not heard, doing your homework, watching out for your constituents, selecting the field of legislative interest which you intend to make your own and cooperating with the leadership of your party. That is what is expected of you.

When I arrived in Washington in 1957, I thought that my principal tasks for the next six years would be concerned with legislation. After the maelstrom of Philadelphia politics and four years of executive responsibility as Mayor, I looked forward enthusiastically to life as a national legislator. There would be time, I thought, to read, to listen, to think, to mull over problems, debate issues and to participate in framing wise laws.

But as so often happens, the world of the Senate was not what it appeared to be from outside the "hallowed chamber." The job of a member of Congress is a fascinating and rewarding one, but it is not what people generally think it is. Congress is not just the nation's legislature. Its job is not merely to pass new laws, amend or extend old ones and oversee executive administration. Perhaps its major business, at least in terms of time and energy expended, is to take care of the small but pressing needs of millions of American citizens.

Few people appreciate how large a part of the Congressman's day is spent not on grand affairs of state but on ministering to the inexhaustible requests of the people who elect him. His life is hardly one of splendid isolation, for his contacts with the world outside of Washington are continuous and time-consuming. He has too little time for sustained thought, for the demands upon him outmatch his capacity to meet them. Few Congressmen do many things which ought not to be done, but almost all of us leave undone things which ought to be done every day. Perhaps as a result, there is, in the words of the Book of Common Prayer, no health in us—miserable offenders that we are.

Senators are somewhat more insulated from constituent pressures than members of the House. Their larger staffs shield them from a good number of the demands that require the personal attention of a Representative. Yet members of both legislative bodies must devote a major part of their energies to constituent problems.

There are 5,673,497 registered voters in Pennsylvania out of a total population of some 11,500,000. My mail fluctuates from one thousand to ten thousand pieces a week. In an average year I receive fifteen thousand pieces of bulk mail (newspapers, magazines, reports, brochures, etc.) and 110,000 letters and postcards. Obviously, it would be physically impossible to read personally and answer any significant proportion of this flow. Much of it is repetitive, as when a lobby mounts a campaign to "snow" a legislator with pleas to enact or defeat a particular bill. Much of it requests assistance or information which can be answered adequately by staff. Some of it, alas, is full of hate and venom, signed and unsigned, printed and hand printed. A small part of it is crackpot, and another part is from schoolchildren who have been given the mistaken idea that their Congressman is a librarian. A colorful description of the mail has been given recently by Representative Clarence D. Long of Maryland:

> A letter from PRAY (Paul Revere Association, Yeomen, Inc.) predicts that the nuclear test ban will end up with "the Russians and Zionists ruling the world, all Christianity wiped out, and all wives, mothers, and daughters in the brothels of Asia, China and India." George W. ("Wake up Humanity") Adams demands that I "banish organized religion damned quick lest organized religion banish the world a hell of a lot quicker." A neighbor wants to know, "What are you clowns doing in Washington?" A 13-year-old boy asks me if I have ever taken a bribe. A woman timidly seeks help in getting veterans benefits, since she just learned that her husband, who years ago abandoned her with 10 children, had recently died after living with another woman in Brazil.[1]

From time to time, people make demands that are so extreme that many of us have the desire to follow the example of former Congressman John Steven McGroarty of California, who wrote back to a constituent:

> One of the countless drawbacks of being in Congress is that I am compelled to receive impertinent letters from a jackass like you in which you say I promised to have the Sierra Madre mountains reforested and I have been in Congress two months and haven't done it. Will you please take two running jumps and go to hell.[2]

Sometimes letters are remarkable in their senseless abuse, like the hate mail sent that fine Republican Senator, Thomas Kuchel of California, by members of the right-wing lunatic fringe, or the one sent by a citizen of Ohio to Senator Stephen Young. In a lengthy diatribe, the poison-pen artist viciously took to task, among others, welfare recipients, labor unions, the minimum wage, foreign aid, Chester Bowles, Nelson Rockefeller and Earl Warren. Young's reply was simple and to the point. "Dear Sir," the Senator wrote, "What else is new?"[3]

The volume of the mail, as well as the importance attached to it both by members of Congress and constituents, is what strikes the new legislator first, last and always. Of the twenty-five or so people on my staff, each and every one of them is concerned with the mail in one phase or another, half a dozen are preparing letters for my signature, and about a dozen spend their entire working day coping with it.

As Mayor of Philadelphia I personally read, approved and signed almost everything that went out of my office over my signature. After one week in the Senate I made the administrative decision that since I would have to rely on the judgment of my staff to screen my mail for me, I would give them virtually complete responsibility for processing the mail and restrict my own mail-reading to what was obviously and absolutely necessary. This is the way it still works.

The mail is opened and sorted into categories. Volume mail on major issues, those on which fifty to a hundred letters come in every week, is answered by form letters on robotypers. Robo machines are semiautomated electric typewriters which will type a form letter at the press of a button. There is a newer, more expensive model which is fully automated. The robos will produce hundreds of perfectly typed letters in an afternoon; the super-robos will produce thousands of letters all night, while the staff and the Senator sleep! And the beauty of it is that only a real expert can tell a robotyped letter and signature from one personally dictated and signed.

These machines are used to cope with a large percentage of the mail, from half to two-thirds of it. The form letters used must be kept up to date as the legislation to which they pertain changes status in Congress or the problem to which they refer is resolved or dropped or forgotten. I rarely, if ever, write the form letter, but I do edit, change and then approve the draft prepared for me by the staff member most familiar with the subject and area of concern. Occasionally a letter I have personally dictated will be adapted or used as a robo form.

Additionally, dozens and dozens of so-called form letters (the distinction is almost meaningless nowadays) are prepared to answer mail which comes in dribs and drabs throughout the session —not enough, in other words, to warrant a mechanized operation. These are hand-typed by secretaries after they have been opened, read and marked in the mail process to designate their category: "education—pro"; "Bible reading—con"; "general views—for schoolchildren"; "Lithuanian Independence"; and so on. More than one hundred form letters are used in an average session of Congress, perhaps half of them prepared for "robo." These forms and "robos" are used to answer 80 to 90 percent of the mail.

That remaining 10 or 20 percent of the mail, however, takes as much or more time than all the rest put together. These are the letters which require individually prepared and hand-typed responses, as much because of who writes them as because of what they say. This mail is distributed among the professional or executive staff members, and may require more than just information or expertise. It may raise questions of policy or action to be taken; it may lead to a cable to the consul's office in Tegucigalpa or the drafting of new legislation; it may require a message of greeting or a picture and a biography. Whatever it requires or leads to, individual attention and time are necessary. Some of it is relatively routine and can be supervised and approved by my office manager. But a good deal of it is not routine and must be handled by those assistants, legislative and administrative, who work directly and fairly constantly with me, who thoroughly understand and can explicate my views, and who participate in the decision-making process. And while I can personally approve, and do, all form letters, I cannot take the time to read the hundreds of letters turned out each week by my top assistants. But I have perhaps the best staff on Capitol Hill and I trust its members implicitly. In seven years of dealing with my mail, they have never made a serious blunder and the minor mistakes could be counted on one's fingers. I am their willing captive.

In an average week I personally read and sign perhaps fifty letters.

How does the rest of the mail get signed? There is still another gadget widely used on the Hill for coping with this problem. I have one right in my own office, and it cost me $1,200 out of clerk-hire—i.e., my office allotment.

My signature is reproduced, or forged if you will, to practically all my letters by a device known as an "autopen"—a wonderful product of automation which saves precious hours each week. There are three forged signatures. Most answers get the formal "Joseph S. Clark." Politicians who are not intimate get "Joe Clark." Friends get "Joe," as do a fair number who are not friends but call me "Joe" when they write.

If this sounds disheartening to all those good people who write their Congressman, and want their views to be known to their Congressman, it is not meant to be, and should not.

First of all, the constituent's views are counted, noted and registered. I receive a monthly mail report informing me of the number of people who wrote and what they wrote about. I know that ten thousand Pennsylvanians wrote to me this year asking me to support federal aid to private schools, and the fact that I did not read each and every one of their letters does not make their position count for less. At the same time, the reply they received is an accurate account of my position on the subject of interest to them, very possibly in my own words. If I did not dictate the letter myself, the draft that was prepared for me in all likelihood included language I used in discussing this legislation in committee, or on the Senate floor, or in a speech, or in a staff meeting. Moreover, the staff members who have actually read the mail represent to me with objectivity and clarity the views and attitudes expressed in it on every issue under discussion. So in the end, the mail does what it is intended to do, and I make my decisions fully aware of that intention.

How much attention do I pay to my legislative mail? Some, but not much. It is useful as an indication of how certain groups of constituents feel, but to rely on it as an accurate guide to opinion would be folly. On the whole, mail is more trouble than it is worth as a reflection of public opinion. Public sentiment can be more accurately checked by reading the newspapers, talking or corresponding with political and leadership groups and conducting or following public opinion polls.

Many Senators and some Representatives follow the procedures respecting mail just outlined either from necessity, if they are from populous states or districts full of letter-writers, or, anyway, from a desire to save time for more important official duties.

Some Senators, particularly those from small states, and most House members read all their mail and personally sign all the answers. Those who follow this procedure condemn themselves to devoting several hours each day to their correspondence.

Although comparatively few citizens, out of a staggering potential in a large district or state, come to see their Representative or Senator, many do—particularly if they live fairly close by. There are always more visitors seeking to shake hands or chat with their Congressman than he can possibly find time to see. Especially during vacation periods, whole families flock to Washington, swarming through the Capitol and calling legislators off the floor of the two chambers or "just dropping in" at the office to be recognized by the men who represent them on Capitol Hill.

Despite the time factor, the effects of face-to-face meetings with constituents are often rewarding. There is real satisfaction in discussing current issues such as disarmament, Congressional reform or educational needs with the student and civic groups that visit with me. It often clarifies thinking to talk with Pennsylvania businessmen and labor leaders about issues with which they are concerned. There are also, however, the daily instances of being collared by constituents whose chief purpose is to say "Hello," usually with the added good news that they voted for me and I haven't done anything for them lately.

The difficulty is that there are only twenty-four hours in a day. As a result of these persistent demands from one's constituency, the Congressman has become in large part a delegate responsible for rendering personal service. One former member of the House expressed this aspect of the Congressman's role accurately when he said:

> A Congressman has become an expanded messenger boy, an employment agency, getter-out of the Navy, Army, and Marines, a wardheeler, a wound healer, trouble shooter, law explainer, bill finder, issue translator, resolution interpreter, controversy-oil-pourer, glad hand extender, business promoter, veterans affairs adjuster, ex-serviceman's champion, watchdog for the underdog, sympathizer for the upperdog, kisser of babies, recoverer of lost baggage, soberer of delegates, adjuster for traffic violations and voters straying into the toils of the law, binderup of broken hearts, financial wet nurse, a good samaritan, contributor to good causes, cornerstone layer, public building and bridge dedicator and ship christener.[4]

Here again the staff is helpful, both as a screen and as properly trained and qualified representatives of the Member himself. The visitor whose primary purpose is to meet or greet the Congressman may very well be disappointed if he doesn't get to see him "in person." But those who want something done can usually be satisfied with efficient and courteous treatment from a staff expert experienced in dealing with such problems. A surprising number of people drop by my office just to get passes for the House and Senate gallery, or tourist information, or just to touch base with their home-state Senator without asking or expecting to see me or anyone else. They sometimes leave notes. More frequently they tell my receptionist to "just say hello." But there are always enough visitors, singly and in groups, to keep me busy greeting people all day long if I chose to do so.

The choice varies among members of Congress. A few may see all visitors, even take many of them to lunch or on personally conducted tours of the Capitol. Most see as many as they feel they can. A few Senators—Paul Douglas and Hubert Humphrey among them—have given themselves a daily quota which they usually meet.

The reason a Congressman spends so much time on these routine tasks is largely that he is gregarious and also that he is a politician. The Congressman thinks, with good reason, that proper performance in his contacts with constituents will help him win re-election. The birthday and condolence letters to constituents, the copies of the government publication, *Child Care*, that are sent to new mothers, the research materials that are mailed to high school students, the endless congratulatory notes to those who distinguish themselves back home, all constitute part of a continuous selling job. The Congressman is always trying to impress upon his electorate not only his name, which is more difficult than may appear at first glance, but also the idea that he is faithfully servicing their individual needs and forwarding their individual aspirations. The better these jobs are carried out, the more leeway he has when it comes to the business of legislation.

While a Congressman is rarely called upon to give advice to the lovelorn, it is extraordinary how often he acts as a father confessor to his constituents. "Please listen to my story and tell me what to do" comes in the mail every day and over the phone several times a week, and often in the evening or over the weekend when one is trying to get away from it all for a little relaxation or sleep.

Some of the personal services are vital to the citizen who suffers injustice or undue delay at the hands of the executive bureaucracy. Rules and procedures of executive departments lead to injustices to individuals more frequently than one might think. Here the Congressman or his staff must intervene in an effort to humanize what is inevitably a hardened bureaucratic process.

A goodly portion of the work that comes to my offices consists of "cases," requests for a wide variety of services requiring me to go to bat for citizens with the administrative agencies of the federal government. Not all the requests are valid, but many are.

The very knowledge by executive officials that some Congressman is sure to look into a matter affecting his constituents acts as a healthy check against bureaucratic indifference or arrogance. Congress performs a useful function in acting as errand boy, correspondent and father confessor.

The mail and the visitors have to fit into a schedule. And so do a good many other things. Here is Congressman Long's description of his schedule:

> My "rubber-chicken" calendar for a not untypical week included the following: Addressed students of three high schools visiting the House floor, veterans groups from two counties, officers club in Army Chemical Center, and civil-defense officials of seven states; attended meeting of 13th District Community Council, and various meetings on urban renewal, alcoholism, and relocation of a post office; attended a bar mitzvah, two bull roasts, and dedication of a school; went to a Democratic club dinner, a political cocktail party and dinner for a visiting Indian industrialist.
>
> This routine—on top of legislative and administrative work—goes on seven days and five nights a week, except in July and August. Holidays are busiest. On July 4, I marched in four parades, smiled at 200,000 people, spoke to 5,000 more in the evening, attended a party, drove 100 miles.[5]

My own typical schedule for one day would go something like this:

Up by seven, skim the *Congressional Record*, read the Washington *Post*, breakfast, off to work by eight, walking the first mile, then picking up my secretary and a cab, reading *New York Times* and sometimes dictating a letter or two en route; arrive at office 8:30, read Philadelphia *Inquirer*; read testimony to be presented at ten-o'clock committee hearing or start on "incoming" box; go over day's schedule with secretary; staff meeting at 9:00, giving assignments, hearing reports, discussing advance schedule for speeches, appearances, etc; committee meeting 10:00-12:00, sometimes shuttling back and forth between two, occasionally three, committee hearings scheduled simultaneously; lunch with journalist, official of executive branch, members of Congress, staff, constituents, or—rarely—family and friends; check Senate floor, perhaps insertion in record or brief "morning hour" remarks, put name on list for speech later in day, talk with other Senators and Majority Leader about various problems and pending legislation; thirty-minute rest or nap; seclusion in private Capitol office (first obtained through seniority in 1963) to read reports, memos, studies, or perhaps to write; to Senate floor to participate in debate, offer amendments, make speech; radio or television program or press interviews; return to Senate Office Building office around 5:00 for desk and paper work, individual meetings with staff members, visitors, Pennsylvania politicians until 6:30; home to bathe and change for dinner, perhaps at home but more likely with my wife at an embassy, a colleague's, an official function, a Cabinet officer's or, occasionally, just a friend's; where in each case almost always I pick up something worth knowing and meet under informal circumstances people who contribute to my education. Weekends are frequently interrupted by politics, speeches, visits from constituents; but we keep a good part of them to ourselves for tennis, reading, writing and fun with friends.

During the course of the day I will have received a hundred phone calls, ten of which I may have picked up; phoned my secretary and administrative and legislative assistants from the Capitol several times each; talked to my Philadelphia office; and talked with my wife to check on our engagements and schedule.

Almost every Friday afternoon we go back to Philadelphia by train in time for dinner, getting some paper work done en route. Most Monday mornings I come back to Washington on the morning Congressional, arriving at the office at 10:30. But if there is a committee meeting or early Monday morning appointment, I get up at 6:30, take a commuter train to Thirtieth Street Station, then a taxi to the airport for a plane that gets me to the office by 9:00.

All of this takes time—lots of time. Where does the member of Congress find it—even enough time to do a small part of all this?

The answer is that he has to. He must order his life with rigorous self-discipline. And he must hire the best staff he can get on the rather generous allowances given to him for this purpose and then delegate every nonessential and many fairly important duties to his qualified assistants instead of trying to do it all himself. When he has accomplished this task, he should be well on the way to becoming an effective Representative or Senator.

In a recently published study of the Congress, Charles L. Clapp notes the common complaint of Congressmen that they lack time to perform their job, especially the legislative functions, which should constitute their primary responsibility.[6]

The difficulty of the time factor is compounded by the widely held belief that legislative work is not particularly noticed or appreciated by the constituents, and that it does less to help the Congressman get re-elected than "bringing home the bacon"—providing service to constituents—and good public relations.

This is perhaps less true of the Senate than the House, but it is all too true. Yet the legislative work must be done, and it becomes more complex and more crucial with each passing year. The way out of this dilemma for most Congressmen is to seek refuge in specialization, to place heavy reliance on the committee system, and to go along with the recommendations of senior colleagues or the leadership on matters on which he is not an expert.

In the House some members get two major committee assignments, more only one. In the Senate each Senator gets at least two legislative committee assignments, and sometimes three or four major ones.

After he gets his committee assignment (and he may be lucky enough or smart enough—i.e., play his cards right with the ruling clique—to get the committee of his first choice, his first term), the Congressman is encouraged by his chairman and senior colleagues to select one or two aspects of the committee's work in which to become expert. Then, as Clapp puts it:

> The emphasis on specialization simplifies significantly the task of the representative. Colleagues turn to him for aid in determining their own position on legislative matters which arise within his field of competence; he, in turn, settles on one or two trusted colleagues on each committee to whom he can turn for clarification or advice regarding proposals falling within their committee's jurisdiction.[7]

Useful, and even necessary, as this may be, the practice has some questionable consequences. In matters vital to the national interest, including defense, the vast majority of Congressmen must rely on the judgment of a handful of other members without really understanding how or why those judgments were made. Here is the observation of a House member on the subject:

> This matter of the budget, especially the defense budget, and the whole area of executive oversight is a very difficult one. . . . There is a tendency for the average member to throw up his hands in handling such matters. There is also a haunting fear if we vote to cut certain phases of the program we may be hampering national defense.[8]

Despite the endless pieties in Congress about balancing the budget and cutting expenditures, the Defense budget—the single biggest expenditure in the world, by our or any other government—sails through Congress with very little trouble and less floor discussion, much as the executive branch requests it. In the Senate in 1963 it was passed in two hours. In fact, in recent years, the executive branch has had to refuse to spend enormous sums added to the budget by Congress—for nuclear carriers and nuclear planes—which the Secretary of Defense and the President didn't even want.

"Congress in its committee rooms is Congress at work," Woodrow Wilson wrote, in 1885, and this statement is more true today than it was then. It is in the committee room that the Congressman spends a good deal of his time, and there the real legislative work is done.

Thousands of bills are introduced each session. Some Representatives introduce a great many; some introduce none. The fact that he introduces a bill does not necessarily mean the Representative is committed to it; he may be doing it at the request of constituents, an interest group or the executive branch of the government. On the other hand, under the House system a member will often introduce a bill identical to one already introduced by another, particularly if it is a major administration legislative program—an education bill or a civil rights bill—to demonstrate his support for the legislation. Thus a hundred identical bills may be introduced in the House. In the Senate members are permitted to cosponsor each other's bills to avoid duplication. Many bills introduced in the Senate will have ten, twenty or even fifty cosponsors from both sides of the aisle.

All bills are referred to the appropriate legislative committee—that is, the committee having jurisdiction over the area covered by the bill. There are sometimes jurisdictional disputes, and a bill may then have to pass through more than one committee before passage. In addition, after passage, an appropriation must often be obtained before its provisions can become effective. The Communications Satellite bill, for example, went to the Commerce, Space, and Foreign Relations Committees. Thereafter the Appropriations Committees had to agree on the amount to be expended.

Most of the bills on which the committees actually hold hearings are those sent down to the Hill by the administration, those introduced by the chairman of the committee, those introduced by senior ranking members and those sponsored by a large number of members. Occasionally an individual Senator's bill may become law, as when he fathers the idea for a brand-new program or concept such as the Fulbright Scholarship Program, but this does not happen very often.

When I ran for the Senate the first time, I took a look at my incumbent opponent's record and saw that no legislation of any importance bore his name. I went up hill and down dale in Pennsylvania calling this dereliction of duty to the attention of the people of Pennsylvania. And while I was able to get my name on some rather important legislation in my first term in the Senate, I am not sure, knowing what I know now, that I should have said what I did say during that campaign.

I spend more hours in committee meetings than I do on the floor of the Senate. So does everyone else. In the House, where the rules for floor procedure leave little time for debate on legislation, the Congressman can do little more than vote yes or no on the legislation. The House has a rule limiting debate on amendments to five minutes; total time of debate is often limited by the Rules Committee. In the Senate, where unlimited debate prevails, the individual Senators can offer as many amendments as they wish and obtain roll-call votes on them.

When the two houses have passed bills on the same subject which are not identical, meetings are held by representatives of both parties in each House, known as Conference Committees, to iron out the differences in the bills and report an agreed version back to the two houses—or, occasionally, to report that they can't agree. These final steps of the legislative process are very important. Conference Committees are sometimes referred to as the "third house," for while they cannot initiate proposals contained in either the House or Senate versions of the legislation they frequently agree to a compromise which bears little relation to either bill sent to conference.

In 1946, as a part of the Congressional Reorganization Act, Congress passed the Regulation of Lobbying Title requiring the registration of those who seek to influence legislation. By 1963, some 6,500 lobbyists had so registered. This is a rough index of the pluralistic nature of our society. Some of these names, of course, represent duplication. Still others represent organizations whose concerns are quite narrow. A very large number, however, maintain constant vigilance over not only that part of the work of Congress which concerns them but, with varying degrees of concern, most of the major bills.

There was a time when the economy of Pennsylvania meant coal, steel, railroads and farms, and the task of a Senator from the Commonwealth was primarily to concern himself with their well-being. Long before the lobbies were registered these "interests" were amply represented in Washington. But now the economy of Pennsylvania has become so complex and diversified that so simplistic a conception of Senatorial duties is no longer possible. And this is true of most other states in the Union, small as well as large.

The member of Congress, as part of his extra-legislative duties, must serve as a kind of lobbyist himself—a connecting link between government and a wide variety of delegations, groups and interests that have influence in his state or district. In one respect, this is just good politics, but in a more inclusive sense it is one of the reasons why the Congressman is in Washington. Although he cannot always give complete satisfaction and although he sometimes gets annoyed by intemperate demands from vested interests with political muscle back home, he must always be available, ready to lend an attentive ear to almost any problem.

Naturally, delegations visit with me, talk about their problems and suggest how I might help. The result is nearly always to teach me something important and new. In May, 1963, for example, I lunched with Pennsylvania shoe manufacturers, who complained, with some justice, about foreign competition. The next day I was descended upon by a delegation of machinists from a York union, who wanted the government to purchase hydroelectric turbines from their employer to insure their continued employment. Several days later I met delegates of the Pennsylvania Chamber of Commerce, who were unhappy about the small number of defense contracts in the state.

The following week, after requests from city officials and civic groups, I introduced a bill in the Senate to authorize a World's Fair in Philadelphia in 1976 and made, I suspect, a somewhat corny speech in its behalf.

Valuable time and energy, which might otherwise be devoted to legislation, is spent by both the Congressman and his staff in taking care of this flood of organized constituent requests. Yet rarely are the demands of the lobbies entirely unreasonable. Usually, they present a point of view which should be considered in making up one's mind how to act. When the demand is unreasonable, it is more often based on ignorance of the countervailing arguments than on an arbitrary insistence on a point of view known to be untenable.

The word "lobby" has an unnecessarily evil connotation. It is true that some pressure groups "put the arm" on a Congressman, particularly if they have supported him during his campaigns. It is also true that occasionally a lobbyist attempts to wine and dine a Congressman whose support is needed. Certain Congressmen are known as being willing "clients" of the military, of defense contractors, of the AFL-CIO or of the U.S. Chamber of Commerce. The airlines, the railroads, the railroad brotherhoods, the highway lobby, among many others, are active indeed in Washington. But on the whole the direct influence of lobbies on the Congress is not so great as on the average state legislature. While an individual Congressman here and there may be a virtual spokesman for a lobby's point of view, this may be due as much to ideological coincidence as to any dirty work afoot.

This is not to say that lobbies cannot be influential. They can be, but usually they achieve what they want as one part or aspect of a tide or movement that includes a great many people. For example, the savings and loan institutions wanted a change in the House-passed tax bill of 1961 to eliminate the withholding tax on interest, and they got the change they wanted; but they also had the support of a vast—and misleading—newspaper campaign which brought over sixty thousand letters to my office in support of their position. I voted against eliminating the provision anyway, but most Senators, who had received a proportionate amount of similar mail, did not. They did so not because the savings and loan lobby was for the change, but because so many of their constituents seemed to be also.

There is no doubt that many of the lobbies have made influential friends in high places. But the Congress is too large, unwieldy and diverse to be pushed around often even by a very powerful single interest. There are a few rotten apples in the Congressional barrel, as there are everywhere else; but influence-peddling in government, despite the disclosures of the Bobby

Baker case, has been overrated. I do not defend either the lobbies or any of my colleagues for behavior which may be unethical and is certainly sometimes irresponsible, but the relationship between a member of Congress and a lobby—from a lunch to a campaign contribution—is, more often than not, perfectly above-board and legitimate.

Most of the larger and well-organized lobbies have legislative staffs of their own, including in many cases excellent lawyers, well-trained economists, statisticians and the like. It is safe to say that the AFL-CIO and the Teamsters' International know more about a complicated piece of labor legislation than the committee members who worked on and drafted the bill; and that the American Medical Association lobbyists know as much about all the different legislative approaches to the problem of health care for the aged as the White House staff.

In this, the lobbyists serve a particularly useful function. Their fine-tooth-comb study of a bill may reveal "sleepers" in the legislation of which most members have not been aware, or about which they did not understand the far-reaching and long-range implications.

When a committe chairman reports to the floor a hundred-page housing bill or a 175-page tax bill, the average Congressman will not undertake to study every line of the bill. The interested and affected lobbies will, however, and the axes they have to grind will bring to the surface issues helpful both to those who wish to support their position and those who oppose it.

In sum, the lobbies perform a useful educational function for most Congressmen. But like other experts they should be kept on tap and not on top.

A positive responsibility of Congress as an institution and of Congressmen as individuals is to keep the general public informed about the business of the nation. This duty applies to the country at large for the institution and to his own constituents for the individual Congressman. It is performed in many ways.

The legislative functions of Congress have important educational aspects. So does the oversight function, of which more hereafter. The publicity attendant on the introduction of a bill, the public hearings before committees both legislative and investigatory, committee reports, floor debate and the daily publication of the *Congressional Record* are all methods by which Congress, the institution, keeps the public informed.

So long as the educational work of the institution is done in committee it is done fairly well. There are exceptions where committee members browbeat witnesses, where witnesses drone on with little to contribute, where reports are badly prepared, where, in the case of investigations, one wonders why they were ever started. But on the whole a Congressional hearing or committee report is a mine of useful information to those who seek to be informed.

The late Senator Estes Kefauver's reputation was made and will long survive in history for his educational efforts. He was the first to turn the spotlight on the connections between interstate and international gangsters and crooked local politicians. Through his efforts a score of law enforcement agencies bestirred themselves and sent a hundred crooks to jail. The efforts of the Antimonopoly Subcommittee of the Judiciary Committee of the Senate, which he chaired, was responsible for more vigorous prosecution of the antitrust laws, including the conviction of top officials of the General Electric Company, Westinghouse and others for conspiring to fix prices. It also collected the data necessary to push to passage the Drug Act of 1962 after the country became aroused over the Thalidomide scandal.

Senator Henry Jackson's Subcommittee on National Security Organization has made a valuable contribution. So have Senator Humphrey's Subcommittee on Disarmament, Senator Paul Douglas' hearings on the Truth in Lending Bill, Senator Eugene McCarthy's Special Committee on Unemployment of 1959-60, and Senator Pat McNamara's Special Committee on Problems of the Aging.

The Joint Economic Committee annually conducts educational hearings on the various matters raised by the President's Economic Report under the alternative chairmanship of Senator Douglas and Congressman Wright Patman of Texas.

On the House side, the Subcommittee on Government Information chaired by Representative John Moss of California has made a useful contribution through hearings on the knotty problem of how far the public's "right to know" extends as against the need for keeping secret information which might aid a potential enemy.

While some of these Congressional hearings are conducted on specific bills and are intended as a preliminary to direct legislative action, most of them are not. Their primary purpose is educational, i.e., to inform the public of conditions which exist in the hope that efforts to remedy abuses will result.

But the wearisome and irrelevant talk on the floor of the Senate contributes little to the job of education. Few qualified observers refer to the Senate today as "the greatest deliberative body in the world" without a twinkle in the eye. And while the House has a strictly enforced rule of germaneness and a time limitation on speeches, there are few dedicated readers of the record of its proceedings. In fact, there are those who consider the *Congressional Record* one of our more comic magazines.

This is not to say that debate does not sometimes rise to high levels, particularly in the short, sharp clash of minds in colloquy just before a controversial bill goes to the vote. It does. But these occasions are small oases in a desert of tediousness.

The educational function of the individual Congressman is different. In order to educate, he must communicate off the floor and out of committee. One difficulty with some Congressmen, it must be admitted, is that they often attempt to communicate when they have nothing to say. This has resulted in those devastating reprints from the *Congressional Record* appearing from time to time in *The New Yorker* under the heading "Wind on Capitol Hill." It has also made the Congressman the butt of many a cartoon, Lichty's "Senator Snort" being the prototype.

All Congressmen will periodically have a message they want to get across to the voters back home. There are a number of ways of doing this. Correspondence, newsletters, speeches on and off the floor, press releases, radio and television broadcasts are the media every Congressman uses. And occasions frequently will arise where reporters will seek out a Congressman to elicit his views on a particular subject on which he is thought to have some special competence.

It is a rare Congressman who is not anxious to have his thoughts and actions reported in all areas of the communications media. All things considered, the coverage is good; yet there are conspicuous failings. Nobody has stated them better than the late Clem Miller, until his death Representative from the First California District, in his newsletters, published in 1962 under the title *Member of the House*.[9]

Congressman Miller pointed out that major stories are sometimes not covered at all. For example, on one occasion the chairman of the House Rules Committee tried to chastise a Congressman for being critical of him on a radio broadcast. As a result, the subsurface feud between Northern Democrats and the Rules Committee broke into the open. The incident might well have been heralded as an historic turning point in the development of the House. "Yet," Mr. Miller wrote, "there was not a line, *not a line*, of this 'effort to censure' in the newspaper the following day. A complete blackout . . . So concerned is the press with the surface events of the day that the meaning of life in Washington is many times all but obscured or actually distorted beyond resemblance."

The dilemma of the Congressman is obvious. "If the press did not report Congress," Mr. Miller said, "Congress could hardly function. If the sound of congressional voices carried no farther than the bare walls of the Chambers, Congress could disband. We know this; it is brought home to us every day. Reporters appear very aware of their powers. . . . This suggests a basic rivalry between the press corps and Congressmen."

One difficulty is that, since the press operates under the constant pressure of meeting a deadline, the reporters are tempted to think in clichés and to write slogans. Therefore they prefer to have Congressmen do likewise. The press, as a rule, has no time to listen or discuss and, on occasion, not even the time to think. The result is an inevitable distortion that comes from oversimplification and compression. Moreover, most of the trouble is not with the reporters. It is with the editors and publishers back home. Too often they reflect an ill-informed attitude toward national affairs. Too often they present biased news coverage because their editorial policy is partisan. The pernicious influence, conscious and subconscious, of advertisers on editors and broadcasters may also be a real evil.

The wide variety of ability and performance of both reporters and the publications they work for should be stressed. They range all the way from superlatively good to pretty pathetic. An astute Congressman will promote his relations with the former and hope the latter will let him alone.

However good the press coverage in Washington may be, the important thing to the member of Congress is what gets printed and reported on TV and radio back home in his district. Copy that is written and filed but never appears is not much help. Most members of Congress, therefore, establish direct contact with the papers in their district, phoning and wiring news of contracts, postmaster nominations, awards, hospital grants and so on. This purely local news will receive more play in the local press, particularly the smaller papers and the weekly press, than some major statement of policy on a grave national issue. I have made long speeches in the Senate on disarmament, civil rights and the manpower revolution which inspired either a few paragraphs from the wire services or nothing at all in many a paper with less than 25,000 circulation in Pennsylvania. But when I have forwarded the announcement of a new post office or a million-dollar contract award, I have been blessed with streamer headlines, even pictures, and once a special box on the front page of the Pottstown *Mercury* headed, "Thank You, Senator!" And, usually, I had little, if anything, to do with the award.

Many Congressmen write newsletters to their constituents which are released to the press and appear as a regular column in local papers, again primarily in weeklies and smaller papers.

Press releases—the well-known Washington handout—are legion from all offices in the Capitol, and while the metropolitan press and individual reporters may look down on them, or consider them worth only a paragraph or two, many papers will print them, especially if they favor the member's politics. Because of the time factor, the press release is not much good for spot news, but can be useful for a weekend story and as background for future stories on the same subject.

There is a radio and TV gallery just above the chamber floor in both houses where tapes are made for later broadcast. The Congressman interested in his educational role, or his administrative assistant acting on his behalf, will solicit opportunities to use the gallery when he has something worth saying. And outside the doors of each chamber lurk daily the portable-tape-recording radio reporters anxious for anything, or almost anything, a Congressman wants to say in one minute about issues pending in committee or on the floor. This is sold as spot news for the local stations back home on a syndicated basis outside the network systems. The Congressman will do well to patronize them.

For radio and TV most members of Congress also provide, as with the newsletter, special services of their own, most often regularly produced programs or reports to be carried on local radio and television stations. There are TV and radio studios in the basement of both the House and the Senate where for a nominal charge tapes can be cut and mailed home. Since 1959 my Republican Senatorial colleague, Hugh Scott, and I have, every two weeks during the session, appeared on a half-hour TV program, "Your Senators' Report," to the people of Pennsylvania. For political reasons we are off the air whenever one of us is up for re-election.

Senator Scott and I believe the program has a dual value. It helps educate our constituents in the issues and controversies of the day, and it gives a platform from which to enunciate our respective party and personal positions on those issues. We believe it helps us as Senators to play a positive role in national affairs.

There are, then, innumerable ways in which a Congressman can utilize the media of communications both to educate his constituents and, in that ghastly Madison Avenue phrase, "project his image." The media are not perfect. But they are very good. How skillfully a Congressman uses them will have a real bearing not only on his chances of surviving but on the contribution he will make to the public performance of the United States Congress.

There is nothing self-evident about the proper role of Congress. But it is clearly high time that the Congress makes the effort to figure out what it is doing. Perhaps its representative function has been carried out in the best possible manner. Certainly as a personal representative of his constituents, a mediator between governmental bureaucracy and the rank-and-file citizen, a case worker or errand boy for the folks in his state or district, the Congressman today performs indispensable service. And it is service that cannot be done by any other agency of the federal government.*

As an educator and leader of his constituents the performance is spottier. Some do, some don't perform the task well. But when we deal with Congress in its relationships with the executive there is real difficulty. The problems here are twofold: first, how can Congress keep a watchful eye on the operating conduct of the executive departments and agencies without interfering in day-

* Representative Henry S. Reuss has recently suggested that we institute a new type of Administrative Counsel who would handle many of the service functions of Congressmen. The Ombudsman, as he is called in the Scandinavian countries, deals primarily with constituent problems with the bureaucracy, thus allowing Members to spend more time on the study of legislation. See *Congressional Record*, July 16, 1963 (daily ed.), p. 12067

to-day administration and without usurping executive functions; and second, how can Congress responsibly participate in the formulation and consideration of national policy?

Congressmen must wear two somewhat different sets of lenses in viewing their responsibilities. They have to look to their states or districts, since they have the duty of representing the people back home. But they have also to look to the nation and its needs, which are not always identical with the sum of the needs of the separate states and districts. In this second capacity, they must work hand in hand with policy makers in the executive branch, enacting legislation and checking on its administration, in the interests not of diverse and separate constituencies but rather of the general public.

V

TUG OF WAR WITH THE WHITE HOUSE

All Presidents have to deal with the Congress in one way or another. There has developed over the years of our history a tug of war between the executive and legislative branches.

Our schoolday maxim of the marvel of checks and balances, how each branch of government can go so far and no further without colliding with the restraining influence of another branch, is a cheerful, but defective, account of our system. The happy equilibrium of the executive, legislative and judicial powers is as faulty a theory as Adam Smith's doctrine that economic man, each pursuing his own self-interest, is guided to the general welfare by an invisible hand.

The facts are that our politics have evolved continuously from the birth of our Constitution and that each step in the process has had its dramatic effect on the separated and balanced powers the framers of the Constitution created. The result today is substantially different from what they contemplated.

The issues which have divided us have been to some extent ideological. But the debate has more often than not been translated into institutional collisions.

The executive-legislative tug of war is reflected in our political history and has its origin deep in our political system. The President is the sole spokesman of all the people. The Congress *in toto* is supposed to represent all the people, but in fact does not. The national outlook of a President in the White House is pitted against the gerrymandered views, enshrined in the Constitution, of Senators from fifty states of vastly unequal population and the parochial viewpoints of 435 Representatives from very diverse districts which command their fierce loyalty.

On the Hill this gives rise to the oft-repeated claim that the President's program is not widely supported by the public, the evidence usually being the Congressman's mail from his district, his contacts and visits back home and, in many cases, his continued re-election despite his opposition to the President's program. This view gives pockets of selective, and on the whole negative, mail equal or greater weight than scientifically conducted national public opinion polls. It conveniently ignores the wide and unequal disparities of population from district to district, and the important fact that those lowest on the economic ladder (and most directly affected by government programs for the domestic welfare) are the least likely to write their Congressman—and, alas, least likely to vote except in Presidential elections.

The conservative press is prone to support the view from the Hill. The unreliable habit of gauging popular sentiment by checking Congressional offices for a mail count persists in all segments of the press. The post-Easter-recess story on what "the folks back home" think of the President's program is shopworn, but universal. This exchange at President Kennedy's press conference on April 24, 1963, sums up the problem:

QUESTION: Mr. President, this has to do with the *Wall Street Journal* survey on grass-roots apathy which has just been published. Do you agree, sir, that such apathy exists, and if so, how do you account for it, and if it does exist, what do you plan to do about eliminating it?

THE PRESIDENT: Every April the *Wall Street Journal* writes a story on the left-hand side of the paper, reporting that Congressmen have come back and found great apathy about the President's programs.

Some months later the *Wall Street Journal* printed an editorial piece by Alan Otten opposing Congressional reform on the grounds that the Congress was accurately reflecting public opinion and correctly holding up the President's program because the mail indicated it wasn't popular with the people back home.

In the absence of a national crisis and/or a strong President of contrary views, the Congressional view of public issues, supported by the press, is likely to prevail. The limits of the political dialogue will then be set by Congress around those issues over which it has the greatest control and the most to say. Since it is the power of the purse which rests with Congress, it is a natural result that "spending"—the President's budget—is the issue about which Congress is most intent. A balanced budget and federal spending have dominated the political debate and political campaigns in this country for a generation. This brings despair to every economist educated beyond the fallacies of Adam Smith and his heirs, who represent what John Kenneth Galbraith calls "the conventional wisdom." Until President Kennedy had the courage to ask for a tax cut at a time when the country was running a deficit, it was an article of political faith that all candidates for public office had to be in favor of a balanced budget. (A very few of us were willing to say publicly, "balanced for the business cycle.") President Kennedy's death is tragic for nobler reasons than that he did not live to see Congress pass his tax program. But his enlargement of the political dialogue on the issue of the government's economic policy is a legacy for which he will be long and gratefully remembered by literate economists.

Every President sees his program in terms of national needs and international commitments. But the same conservative element in Congress that controls the committees handling the budget appropriations and espouses the conventional Congressional wisdom sees these programs in terms of spending. The Congress—except in matters of national security—does not ask: What must we do? It asks: How much will it cost?

The two major responsibilities of Congress under the Constitution are the legislative function and the oversight function, i.e., making certain that legislative programs are being properly administered by the executive branch. The oversight function is performed by the Congress through both legislation and the appropriations process, the power of the purse. To shore up this strongly, indeed constitutionally, entrenched position, the Congress has added a few committees for the specific purpose of overseeing federal spending, taxes and the executive budget. These are: the Joint Economic Committee, the Joint Committee on Internal Revenue Taxation, and the Joint Committee on Reduction of Nonessential Federal Expenditures. Of these the first is necessary and important, the second is wise and useful, and the third is primarily a propaganda organ of the conservative coalition.

Oversight of the budget and the President's economic and spending programs is not to be underestimated, however. The principal difficulty at present is not that Congress has the function of reviewing the budget and the power of the purse—it should and must—but that the powers of Congress are too frequently used in an antagonistic way against the recommendations of the executive branch rather than in cooperation with it. "Let us reason together," President Johnson likes to say. But the view from the Hill is more one of recalcitrance than of reason.

To solve the problem of this legislative-executive tug of war, the Constitution gives us little guidance. It states only that all legislative powers shall be vested in a Congress and that "the executive power shall be vested in a President," who "shall take care that the laws are faithfully executed." The cliché has been that the President proposes and the Congress disposes. But even were it as simple as that, there is the further step not accounted for in the stereotype and only partly in the Constitution. How do we make certain that the executive is faithfully executing the laws passed by the Congress?

The power of the purse, the appropriations process, is our first answer. But while it sets the limit on what may be spent, and to a large degree how it may be spent, it cannot guarantee how *well* it will be spent. In our vast and complex executive structure the problems of administration go wider and deeper than mere budget-cutting.

In his famous work *Congressional Government,* written eighty years ago, a future President, Woodrow Wilson, said that it was the proper duty of the legislative branch to look diligently into the conduct of administration. "Discussed and interrogated administration," he concluded, was "the only pure and efficient type." On this there is quite general agreement. There is also general agreement that the oversight function has two main purposes: (1) seeing to it that the policy objectives agreed upon in legislation are properly carried out; and (2) preventing and uncovering malfeasance and negligence.

Collaboration between the President and Congress is difficult enough in legislating. It is even more difficult in the area where Congress must distinguish between scrutiny of the executive branch's performance and interference in administrative operations. Where much discretionary authority is delegated to the executive under broad terms of statutes, it becomes even more important for the legislative branch, on behalf of the nation, to hold the executive responsible.

Oversight, by legislative and investigating committees, through the annual appropriations process and the almost daily contact of individual Congressmen with the bureaucracy, enables Congress to maintain at least some control over what is going on in the far-flung and enormous executive branch. It has also become—in the use of the investigating committee—one of Congress' chief weapons in the rather immature but constant contest with the executive branch for power, prerogatives and public favor.

The Congressional investigating committee has developed in our day into something resembling an institution in its own right, with a domain as wide as the horizon. The House Committee on Un-American Activities and the Senate Internal Security Subcommittee are not just watchdogs of the executive branch, though they are certainly that; they are also the scourge of the individual citizen whose loyalty to his country the members of the committees may suspect. They more often make headlines than recommendations to the Congress for constructive legislation.

In recent years they have had to compete for public attention with widely publicized Congressional investigations into crime, racketeering, scandals in the broadcasting industry, defense contract awards, the price of drugs and the affairs of such assorted characters as Jimmy Hoffa, Billy Sol Estes and Joe Valachi.

Most of the latter were conducted by the Senate Government Operations Committee, which with its House counterpart has specific jurisdiction of the executive branch conduct. But so far from mere executive branch oversight have the Senate committee's operations gone that it is best known merely as the McClellan Committee (after its chairman, Senator John L. McClellan of Arkansas), or in some years as the Senate rackets committee.

The most famous investigation by this committee, of course, took place when Senator Joseph McCarthy of Wisconsin was chairman of the Subcommittee on Permanent Investigations. He held hearings, it will be recalled, which made all previous investigations and all other investigating committees seem tame and colorless indeed.

While I do not underestimate the damage to our government, our country and our people done by McCarthyism, it was only the worst example of what had frequently happened before in the legislative-executive struggle, and no different in kind from previous examples of Congressional attack on agents of the President. More than one hundred years ago the Joint Committee on the Conduct of the War, created in 1861, questioned the strategy of particular military campaigns, forced the resignation of one Cabinet officer and the firing of innumerable generals, issued eight volumes of hostile reports, and made its chief claim to fame the harassment of that most patient of all American heroes, President Abraham Lincoln.

Such aggressive threats to constitutional government and the national welfare were, no doubt, extreme. But in our time Congress has recourse more and more to the use of the investigating committee as it becomes more and more frustrated in its battle for power with the executive branch. Whether for petty or hostile purposes, the conditioned reflex of the Congress to slights imagined or real is to hold a hearing, if possible to conduct a full-scale investigation. Quite often the legitimate oversight function is used by appropriations subcommittees to embarrass and demean patriotic officials of integrity, such as Roswell Gilpatric, former Under Secretary of Defense, or to make petty use of insignificant budget details to slash a program, as when the cost of a State Department wastebasket was made the excuse to cut its representation allowances for our foreign officers abroad. Sometimes it is used to chasten an officer of the executive branch for an ill-tempered or ill-advised statement, as when the USIA budget was slashed to bits in 1957 because Arthur Larson, the administrator, made a speech in which—no doubt unwisely—he said, "Throughout the New and Fair Deals this country was in the grip of a somewhat alien philosophy imported from Europe." The Democratic majority in the House and Senate, mostly Roosevelt and Truman men, took affront. Mr. Larson, a most useful public servant, left the government shortly thereafter—but not before the important program he headed was dealt a staggering, if temporary, blow.

In these instances Congress is only suggesting an answer to the old, old question: "Who's in charge of the store?"—the answer being "Us!" But whether it is a $25 wastebasket "scandal" or a frontal attack on the entire Department of Defense, the view from the Hill of the White House is fundamentally the same: subconsciously it would like to see the executive branch helpless and dependent on Congressional largess. Consciously it knows the President is pre-eminent and commands an army so enormously large it can scarcely ever be wholly subjected to Congressional scrutiny.

Of course, not all Congresses and not all executive oversight investigations have been irresponsible. While the response of the Congress to the excesses of McCarthyism has been far from adequate in terms of improving investigative procedures and protecting the constitutional rights of witnesses, there has, with the aid of the Supreme Court, been some improvement. There is generally a heightened awareness of the importance of fair proceedings. There is in more mature Congressional circles, particularly among former governors and mayors, a tolerant understanding of the enormous difficulties of federal executive administration. While civil libertarians have no cause to roll over and go to sleep, there is in the Congress today a healthy disposition toward responsible use of the investigatory weapons of the oversight function.

Naturally, some committees perform oversight functions more responsibly than others. When conducted in a judicious atmosphere with the purpose of uncovering the facts rather than punishing the culprits, Congressional investigations of administration are indispensable for an informed and vigorous legislature. President Truman, who had much experience chairing a constructive Senate investigating committee during World War II, told the Senate in 1944, "The manner in which investigating power is exercised will largely determine the position and prestige of Congress in the future."[1] His Special Committee Investigating the National Defense Program might profitably serve as a model for the conduct of contemporary Congressional oversight committees.

There are always difficulties and risks in vigorous oversight of administration. The President's responsibility under the Constitution for the operations of the executive departments and agencies is sometimes disrupted and interfered with to the point of direct challenge. Congressional committees, which can never be held directly accountable, individually or jointly, for the performance of the executive bureaucracy, try to direct administration officials in the day-to-day management of their duties. This tendency to interfere in the details of administration should be resisted by Congress.[2] On the whole, it is not so resisted by those for whom it is most important to do so—the committee and subcommittee chairmen. Partly this is because the group of men who have the principal power of Congressional oversight are the very ones who most resent executive growth in size and power and are most anxious to keep as tight a rein as possible on the President—the conservative Congressional Establishment. These are William S. White's "true Senate types"—and one might add true House types—who regard the Presidency as a different but not a higher office.

This interference with administration can go pretty deep, to the point where it produces a direct conflict with Presidential policy. For example, one of the departments of the executive branch in 1963 decided that it would cancel certain programs being operated in Southern states on a segregated basis, and withdraw its proposals for new programs until desegregation of the program could be accomplished. The right of the executive branch to withhold federal funds from segregated activities even without specific Congressional approval is not, to most constitutional lawyers, questionable. But to a Southern Senator there are a good many questions indeed, including the basic one of whether an executive department is entitled to its budget appropriations when it makes such decisions. The Southern chairman of the appropriations subcommittee handling that agency's budget decided that its budget needed a careful and slow examination and that it was asking for all kinds of new programs of dubious merit. In a relatively brief time, the department made a new decision regarding its attitude toward the use of money in segregated programs. For face-saving purposes it remained consistent in principle while in reality accepting the merest token of integration. The Southern Senator was gracious, realistic and appeased. The program, segregated in fact, continues; the department has its budget.

The contest between Chairman Carl Vinson of the House Armed Services Committee and the Secretary of Defense, Robert McNamara, on whether the government should spend billions of dollars to produce the RS-70, a manned bomber which the Secretary of Defense considers obsolete and Chairman Vinson considers vital to the national security, has been going on for years. This was a major policy decision. Mr. Vinson has the right and duty to examine, argue against and even oppose Mr. McNamara's decision not to build these planes, but he cannot make the Secretary build them by authorizing and appropriating funds. The executive horse can be led to water, but the Congress cannot make him drink. Yet the fact that the Defense Department continues to keep the program alive through experimental research, studies, mock-ups and other devices despite its announced opposition is an indication that the Secretary of Defense understands Congressional realities which, in the absense of great tact, could hurt his program in other areas.

Some distinction has to be made between investigating the business of the administrative branch and actually attempting to conduct it. The President and his subordinates are responsible for executing policy; Congress and its committees can and should watch closely and criticize where appropriate. But neither Congress nor its committees is qualified to "run the government."

Congressional enlargement of its oversight powers to humble and even control the executive is nothing new; in fact, it is just about as old as Congress itself. Whenever the President permitted it Congress was ready to move in and exert supremacy; to try to run the country. During very long stretches of our national history we have had Congressional rather than Presidential leadership, and therefore Congressional instead of Presidential rule. But a quick survey is apt to convince us that these were the periods of our history of which we are least proud.

To a very great extent the ascendancy of Congress depends on the character, temperament and personality of the man who is President. George Washington's administration, for example, was unique in that the first President stood above the political crowd, meticulous in his interpretation of the doctrine of separation of powers as then understood. He deliberately abstained from pressuring Congress or pushing specific programs. His two principal Cabinet officers, however, had an entirely different attitude. Jefferson and Hamilton were frequently at each other's throats advocating conflicting measures before the Congress, which in a sense was a pawn over which they quarreled. The Washington years were a shakedown cruise in the relations between Congress and the executive branch.

John Adams, our second President, was a strict constructionist in his relations with Congress. Having presided over the Senate for eight years and cast many a vote to break a tie, he did not attempt to interfere with legislative discretion. In fact, he is one of only seven Presidents who never vetoed a bill—not even the iniquitous Alien and Sedition Acts which so clearly violated the Bill of Rights amendments to the Constitution.

He was concerned, however, that "the House of Representatives have discovered an incessant hankering for Executive power";[2] and he was firm in asserting the constitutional powers of the President. He was a Federalist whose party controlled both Houses during his term. Since he never tried very hard to lead the legislature, there is little evidence of an executive-legislative conflict during his term. The separation of powers doctrine was under no strain.

In 1781 Thomas Jefferson wrote John Adams a letter about the dangers of executive despotism, comparing the peril of a re-elected President to that of the Polish King. "I am not," he wrote, "a friend to a very energetic government. It is always oppressive."

Twenty-five years later John Adams' son, John Quincy Adams, had this to say about the then President of the United States, Thomas Jefferson, author of the probably unconstitutional Louisiana Purchase:

> His whole system of administration seems founded upon this principle of carrying through the legislature measures by his personal or official influence. There is a certain proportion of the members in both Houses who on every occasion of emergency have no other enquiry but what is the President's wish. These, of course, always vote accordingly. Another part adhere to him in their votes, though strongly

disapproving the measures for which they vote. A third float in uncertainty; now supporting one side of a question and now supporting the other, and eventually slinking away from the record of their votes. A fourth have the spirit even to vote against the will of their leader. . . .

Jefferson was a leader, and a strong one, who demonstrated uncanny political adroitness in dominating the Congress. He exerted influence on the selection of the Speaker and the chairmen of committees. The floor leader was dubbed Jefferson's "premier." The President took a direct hand in drafting legislation. He sailed triumphantly through two terms in the White House with Congress tucked under his arm.

In this he was more adept or luckier, or both, than many another President.

Jefferson was constantly confronted with opposition in Congress, despite the fact that his election victories had shattered the Federalists and given him majorities in both the House and the Senate. He had the "bitter choice" of permitting internal weaknesses to wreck his party or of throwing away his theories and taking full charge of the management of the legislature. Grand theory gave way to hard facts; Congress during the years 1801-8 was too fragmented to develop and enact a coherent program. The President had to move in and take charge. And so it has been ever since when Congressional action was required in the national interest.

The scales were soon to tip the other way. Jefferson was hardly out of the White House before Congress took over national leadership. The very institutions which he had used to impose his leadership now became the weapons for Presidential harassment. Henry Clay, as Speaker, used the committee system and the caucus to dominate the legislative process. John C. Calhoun was his able coleader. Webster was not far behind. The "War Hawks" confounded President Madison and forced the country into the quite unnecessary War of 1812. For the next sixteen years, under the Presidencies of Madison, Monroe and John

Quincy Adams, American government was Congressional government.

The tide turned again in 1828 with the election of Andrew Jackson to the Presidency. Jackson actually received more popular votes and more electoral votes than any of his three opponents in the election of 1824, but because he did not have a majority the choice of a President was thrown into the House of Representatives. And the last thing Congress wanted was a "strong" President of Jackson's caliber. Speaker Henry Clay engineered the victory of John Quincy Adams in the balloting in the House and then became Adams' Secretary of State. Jackson protested loudly against this "corrupt bargain" and overwhelmed Adams in the next election. Naturally, he entered the White House with a deep suspicion of Congress and all its works.

Jackson thought of the President as "the tribune of the people" and proceeded to act as such. His campaign against the "special interests" of his day and his conviction that those interests controlled Congress drove him to rough measures to fend off his opponents. When Clay, the symbol of Congressional supremacy, joined Nicholas Biddle of Philadelphia, president of the Second Bank of the United States, in securing legislation to renew the bank's charter four years before it would expire, Jackson vetoed the bill. Clay opposed Jackson in the Presidential campaign of 1832, and made the charter of the bank—which Congress did not try to pass over the President's veto—the principal issue of the campaign. Jackson was overwhelmingly re-elected and the bank died when its charter expired in 1836. This was but one example of the popularity of a strong President with the people. Jackson reigned almost supreme for eight years.

Once he was out of the way Congress reasserted its supremacy over the Presidency. With the exception of James K. Polk's four years in the White House from 1845 to 1849—most of them Mexican War years when the role of Commander in Chief enhanced Presidential powers—Congress held the upper hand until

Lincoln and the Civil War briefly restored Presidential primacy.

During this period both the Whigs and the Democrats elected Presidents who regarded themselves with humility and took very literally the Constitution's description of the substantial powers of the legislative branch. The nation's conservatives, in control of both parties, slowly but surely reduced the qualifications for the office of President. There seemed a tacit conspiracy among both proponents and opponents of slavery to refrain from sending to the White House men capable of solving the controversy which finally erupted into the Civil War.

So Van Buren, Harrison, Tyler, Taylor, Fillmore, Pierce and Buchanan abode their destined hours and went their way. It is interesting, and not insignificant, that six of those seven men—all but Taylor—had been Senators before they became President. In my view, unlike Presidents Kennedy and Johnson they always remained Senators and were hence incapable of executive and administrative leadership.

But the Presidency, because of its potential, was still a great prize. So great a prize that when the South lost it to Lincoln, a Northern man *without* Southern principles, South Carolina seceded and the war was on.

With catastrophe came another strong President. But Congress did not give up easily. Lincoln was so fearful of his own Republican party's Congress, split between radical and conservative factions, that like Jefferson sixty years before he resorted to every trick in the political book to establish and maintain executive supremacy in order to win the war and save the Union. By proclamation he increased the size of the Army and at the same time called a special session of Congress to convene three months later to ratify his actions. While Congress was out of session he issued the Emncipation Proclamation. He suspended the writ of habeas corpus and declared martial law. Fearing passage of a confisction bill that he felt unwise, he sent a proposed veto message to Congress before the bill was passed. Congress pushed through an explanatory joint resolution "interpreting" the measure in a way which met the President's objectives and enabled him to sign the bill. Without Congressional appropriations he directed the disbursement of Treasury funds. As Clinton Rossiter has put it, "Lincoln did not attempt to break down the barrier between the legislative and executive branches; he merely ignored it."[3]

The Reconstruction Congress, by imposing impossible conditions on the South, lost the peace Grant's armies had won. A hundred years later we still suffer from the folly of Thaddeus Stevens and Charles Sumner. Andrew Johnson struggled valiantly. He defended Western settlers against land speculators. He advocated tariff reduction and business "lost confidence" in him. Railroad promoters found Congress easier to deal with than the President. Bondholders were frightened at Johnson's plans for debt reduction. The Congressional party was known as "radical" because of their views on Reconstruction. But in economic as in social matters they were conservative if not reactionary. And in terms of encroachment on executive powers Congress moved further than ever before or since.

In the end Congress was too much for the President. Veto after veto was overridden. The notorious Tenure of Office Act forbade the President to remove members of his own Cabinet and other administrative officers without the consent of the Senate. Impeachment failed by one vote, thanks to the political courage of Senator Edmund Gibson Ross of Kansas.[4] Johnson served out his term, but Congress ran the country.

After Johnson came Grant and eight more years of Congressional rule. It was during his administration that an Ohio Congressman described the House of Representatives as "an auction room where more valuable considerations were disposed of under the Speaker's hammer than any other place on Earth." Sordid corruption was the order of the day in business, in finance, in local, state and national government. It permeated the halls of Congress and, in the White House, reached as close to the President as his private secretary.

But it was not the corruption of strong men who, despite their loose ethics, got things done. Grant took no initiative with the Congress. He merely reacted to problems as they arose. Samuel Eliot Morison and Henry Steele Commager in their *Growth of the American Republic* describe the Grant era as one of "Scandal and Stagnation."[5]

Some of the later Presidents fought back. Hayes got Civil Service reform under way despite a hostile Congress whose attitude was well summarized by a remark of Senator Roscoe Conkling of New York, the prototype of the machine politician of the day: "When Dr. Johnson referred to patriotism as the last refuge of a scoundrel, he ignored the enormous possibilities of the word 'reform.' "[6] The assassination of President Garfield by a disappointed job holder forced Congressional action. The Pendleton Act was passed and, to the disappointment of the spoilsmen, signed by President Arthur. It was effectively implemented by Grover Cleveland, who in addition, after a number of setbacks, finally got the Tenure of Office Act repealed, thus re-establishing some executive control over executive administration.

But by the end of his second term in 1892 Cleveland had become the prisoner of a hostile Congressional majority—part Populist, part "Silver Democrats" and part Conservative Republicans—confidently waiting for a resumption of control of the White House in the election of 1896.

Things did not improve under McKinley. While politics of the period ranged over a wide variety of subjects, foreign as well as domestic, the major Congressional achievement of his term in retrospect was to force the country into a totally unjustifiable war with Spain. It is related that Theodore Roosevelt, then Assistant Secretary of the Navy, coming out of the White House in a towering rage after the sinking of the battleship *Maine* in Havana Harbor, exploded to a friend: "Do you know what that white-livered cur up there has done? He has prepared *two* messages, one for war and one for peace and he doesn't know which one to send in."[7]

Two years later a meteoric career in that same Spanish War shot the hero of San Juan Hill, via the governorship of New York, into the Vice Presidency to get him out of the hair of conservative New York Republican politicians. An assassin's bullet did the rest, and the White House suddenly had in Theodore Roosevelt its first President capable of handling Congress on even terms since Lincoln.

Leadership with flair, plus a keen understanding of the legislative process, pushed the President's program through a Congress which viewed T. R. with a mixture of admiration and alarm. When, at the end of his seven years in the White House, he went off to Africa to shoot big game as a substitute for demolishing political opponents at home, Roosevelt could point with pride to a series of administrative and legislative achievements ranging from the acquisition of the Panama Canal Zone to the establishment of sound conservation policies and the beginnings of the regulation of business and the economy in the national interest.

Under Taft, an able man with administrative ability but no ambition to exert executive leadership, Congress moved back into control. For two years practically no legislation of importance was passed other than the protectionist Payne-Aldrich tariff act which Taft reluctantly signed. The Old Guard under the control of "Uncle Joe" Cannon in the House and Nelson Aldrich in the Senate was in command.

Yet the country was not content. The election of 1910 resulted in a Democratic-Progressive sweep. The elder La Follette and his allies made life so miserable for Aldrich he decided not to run for re-election. Under the leadership of George Norris, Speaker Cannon's autocratic powers over the House, inherited from Thomas B. Reed, were stripped from him. During Taft's last two years the anti-Old Guard coalition passed a not inconsiderate body of useful legislation, which the President signed. But it was still Congressional control.

When as a result of a Republican party split Woodrow Wilson became President in 1913, his supporters in Congress were able to reorganize the national legislature and complete the rout of the Old Guard. The major planks in the Democratic "New Freedom" platform were enacted into law before the tensions of war turned the nation's attention to foreign affairs. Many of these achievements were possible only because the progressive Senators of both parties (who were a majority of the Senate) modified the rules to prevent the minority from blocking needed legislation.

With his own men in control, Wilson mastered the system from the beginning. For five years he could do no wrong. He dealt persuasively with recalcitrant chairmen, even by-passing Speaker Champ Clark, his rival for the Democratic nomination in the long-drawn-out Baltimore Convention of 1912. The austere appearance of the ex-college president belied his not inconsiderable political skill. He utilized postmaster patronage in the interest of his legislative program as effectively as any of his predecessors.

For the first time in over a hundred years, the President addressed the Congress in person. He pleaded for party unity and it worked. When Wilson sought tariff revision, he used every tactic ever devised by a President, even to dropping in on legislative committee meetings. When the Underwood reform tariff bill received the vote of every Democratic Senator, it seemed as though the scholar turned politician had found the elusive cure for executive-legislative ills. His legislative accomplishments were impressive. In addition to the tariff, the Federal Reserve Act, the Clayton Act, the Federal Trade Commission Act and child labor legislation were a few results of Wilson's executive leadership.

But the old antagonisms between any Congress and any President were not dead. Always latent, Congressional impatience with executive leadership erupted again. When Wilson sought Congressional sanction to arm merchant vessels, the measure passed the House 403 to 14. Twelve Senators filibustered against the House bill until Congress adjourned, its session having expired. And they had their way, temporarily, despite the extraordinary statement by seventy-five Senators that they favored the measure and that it would pass the Senate "if a vote could be had."

Wilson demanded that the Senate revise its rules so that the government would no longer be rendered helpless by "a little group of willful men representing no opinion but their own." The result was the first cloture rule (Rule XXII) adopted under the leadership of Senator Thomas J. Walsh of Montana. But a more immediate result was Wilson's insistence that the power to act was his in the absence of Congressional action. And act he did. He armed the merchant ships anyway by executive order.

The power of the President, as always, grew in response to the crisis of war. Wilson defeated the effort, successful in Lincoln's day, to create a joint Congressional committee to oversee the conduct of the war. The threat of a wartime railroad strike brought about the Adamson Act and still more executive power. So many other acts increased Presidential authority in wartime it seemed as though the Congress were giving Wilson statutory authority to be a wartime dictator. "The lash, forever and eternally the lash, is laid across the legislative back. More and more we cringe," lamented Senator Jim Reed of Missouri.[8]

Almost automatically a violent reaction set in as soon as victory was in sight. The election of a Republican Congress in 1918, Wilson's unsuccessful fight for the League of Nations, its defeat in the Senate while an invalid President watched helplessly, marked a resumption of Congressional supremacy which was to continue through the administrations of Harding, Coolidge and Hoover until the days of the New Deal.

While Congress was in charge in the 1920s the rate of progressive legislation slowed down to less than a trickle. Almost all the early New Deal economic reforms were overdue *before* the Wall Street crash. Quite possibly forward-looking legislation might have prevented the entire depression. Yet the so-called Jazz Age produced practically nothing from Congress save two really bad tariff bills, a long inconclusive squabble over farm legislation and a long-delayed investigation of the Teapot Dome

Scandals, as a result of which former Senator Albert B. Fall went to jail for taking a bribe while serving as Secretary of the Interior.

The Stock Market crash of October 16, 1929 marked the beginning of the worst financial and economic collapse in the history of the country. Two years of President Hoover's term remained. Yet neither Congress nor the President did anything effective to stem the tide of disaster other than to create the Reconstruction Finance Corporation—which did do much effective work in saving some large corporations from bankruptcy. Yet banks and businesses continued to go to the wall. The election of 1932 took place in an atmosphere of crisis. Hoover was defeated. Franklin Delano Roosevelt went to the White House with Democratic majorities in both the House and the Senate pledged to support him, but on a platform which was to prove entirely inadequate to the needs of the day.

The day he was inaugurated Roosevelt closed the banks by executive order. There followed the "Hundred Days" during which the Congress of the United States in fact, if not in theory, abdicated its constitutional authority to the President to an extent unknown in peacetime and hardly rivaled during the Civil War and World War I.

The Hundred Days included some of the nation's brightest and several of its darkest. The atmosphere of panic led to much significant legislation, but under circumstances which should warn us against complacent, uncritical admiration of our institutions. "It is to be hoped that the normal balance of executive and legislative power authority may be wholly adequate to meet the unprecedented task before us," Roosevelt said in the First Inaugural. "But," he warned, "it may be that an unprecedented demand and need for undelayed action may call for temporary departure from that normal balance of public procedure." He further warned that unless Congress acted affirmatively, he would ask for "broad executive power to wage war against the emergency, as great as the power that would be given to me if we were in fact invaded by a foreign foe."

Congress was overwhelmed. Its leaders became Presidential lieutenants, participating with Cabinet members in the drafting of legislation and then marching it to a vote. Committee action was but a momentary pause. Senators and Congressmen voted for bills they had never read and of whose contents they had only the foggiest notion. An emergency banking bill was debated for forty minutes; eleven of the President's most important bills were passed with an average of three and two-thirds hours' debate.[9]

All the old Presidential tools of Jefferson, Lincoln, Theodore Roosevelt and Wilson were used. New skills and new tactics were found. Roosevelt was a man of great personal magnetism. He used his charm to the hilt. Friendly telephone calls were made. Reluctant Congressmen basked in the Presidential limelight. The courteous note was written. The warm Rooseveltian smile, the hearty handshake, the jovial wisecrack were brought into play as never before. But the stick followed the carrot. Radio fireside chats and press conferences kept reminding Congress that a tired, desperate nation would tolerate no interference with recovery—and recovery planned and directed by the President and his executive advisers. At the end of the Hundred Days, Roosevelt had sent fifteen special messages to Congress and guided fifteen major bills to enactment.[11]

There were, to be sure, many laws passed which had vigorous Congressional proponents. Senator Robert Wagner of New York had long been pressing for the National Labor Relations Act which bears his name. Senator George Norris of Nebraska was the father of the Tennessee Valley Authority. Yet even strong Congressional support for such measures would not have been enough without F.D.R. behind them.

The panic was conquered, but recovery was not just around the corner. Things were to be bad for the rest of the thirties. Roosevelt retained executive primacy with a workable Congressional majority until in 1937 he lost his fight to "pack" the

Supreme Court.* But the honeymoon was over by the end of 1934. Congressional opposition raised its head again, sometimes successfully.

Majority Congressional sentiment was, nevertheless, so tied to Presidential leadership that in 1935 the House changed its rules, increasing from 150 to 218, or a majority of the whole House, the number of signatures necessary to discharge a bill from a stubborn committee. This move simply assumed, ironically in the light of later developments, that representatives of the Presidential party in charge of the committee structure needed protection from a possible Congressional minority interest which could, under the old rule, force the House to vote on popular but unsound bills.

As the atmosphere of crisis receded, the cold war between the executive and the legislature was resumed. But the relationship has never been quite the same. From Franklin Roosevelt on, no President and no Congress could ignore the elementary fact that our economy was a national entity, no element of which could suffer for long without affecting the whole country's well-being.

In 1935 the Congress was up to its old tricks. The Senate was tied up by a filibuster on an antilynching bill. Senator Huey Long's talkathon against extending the NRA also paralyzed the Senate. F.D.R.'s victory over the veterans lobby when Congress sustained his veto of the bonus bill was narrow. The continuous strength of local, organized lobbying was again in evidence. Despite the astounding size of Roosevelt's victory in the Presidential election of 1936, the President's bid to "extend the frontiers of social progress" by a Fair Labor Standards Act bogged down in the House Rules Committee dominated by a Republican–Southern Democratic coalition. The bill never emerged during the session in which it was introduced and became law in 1938 only after another struggle with the Rules Committee and still another discharge petition. When in 1938 a new Senate filibuster on the antilynching bill

* The shift of Chief Justice Hughes and Justice Roberts in their judicial votes on New Deal legislation achieved many of the results which would have come from increasing the membership of the Court with Presidential appointees.

developed, Senator Barkley, the Majority Leader, described the rules of the Senate "as the most archaic conglomeration of contradictory decisions that ever prevailed in any parliamentary or legislative body." They still are.

The President's continued popularity with the people could no longer be translated into effective leadership of Congress. After 1938, the power to control legislation settled in the laps of Congressmen whose seats were so safe that they could not be reached by even the most stirring of Presidential voices. The effort to "purge" them failed.

Of course, with World War II, Presidential power rose again. Harry Truman's Committee on the Conduct of the War bore little relationship to the Joint Committee of Lincoln's day. But it was obvious then as now that the same electorate which could give a President a mandate could also produce a Congress which could negate that mandate, particularly when the rules and customs of the Congress were skillfully employed.

During the seven years of Harry S. Truman's Presidency, Congress was continuously off the reservation in domestic affairs. In 1946 an administration bill to increase the minimum wage passed the Senate, but died in the House Rules Committee. The Truman proposal to give home rule to the District of Columbia died in the Senate District of Columbia Committee. It was later to pass the Senate three times, only to die in the House District Committee. A filibuster killed the fair employment practices bill. Presidential recommendations on unemployment compensation, medical care and civil rights all languished, then died in committee. Even the proposed full employment bill, which was finally passed as the Employment Act of 1946, bore so little resemblance to the Presidential recommendation that the term "full employment" appears nowhere in it.

In fairness it should be noted that Congress responded well to Presidential leadership in foreign affairs, as the Marshall Plan and aid to Greece and Turkey attest; and during the Korean War (despite Congressional uproar over the removal of General

MacArthur) the Congress gave the President what he needed as Commander in Chief. But Congress was clearly both unwilling and unable to tackle domestic problems in the manner recommended by the President. Indeed, the most significant pieces of domestic legislation of the period were the Taft-Hartley Act and a tax reduction bill favoring those in high income brackets, both passed over Presidential vetoes. When President Truman confronted a Republican-controlled Congress in the summer of 1948 with the demand that it take action on the recently adopted GOP platform, the Congress came and left, with Truman's fourteen specific proposals destined to become a magnificent campaign document in the ensuing election, but never a legislative agenda taken seriously by Congress.

With the election of Dwight Eisenhower in 1952, old problems re-emerged in new forms. It is too simple to suggest that the years 1953-60 neglected many of our worst domestic problems because the Whig concept of the Presidency had returned to the White House. The President established formal liaison with Congress; he met the press frequently, if not enthusiastically. He worked constantly with the leadership in both Houses. And the platform on which he ran was a document generally suited to the needs of the country. Moreover, the politics of Presidential elections loaded the dice against those who symbolized the Congressional status quo. The country wanted some forward movement but not too much, and it wanted, very badly, peace in Korea. The President provided both.

The Eisenhower problem was that when he cared, he cared not too deeply. When he tried, he tried not quite hard enough. When he said "Yes," it was without conviction; when he said "No," it was difficult to be sure he meant it. And his habit of withdrawing support from his Congressional leaders by retreating when they were prepared to advance became chronic.

The Republican Congressional leadership found it difficult to go all out for Eisenhower proposals because of the fear that they might suddenly find themselves cast as troops without a general just as the serious shooting began. And when the Democrats resumed control of Congress in 1955, the Republican task of leadership was rendered far more difficult. This meant that the real leadership of the Congressional committees was in the hands of its senior Southern conservative members, a group hardly noted for building legislative bonfires under a hesitant President.

With the election of 1958 liberal Democratic strength increased substantially and efforts were made, often over the opposition of committee chairmen, to enact parts of the 1956 Democratic platform and the recommendations of the Democratic Advisory Committee. In an extraordinary and perhaps unique fashion the Democratic Majority Leader of the Senate, Lyndon Baines Johnson, announced his party's legislative goals each year in what amounted to State of the Union messages from the Hill. He then proceeded to steer at least some positive legislation through the Senate, and with the help of his Texas friend, Speaker Sam Rayburn, through the House as well.

The Democratic "opposition" to President Eisenhower during the period when there was divided government—six years from 1955 through 1960—was responsible, but incapable of passing the legislation supported in the party platform. Even a dazzling Majority Leader is no substitute for a President who is willing to lead.

Things changed at the White House in 1961. John Fitzgerald Kennedy was a President who tried hard to lead. He used the carrot, not the stick. Addressing the Congress on executive-legislative relations he suggested that the Constitution makes us "not rivals for power but partners for progress." Yet he understood the problem of a recalcitrant Congress. He and his staff led the fight behind the scenes to enlarge the House Rules Committee in January, 1961, in the hope that his program could be brought to a vote on the floor. Though he was successful in that fight, and some progress was made as a result, much of his legislative program was buried in committee at the time of his death and he was never willing to help remove the procedural roadblocks to action in the Senate.

We now have a President who is thoroughly educated in all the intricacies of Congressional maneuver and leadership. But Majority Leader Johnson and President Johnson can never be quite the same; their constituencies, their responsibilities, their goals and points of view must inevitably differ. President Johnson's approach to Congress will be the same as that of all his strong predecessors, from Thomas Jefferson to John F. Kennedy, namely, to assert his executive prerogatives and try to bring Congress into line as an equal, positive partner in government.

Franklin Roosevelt once noted that in the relationship between Congress and the President the letter of the Constitution "wisely declared a separation, but the impulse of a common purpose declares a union." The burden of historical proof is clear that legislation designed to serve the general welfare must be executive-inspired and pressed with all the power of the Presidency or it will not pass. And to get it passed takes all of the varied techniques of persuasion and power which have accumulated in the Presidency since 1789. In times of peril the President can act because the Congress will recede. If he can cite statute he will, if not he will act anyway, as Lincoln and F.D.R. did. As the sense of danger recedes, Congress rises again to reassert its constitutional prerogatives. In the absence of crisis, Congress cannot and will not act affirmatively except under a strong President who has a clear mandate from the people, not only because of the separation of powers and the way Congressmen and Senators come to office, but also because of the congeries of rules and customs which favor inactivity.

The historical record compels the conclusion that Congress has been a junior and unwilling partner, with a greater capacity for petulance than participation. The task of the moment is to change that historic role.

Modern times have not been congenial to Congressional pride or Congressional power. Congress has been nudged into the shadows, in part by the radiance of the Presidency, perhaps more by its own abdication of responsibility for positive action. The results have been far from reassuring. Yet we have not discovered how, except in time of war or a crisis such as 1933, the President can lead the nation effectively without outraging the sensibilities of Congress. Nor have we found a way to permit the luxury of Congressional government without depriving the President of essential power. The need is to end the tug of war and fashion a workable balance between President and Congress, one that can meet the challenges of contemporary life. Congress perennially seeks to restore equilibrium by refusing to follow the President's positive lead, yet the job of Congress can be performed well only as it is assisted by the strength of the President. A sound balance will be achieved not by weakening the executive but by strengthening Congress so it can perform its constitutional duties. A sit-down strike is not good enough.

Too often the men on Capitol Hill and the man in the White House and his staff confront one another in a posture of competition and rivalry. It is not that President and Congress never collaborate. They frequently do. But the overriding spirit is one of antagonism. And, curiously, the philosophy of the antagonists is not what the Founding Fathers predicted. No longer do we have a conservative executive restraining an impetuous Congress. Now a fragmented Congress, dominated by a conservative oligarchy, restrains a more venturesome President.

Ironically, the continuing struggle by Congress to assuage its damaged pride and recapture its ancient glory has not helped to repair the imbalance between a creative executive and a negative legislature. From pride, not policy, Congress ever keeps in mind its days of alleged greatness in the days of the War Hawks of 1812, of Webster, Clay and Calhoun and the era from Andrew Johnson through William McKinley. It reminds itself constantly that its main antagonist is the President, not poverty, injustice or the threat of nuclear holocaust. The threat of Congressional paranoia is constant. Senator Burton Wheeler accurately expressed it when he said in 1937, "We must teach that man in the White House a lesson."[10]

The way Congress can overcome its complexes is to perform its proper and major role—a role that complements rather than conflicts with that of the President. This includes acting with reasonable promptness on his legislative recommendations; initiating important policies and legislation of its own; serving the special needs of its constitutents; and exercising a continuous but not wholly hostile scrutiny of all areas of administration. To do this effectively it must revamp its creaking machinery, its archaic organization, procedures and rules. It must be prepared to act when a majority is ready for action. It must accept and establish some measure of national party discipline. Congress, and especially the President's party in Congress, will have to look in the first instance to the program and leadership of the executive, which in turn spring from the platform of the successful party in the last Presidential election.

A certain amount of localism, because of our election process, is inevitable. But if our national legislature is ever to act responsibly, democratically, efficiently and in time to head off catastrophe, Congress will have to alter its collective habit of looking in 535 different directions for cues.

This is not to say that Congress need become a pliable rubber stamp for the President. Far from it. If Congress plays a creative and responsible role in the process of governing, it will be less subservient and less paranoid than it is today. The Presidency is the most effective focal point for formulating national legislative policy. In our complex and danger-ridden world most policy recommendations will necessarily emanate from the White House, regardless of the party in power. But Presidential influence is, and should be, something quite different from Presidential control.

Congress today does not fill its proper and major role in policy leadership. It is too absorbed in the silly game of continuously applauding its unique identity as "an Institution that lives in an unending yesterday where the past is never gone, the present never quite decisive and the future rarely quite visible,"* about as inept a role as a group of grown men can be asked to perform. It is less interested in the content of policy than in dogma, ritual, routine and the mechanics of legislative maneuvering. In Congress, power, knowledge and effective action are rarely combined. By comparison the executive is unified, decisive, expert and responsible.

The role of Congress in reviewing executive proposals is a vital one, for a representative legislature should bring important political qualities to bear on the consideration of policy. There is every opportunity for Congress to leave a positive imprint. It can thoroughly discuss, criticize, add or delete, vote a Presidential proposal up or down and suggest alternatives of its own. Executive initiative, after all, does not preclude Congress from putting its own foot on the accelerator. The Constitution bestows legislative power on Congress, not the President. There are many times when Congress should initiate proposals and try to persuade the executive to adopt them as its own, especially when government is divided—one party in control of the White House and the other with majorities in one or both Houses of Congress.

As Walter Lippmann put it recently, "We have here in its American form the critical disease of democratic government; namely, the paralysis of the executive by the elected assembly . . . [a] government in which the chief executive cannot induce the legislature to consider his proposals is dangerously weak."[11]

Although it is far from easy for Congress to secure adoption by the President of a policy toward which he is lukewarm, as President Eisenhower's repeated and successful vetoes of legislation passed by a Democratic-controlled Congress demonstrated, legislative initiative by Congress is both useful and feasible. At worst, issues are sharpened and the choice before the electorate is made clearer. At best, Congress may succeed from time to time in

* William S. White, prophet of the politics of nostalgia, describing the Senate and not both houses of Congress. *Citadel: The Story of the U.S. Senate*, p. 2. Mr. White extols this type of antiquarianism.

turning the President's attention slowly but surely to the need for a new policy. In exceptional and sometimes unhappy instances, such as the Taft-Hartley and McCarran-Walters Acts passed over President Truman's vetoes, Congress actually prevails.

Congress can serve as a seedbed for the breeding and maturing of new legislative ideas. Little is ever accomplished overnight. Before a bill becomes law the chances are that it has been kicking around for some time, often too long. Senator Norris' idea for TVA, Senator Wagner's proposal for collective bargaining, Justice Black's wage-hour legislation, the more recent example of medical care for the aged, the Area Redevelopment Act and various housing proposals all germinated and grew within Congress. In each case, constant prodding of the executive from Capitol Hill helped and indeed paid dividends.

Concentration of power and coordination of effort toward common ends is sorely lacking in the Congressional system. When power does coalesce, it is often wielded to block the desires of a Congressional and national majority. It is infinitely easier to obstruct a major bill than to pass one.

In serving the national interest a member of Congress must often recognize that what is good for a particular district or an individual state is not best for the nation as a whole. There are times —not too often—when to forward the national interest he has, as painlessly as possible, to adopt a course unpopular with a large number of people back home. These are the occasions when political courage is put to the test.

Finally, Congress must be able to act before crises break rather than after they overwhelm us. The less Congress anticipates trouble, the more Presidential power, which invariably expands to meet critical situations, will grow. The way things are, we bounce from one crisis to another, postponing solutions whenever possible. Finally, when things get bad enough, Congress legislates, often too little and too late.

Sometimes potential disaster emerges unexpectedly, as with Pearl Harbor and the Korean War. Then the President and Congress must grapple as best they can. But in other cases trouble can be anticipated. There is no justification for Congress to wait until human and economic problems such as unemployment become unendurable. There was no reason, moral or political, to have failed to meet the needs for justice and equality of our Negro citizens until the nation became engulfed by widespread disorders. There is no good explanation why Congress, despite the lingering threat of nuclear warfare, has not turned its attention to the most thorough analysis of disarmament and proposals for world peace under law. The idea is to get things done while there is still time.

Although the standards suggested here cannot be met under present conditions, they furnish a measuring rod against which to assess Congressional performance.

As members of a representative assembly chosen to forward the vital interests of the nation, Congress falls far short of the mark. The fault is less that of the individual Congressman as he goes about his routine tasks than that of an institution that has become its own worst enemy.

VI

THE CONGRESSIONAL ESTABLISHMENT

An intelligent reader's guide to the Congressional Establishment must begin with a definition of the ruling clique in both Houses. Richard Rovere, one of the ablest Washington correspondents, defines "The American Establishment" as "a more or less closed and self-sustaining institution that holds a preponderance of power in our more or less open society."[1] His definition, applied to the more limited Congressional field, remains accurate.

The two Establishments, American and Congressional, have much in common. For example, the members of each constantly deny there is such a thing. In both cases experts disagree on exactly what the Establishment is and how it works; but, as Mr. Rovere points out, they disagree also about the Kingdom of God—which doesn't prove *it* doesn't exist. Within both Establishments there is a good deal of tolerance for doctrinal divergence so long as the members stand solidly together when the chips are down and the Establishment's power, prestige and prerogatives are under attack.

John Kenneth Galbraith aptly defined members of any Establishment as "the pivotal people." Most writers on the subject, including the present one, exclude themselves when defining the

Establishment and even consider themselves its victims. Douglas Dillon and John McCloy are the prototypes of Mr. Rovere's American Establishment; Richard Russell and Judge Howard Smith are patriarchs of the Congressional Establishment.

The Congressional Establishment is organized in the same easy-going way as its broader national big brother. There are no written bylaws, no conventions, no overt determination of a program. The essential difference is that the Congressional Establishment defends the status quo and views majority rule with distaste, while the American Establishment is content to abide by the principles of democracy along the more liberal lines suggested by the editorial page of its house organ, the *New York Times*.

Within broad limits and subject to some exceptions the Congressional Establishment consists of those Democratic chairmen and ranking Republican members of the important legislative committees who, through seniority and pressures exerted on junior colleagues, control the institutional machinery of Congress. They use this control to prevent a fair hearing and a vote on the merits of the President's program. The official "leadership" group of the Congress—Speaker of the House, Senate Majority Leader, *et al.* —are usually captives of the Establishment, although they can sometimes be found looking out over the walls of their prison, plotting escape.

The Establishment does not always win. It frequently does not use all the parliamentary tools which are available to it. In the Senate it has lost strength consistently since the election of 1958. Its members, almost without exception, are charming and amiable gentlemen, popular with their colleagues, who sincerely believe that the safety of the Republic depends on defeating the "dangerous innovations" in our social life and political economy which are constantly being proposed by the President of the United States.

It is important to note that the views of the Congressional Establishment are not shared by a majority of their own colleagues, who, left to their own devices, would be prepared to bring the Congress into line to cope with the necessities of our times.

In an earlier work I described the Senate Establishment as "almost the antithesis of democracy. It is not selected by any democratic process. It appears to be quite unresponsive to the caucuses of the two parties, be they Democratic or Republican. It is what might be called a self-perpetuating oligarchy with mild, but only mild, overtones of plutocracy."[2]

There are plenty of rich men in the Senate, but only a few of them are high in the ranks of the Establishment; and none of them would admit to a belief that the accumulation of great wealth is a principal object of life. This is another distinction between the American and the Congressional Establishments. The former has, despite its slightly liberal orientation, definite overtones of plutocracy, although its tolerance is much more for inherited than for recently acquired wealth.

The bonds which hold the Congressional Establishment together are: white supremacy; a stronger devotion to property than to human rights; support of the military establishment; belligerence in foreign affairs; and a determination to prevent Congressional reform. The high-water marks of the Senatorial Establishment in 1963 were the two votes on limiting debate in the Senate in order to change the filibuster rule. In response to a question posed by the Vice President, "Does the Senate have the right, notwithstanding its rules, to terminate debate at the beginning of a new Congress by majority vote in order to pass upon a change in its rules?" there were 44 ayes and 53 nays. The Establishment, knowing it had finally rallied enough votes to assure a negative result, permitted a vote on January 21 after a desultory filibuster lasting nine days. On February 7 a cloture petition which would have cut off further debate on the proposed changes in Rule XXII and which required a favorable vote of two-thirds of those present was lost 54-42. Including the announced position of the four absentees, the Senate stood 56-44 in favor of limiting debate (and therefore almost certainly in favor of a more liberal rule of terminating debate), nine short of the necessary two-thirds. But the majority did not prevail.

The low-water mark of the Establishment was the Test Ban Treaty, which came to a vote on September 24, 1963, after more than a month of desultory debate. Under the Constitution two-thirds of those present and voting were required for ratification. The affirmative vote was 80-19. The hard core of the Establishment voted "no."

A typical Establishment line-up occurred on the Mundt bill to block the sale of wheat to Russia (by prohibiting the Export-Import Bank from guaranteeing loans to finance the sales) when all but two of the "anti-test ban" Senators supported Senator Mundt and opposed Presidents Kennedy and Johnson—the vote was on November 26, 1963—in their attempt to further relax the tensions of the Cold War. The Mundt proposal was tabled by a vote of 57 to 35.

Another typical vote showing a similar line-up occurred on approving the conference report on the foreign aid bill on December 16, 1963. The report was approved 61-26, the hard core of the Establishment being in opposition.

Every member of the Senate, except one, Senator Lausche, who voted against the Test Ban Treaty, also voted in the negative on the question posed by the Vice President regarding the right of the Senate to change its rules, and on the motion for cloture. The eighteen Senators listed on the following page represent the hard core of the Establishment and its loyal followers. The senior Senators on this list are designated with an asterisk.

Note the absence on this list of several staunch card-carrying members of the Establishment: Ellender of Louisiana, Hayden of Arizona, Holland of Florida, Johnston of South Carolina, Hill and Sparkman of Alabama, Cannon of Nevada; and on the Republican side Cotton of New Hampshire, Williams of Delaware and Dirksen of Illinois. They all voted *against* cloture but *for* the Test Ban Treaty. Note also that, unlike Wilson's "twelve willful men" in 1917, the hard core of the Establishment did not utilize the

Democrats	*Immediate Vote on Rules Change*	*Cloture*	*Test Ban Treaty*	*Wheat Sale to Russia*	*Foreign Aid Authorization Conference Report*
*Russell of Georgia	no	no	no	no	no
*Stennis of Mississippi	no	no	no	no	no
*Eastland of Mississippi	no	no	no	no	no
*Long of Louisiana	no	no	no	yes	no
*Byrd of Virginia	no	no	no	no	no
Byrd of West Virginia	no	no	no	yes	yes
*Robertson of Virginia	no	no	no	no	no**
*Talmadge of Georgia	no	no	no	no	no**
*McClellan of Arkansas	no	no	no	no	no
*Thurmond of South Carolina	no	no	no	no	no
Republicans					
*Curtis of Nebraska	no	no	no	no	no
*Goldwater of Arizona	no	no	no	no	no**
*Mundt of South Dakota	no	no	yes	no	no
Simpson of Wyoming	no	no	no	no	no
Jordan of Idaho	no	no	no	no	no
*Smith of Maine	no	no	no	no	yes
*Bennett of Utah	no	no	no	no	no
Tower of Texas	no	no	no	no	no

**Paired or announced against.

filibuster to prevent a vote on the treaty or on the wheat deal. It seems clear that it is only in opposition to Congressional reform that the Establishment will play all its cards.

The tolerance of the conservative Southern Democratic members toward their more liberal Democratic colleagues on every subject other than civil rights is very broad. Thus Hill, a charter member of the club, maintains his good standing despite his liberal record on nearly every other issue. Sparkman has been the leading advocate of vast expenditures for housing and urban renewal. So long as a Democrat stands firm against civil rights and cloture, or a Republican against cloture only, his (or her) Establishment status remains unquestionable.

On civil rights the Northern and Western Republican members of the Establishment are permitted some leeway, though it should be noted that when civil rights and property rights conflict—as on the question of public accommodations—they can usually be counted on to support the Southerners. If they vote against cloture, however, they can actually vote as they please on the merits of a civil rights bill if they ever get a chance to do so.

The Establishment strongly supports the Defense program and opposes disarmament. Frequently it goes further than the White House and the Pentagon in its willingness to spend money to build up the armed forces; and it is a solid bloc in opposition to adequate appropriations for the Arms Control and Disarmament Agency. Welfare programs are, on the whole, anathema to the Establishment.

The hold of the Establishment over the Senate is weakening. An increasing number of chairmen and ranking minority members of committees are opposed to Establishment rule. Clinton Anderson of New Mexico, for instance, chairman of the Committee on Aeronautics and Space, and formerly chairman and still ranking member of the Interior Committee, led the fight to change Rule XXII. Warren G. Magnuson of Washington, chairman of the Committee on Interstate and Foreign Commerce, is pushing a change in rules to put the fiscal year on a calendar year basis and straighten out the mess in the appropriations process. John Pastore of Rhode Island, chairman of the Joint Committee on Atomic Energy, floor-managed a rules change in 1964 which now requires debate to be germane for three hours each day. Pat McNamara of Michigan and Henry M. Jackson of Washington are chairmen of Public Works and Interior respectively and have voted to change Senate rules in the past. These liberal Democrats are coming into power in the Senate and most of them are not satisfied with the way the Senate is run.

On the Republican side George Aiken of Vermont and Leverett Saltonstall of Massachusetts, the two senior minority members of the Senate, left the Establishment on the Test Ban Treaty. Saltonstall is taking an interest in Congressional reform. Neither

John Sherman Cooper of Kentucky nor Thomas Kuchel of California, both ranking Republican members of important committees, is a member of the Establishment. Even Everett Dirksen of Illinois, who helped lead its Republican members in maintaining Establishment control of the committees in 1963 and violently opposes Congressional reorganization, left it on the Test Ban Treaty and five-sixths of the administration's omnibus civil rights bill. Nevertheless, he is definitely the Establishment type.

These men understand and respect the traditions of the Senate. But most of them will vote when the time comes for measures which will expedite action in the Senate and make the institution responsive to the will of its majority.

The Establishment no longer *controls* the Senate majority and minority leaderships. Knowland, Bridges, Taft, Kerr, Russell and Bobby Baker no longer *run* the Senate. The new leaders on both sides of the Senate aisle are more responsive to and responsible about the President's program. They must bargain with and sometimes go along with the Establishment, but their hearts are in the highlands.

On the House side the picture is different. Historically, the House has fluctuated from near chaos in the years before "Reed's Rules" of 1890 to the oligarchy he and Speaker Cannon ruled thereafter until 1910. Today it seems to this outside observer that power in the House has long been fragmented. Even so competent a politician as the late Sam Rayburn of Texas, who reigned as Speaker for longer than any man in American history, did not *rule* the House. He could persuade and cajole. His substantial power to give or withhold favor tended to keep backbenchers in line when the time came to vote. But the Speaker shared his power with the chairman of the Rules Committee, the chairman of the Appropriations Committee, the chairman of the Ways and Means Committee and, as military matters occupied a more and more important position in our political and economic life, the chairman of the Armed Services Committee.

Even this is obviously not the whole story. And not every

Speaker has had the advantage of Mr. Sam's remarkable personality and the goodwill he accumulated over the years. Little independent satrapies have been carved out for particular areas of jurisdiction. Wayne Aspinall of Colorado, chairman of the Interior Committee, is in charge of public lands. On the Commerce Committee, Oren Harris of Arkansas, its chairman, is czar of the broadcasting industry. Harold Cooley of North Carolina is sugar daddy and cotton king from his powerful seat as chairman of the Agriculture Committee. Otto Passman rules unchallenged over foreign aid; John Rooney tells the State Department where to get off; Mike Kirwan decides which Congressmen will get public works in their districts. For nearly a generation immigration and "Un-American activities" were synonymous with the late Francis E. Walter of Pennsylvania.

Committee and subcommittee chairmen have more naked power in the House than in the Senate. There is no tax legislation if Wilbur Mills of Arkansas, chairman of the Ways and Means Committee, doesn't want any, nor a wilderness bill against Aspinall's wishes.

While power seems more fragmented in the House than in the Senate, it is probably because the former body is so much larger. Thus it is easier for chairmen to become more powerful. For the same reason there is less cohesion. There appears to be less sense of a "band of brothers." While the South is to some extent in the saddle, it seems less obviously so.

The men who hold the top positions of power in the House do not belong to the same club, as do their counterparts in the Senate. Speaker John McCormack, gray, dignified, ascetic, devout Boston Irish to the core, is quite a different breed of politician from Majority Leader Carl Albert, precise, friendly Oklahoma lawyer and former Rhodes Scholar. Hale Boggs, Majority Whip, the personification of New Orleans urbanity, has in common with the soft-spoken, rural Virginia Judge Howard Smith, chairman of the Rules Committee, and Carl Vinson, chairman of the Armed Services Committee, only the fact that all three come from the South. Elderly, aggressive, Clarence Cannon, chairman of the powerful

Appropriations Committee, and dark-haired, vigorous Wilbur Mills seem in many ways from different worlds.

In the House Establishment these are the charter members, together with their Republican opposite numbers, Charles Halleck of Indiana, Minority Leader Leslie C. Arends of Illinois, Minority Whip John Byrnes of Wisconsin on Ways and Means, and Gerry Ford of Michigan, recently elected chairman of the House Republican Conference. Note that in the House the leadership is part of the Establishment.

There is more partisan cleavage in the House, more committee and floor votes on a straight party-line basis. Yet the conservative Republican–Southern Democratic coalition—whose leaders are the House Establishment—operates on many an occasion even more effectively in the House than in the Senate. It killed federal aid to education there in 1960. It has thrown a roadblock across renewal and strengthening of the Area Redevelopment Act in 1963. It has blocked passage of the Mass Transit Bill and the Youth Opportunities Act. It will not permit health care for the aged even to come out of committee. It crippled foreign aid in the closing days of 1963. On many other measures it has hamstrung the President's program after it has passed the Senate. It cannot stop civil rights legislation because of the urban and suburban Republicans. But it can usually stop if it really wants to what the Establishment likes to call "spending programs."

What makes the House clock tick one day and run down the next is perhaps not understandable to an outsider. And even when it does tick, like its Senate counterpart, it almost always runs well behind time.

Four Democratic party institutions have been effective instruments for Establishment control of the inner working of the Senate: the leadership, the conference, the Steering Committee and the Policy Committee. The misnomers are obvious. The Policy Committee makes no policy. The Steering Committee never steers. There are those who say that the conference never confers and that the leadership does not lead. Nevertheless the nomenclature lingers on.

For a good part of American history the Democratic party caucus in both the House and the Senate was a periodic meeting of all party members for the purpose of determining party legislative policy. The decisions of the caucus taken by majority vote were binding on all who attended, unless special permission to vote against the party decision was given. Discipline was enforced against recalcitrants through the withholding or the withdrawal of privileges and favor. The ultimate penalty was expulsion from the party caucus, a penalty, however, which was rarely enforced. This is still the practice in a number of state legislatures.

The Democratic caucus was a flourishing institution during the sessions of the Sixty-third Congress when the legislative program of Wilson's New Freedom was enacted. John W. Kern, Majority Leader, reported to and took his direction from the caucus. Sometime thereafter, it is difficult to determine when, the name of the caucus was changed to the conference. Over the years its influence declined.

The Democratic Conference has been resuscitated to some extent under the leadership of Senator Mike Mansfield. At a meeting on January 4, 1961 he assured Senator Proxmire that periodic conferences would be called and direct reports made to the members of the weekly leadership meetings with the President. This has been done largely through informal "coffee hours," meetings of small groups of Senators held in the leader's office.

The Democratic Steering Committee, which makes committee assignments, has varied in size from time to time. During the early Wilson days Senator John W. Kern, newly elected Majority Leader, shook loose the Democratic party and indeed the Senate itself from the control of the Establishment of that time by constituting a new Steering Committee. This consisted of nine members, seven of whom were Wilson men, the other two conservatives. Five of the nine members had served for less than two years in the Senate. This committee promptly used its power to assign members and select chairmen for all standing committees so that Wilson administration supporters were in control.

Thereafter, however, the custom arose that once appointed to the Steering Committee members served until they died, resigned or were defeated. As a result, the Steering Committee in 1959 consisted of fifteen senior Senators; seven conservatives from the South, Lyndon Johnson, Majority Leader, and Carl Hayden, President Pro Tempore, giving the Establishment a clear majority of nine. This arrangement could perhaps have been justified prior to the election of 1958. The Senate of the Eighty-fifth Congress, after all, had a preponderance of Southerners and conservatives. But there was no rational excuse for continuing this Establishment control after fifteen new Northern and Western Democratic Senators were swept into office with the Eighty-sixth Congress. I called the need to reorganize the Steering Committee to the attention of the Majority Leader before that Congress convened. My plea fell on deaf ears.

However, there was nothing particularly inequitable about the committee assignments in 1959, the Majority Leader having already established the practice that every new Democratic Senator was entitled to at least one major committee assignment. And because the ratio of Democrats to Republicans on each committee was drastically tilted in favor of the Democrats as a result of our party increasing its numbers from forty-nine to sixty-four seats, there were plenty of vacancies to take care of everybody.

The election of 1960 elevated Senator Johnson into the Vice Presidency. Mike Mansfield became Majority Leader, Hubert Humphrey succeeded him as Whip and George Smathers of Florida became secretary of the conference, thus giving the Southerners another vote on the Steering Committee. The Democratic Senators increased from sixty-four to sixty-seven.

I again raised the question of the composition of the Steering Committee. As a result of informal discussions and a meeting in January, 1961, at which the subject was discussed, the Majority Leader made a commitment to the conference that the composition of the Steering Committee would hereafter reflect the ideology and the geographical distribution of the entire Democratic membership of the Senate. He also agreed to submit his appointments to the conference for ratification. He kept the commitment as vacancies occurred. But he was unwilling to revamp the committee as Kern had done fifty years earlier.

By 1963 Harrison Williams of New Jersey, Thomas Dodd of Connecticut, Paul Douglas of Illinois and I had become members of the Steering Committee. But the Establishment still controlled it, nine votes to six, and through it all committee assignments.

When the Eighty-eighth Congress convened, in January, 1963, the first order of business was Senator Clinton Anderson's resolution to consider a change in the Senate rules. Had this resolution been adopted, Anderson was prepared to move for a change of Rule XXII, to permit debate to be terminated by three-fifths of Senators present and voting, instead of two-thirds as under the present rule. Humphrey planned to offer an amendment to reduce the required number to a simple majority. Those of us who wanted to change Rule XXII in order to put some curb on filibusters believed we did not have the votes to carry the Humphrey amendment, but did have the votes to pass the Anderson three-fifths resolution. The problem was to get the resolution to a vote in the face of the inevitable Southern filibuster.

We had one weapon which had been handed to us by a Republican. Vice President Nixon had rendered an advisory ruling in 1959, and again in 1961, a few days before he left office, to the effect that the Senate could adopt its own rules by majority vote at the beginning of each Congress. This important ruling not only permitted termination of debate by majority rule but also denied the Establishment's argument that the Senate is a "continuing body" whose rules carry over from one Congress to another.

Vice President Johnson in 1963 did not follow Vice President Nixon's ruling. He took the position that any constitutional ruling must be made in the first instance by the Senate itself, not by its constitutional presiding officer. Had Johnson followed Nixon, there is not much doubt his ruling would have been sustained. The Vice President's parliamentary rulings are practically never reversed on appeal.

The Southerners filibustered against the Anderson resolution. At the same time they pressured newly elected Senators anxious about their committee seats and other Senators who wanted new committee assignments. The Establishment Senators did not let the Steering Committee meet until the question of Rule XXII was decided. This held the sword of Damocles over the heads of all Senators hoping to improve their committee assignments. Finally, on January 21 they felt they had the votes to beat the liberals. And they did. The Vice President put to the Senate the question whether a majority of the Senate, "notwithstanding the rules," could terminate debate to change the rules at the beginning of a new Congress. The Establishment moved to table and won by a vote of 53 to 42.

The filibuster continued on the Anderson motion. On February 9 a cloture petition was brought to a vote and failed to receive the necessary two-thirds, although it did secure a majority—fifty-six Senators either voted for or were announced in support of limiting debate. That was the end of the 1963 effort to change Rule XXII. A motion to set aside the Anderson resolution was carried and the Senate proceeded to other business.

A few days later the Democratic Conference met again. I moved to increase the size of the Steering Committee from fifteen to nineteen in order to obtain that geographical and ideological balance which Majority Leader Mansfield had promised. There had been a lot of backstage maneuvering with which I was not familiar. To my chagrin and surprise, Mansfield opposed my motion and Humphrey failed to support it. They told me later Bobby Baker had told them the votes were not there to approve the increase. Perhaps this was right. The ballot was secret and my motion lost by a vote of 21 to 39, seven Senators being absent. A motion of Senator Anderson to increase the Steering Committee to seventeen was then defeated, on a division, by a vote of 23 to 37, objection to the secret ballot having been raised by Senator Russell. Had the Majority Leader and Whip supported Senator Anderson and me, I believe we would have won.

When the Steering Committee met a few days later, the Establishment was still in the saddle. There were many committee vacancies to be filled and a serious question to be settled as to the size and party ratio of the various standing committees. The latter was important because it involved Establishment control of key committees. With sixty-seven Democrats and thirty-three Republicans our party was entitled to a ratio of more than two to one on all committees. It was desirable but not essential not to "bump" minority party members already on committees by throwing them off when the party ratio changed. It was also desirable but not essential to secure at least one good committee assignment for each new Senator. It can be seen that a mathematical and human problem of no small proportions was involved.

The task of recommending to the Democratic Steering Committee and its Republican counterpart, the Committee on Committees, an acceptable solution of this complicated problem was turned over to Bobby Baker and Mark Trice, the Republican minority Secretary. Baker was an Establishment man and I was suspicious of his actions. Coming first to the Senate as a page boy at the age of fourteen, he had a meteoric career. He soon attached himself to the cause of the Establishment, was selected Secretary to the Democratic majority at a salary of $19,600, and made himself indispensable to the leadership as a protagonist of the conservative coalition. His influence, built on an attractive personality, hard work, insatiable ambition and a deep knowledge of the idiosyncrasies and habits of all Senators, was far in excess of the prerogatives of his office. He resigned his position in October, 1963. His activities became the main subject of an investigation by the Rules Committee of the business and financial conduct of employees of the Senate.

I was anxious to increase, if possible, the influence of what

James MacGregor Burns calls the Presidential party[3] as opposed to the Congressional party (the Establishment) on the key committees: Finance, Appropriations and Foreign Relations. This I believed could be done by increasing the size and ratio of these committees. Finance had eleven Democrats and six Republicans, a majority of them Establishment-oriented. A proper ratio would be fourteen Democrats and seven Republicans—adding two liberal Democrats and perhaps a middle-of-the-road Republican. Appropriations had eighteen to nine and should have had at least nineteen and probably twenty Democrats to ten Republicans in order to get at least one more non-Establishment man on the committee and avoid "bumping" Senator Javits of New York, a liberal Republican. Foreign Relations had eleven to six and needed fourteen to seven to avert the threatened loss of control of the committee to the anti-Presidential coalition.

The White House, concerned with the fate of its tax bill and its proposal for health care for the elderly, was initially interested in increasing the size of the Finance Committee and not averse to the other changes I suggested. I handed a memorandum to President Kennedy containing the above suggestions early in January and was later advised by Hubert Humphrey that the President would support the increase.

The Establishment soon counterattacked. Everett Dirksen, Minority Leader, was persuaded to indicate adamant and unanimous Republican opposition to increasing the size of the Finance Committee and his own intention of seeking the one existing Republican vacancy. The conservative Democrats would bolt their leadership on the issue, we were told, in order to support Finance Chairman Harry Flood Byrd. Faced with the possibility of defeat and relying, rather naïvely, on Baker's nose count and Dirksen's ability to control all his troops, the leadership backed away from the fight and the White House decided not to press it. I decided, however, to raise the issue anyway.

When the Steering Committee met in mid-February, 1963, the fight to change the filibuster rule had been lost. The fight within the Democratic Conference to bring the membership of the Steering Committee into line with the ideology and geography of the Democratic Senators had been lost. It was obvious the fight to increase the size of the three key committees in the Steering Committee would also be lost. But I felt it should be made.

As a member of the Steering Committee I moved to change the size of the Foreign Relations, Appropriations and Finance Committees. My motions were voted down by substantial majorities after Senator Mansfield had given his opinion that they could not be ratified successfully on the floor of the Senate. We then proceeded to fill the vacancies, voting by secret ballot. I had Senator Douglas' proxy. Senator Russell held several proxies. All other members were present.

The Establishment demonstrated its power. Whereas seniority is ordinarily a sacred principle in Establishment circles it was ignored in filling the vacancies on eight committees in order to give coveted committee seats to junior Senators who had supported the Establishment in the cloture fight. In three instances seniority was followed, but perhaps by coincidence these three Senators had also voted to support the Establishment during the January floor fight on Rule XXII.

Eight nonfreshman Senators, i.e., elected before 1962, who had opposed cloture submitted eligible bids for new committee assignments. *Seven* of them got what they wanted.

Fourteen nonfreshman Senators who opposed the present filibuster rule applied for new committee seats for which they were eligible. *Only one*—Senator Mansfield, the Majority Leader—got what he wanted. Four others got their second or third choice. *Nine* got nothing.*

In order to achieve these results it was necessary to give most of the new Senators, and all those who voted against cloture, *two* major committee assignments instead of one.

So we lost again.

* For further details see *The Senate Establishment*, pp. 40 ff.; pp. 100-103.

On February 19, 20, 21 and 25, 1963, after considerable thought and knowing the cause was hopeless I took the fight to the floor of the Senate and described in detail what happened in the Steering Committee. The leadership on both sides of the aisle defended the Establishment, and my attempt to regain on the floor some of what had been lost in the conference and the Steering Committee was badly beaten down.

Later, upon the death of Estes Kefauver, two Senators supporting cloture were given committees of their choice; Burdick of North Dakota got Judiciary, Proxmire of Wisconsin, Appropriations. Both had been bypassed for juniors at the earlier meeting to reward opponents of cloture. It should be remembered, however, that Senator Proxmire opposes much of the fiscal program of the President and has less seniority than Senator Yarborough of Texas, an administration supporter, who also applied for the assignment to Appropriations.

The Establishment retained control over the Finance Committee and the Appropriations Committee and made further inroads in the Foreign Relations Committee. Today it controls the Armed Services, Appropriations and Rules and Administration Committees. In each instance the conservative Republican members of the Establishment supply the votes needed for control. With the advent to the Senate of more liberal Senators of both parties since 1958 the Establishment has lost control of the Banking and Currency, Commerce, Government Operations, Interior, Judiciary and Public Works Committees. It never controlled the Committee on Labor and Public Welfare. The measure of how close the Establishment has come to losing its grip on the Senate is perhaps best taken by their genuine fear of Congressional reorganization and rules reform.

A seldom-used but potentially powerful weapon in the hands of the Establishment is the Senate Democratic Policy Committee. This group has had a curious history. It was conceived in the La Follette-Monroney report of 1945 as a committee which would make party legislative policy not only in the Senate but also in joint sessions with a similar group in the House and an executive group headed by the President. It was intended to deal with ways and means of enacting the party platform into law. But it has never even remotely fulfilled that role. The La Follette-Monroney recommendation was discarded in the Legislative Reorganization Act of 1946 because the House did not like the idea of a Policy Committee. Speaker Rayburn is said to have remarked, "I am the Policy Committee!" Given legislative status in the Senate as a committee of seven by a rider to an Appropriation Act in 1946, it has ever since received substantial appropriations for staff which have been spent in mysterious ways not known to most Senators. It is only slightly weighted in favor of the Establishment.* For some years its only ostensible role has been as a "traffic cop" to determine the priority with which a given measure on the calendar will be brought to the floor. It came under attack in 1960 and 1961 from Albert Gore, myself and others as being as stacked against the philosophy and geographical distribution of Democratic Senators as the Steering Committee.

All contested bills have to clear the Policy Committee. Its power to strangle legislation approved by the standing committees of the Senate approaches that of the House Rules Committee, which, however, unlike the Policy Committee is a standing committee of the House, bipartisan in nature. But it has not yet used that power to any substantial extent.

Since the committee asserted until recently, with a good deal of justification, that it never holds up legislation on the calendar indefinitely, the threat may be more potential than actual. Yet by the mere setting of priorities the fate of a bill may well be determined, particularly at the end of the second session of each

* Its members are: Hill of Alabama, Russell of Georgia, Magnuson of Washington, Pastore of Rhode Island, Symington of Missouri, Mansfield of Montana, Humphrey of Minnesota, Smathers of Florida and Hayden of Arizona. There is some controversy as to whether certain other Senators who serve or formerly served on the Calendar Committee and sit with the Policy Committee are entitled to vote.

Congress. Then the sponsors of a score of measures which they have been trying to get to the floor, perhaps for months, are contending for immediate consideration of their bills. If a small group of Senators opposed to enactment can persuade the Policy Committee to withold sending a measure to the floor until the last minute they can then defeat passage by merely talking for a few hours until the leadership, in desperation, sets the bill aside in favor of some less controversial measure. Delay on major legislation could be fatal.

If the Republicans controlled the Senate, they would be confronted with similar problems with their leadership, conference, Policy Committee and Committee on Committees. While the Republicans follow seniority in filling committee posts more slavishly than the Democrats, their party structure is substantially more democratic. Their conference and Policy Committee meet together once each week at lunch to discuss pending legislation and to determine party strategy and tactics.

The minority party in Congress, unless it holds the White House as it did during the last six years of President Eisenhower's term of office, has no authority and not much responsibility. For this reason not much strain is placed on the adequacy of party organization except when votes are likely to be close and the balance can be shifted by a move toward or away from the majority party's leadership position. Accordingly, there seems no purpose in discussing Republican party Senate organizations and procedures at any length.

On November 21, 1963, I spoke in the Senate on "The Senate Establishment Revisited." The failure of the first session of the Eighty-eighth Congress to deal with civil rights or tax reduction or, indeed, even to pass the regular appropriations bills had begun to cause a good deal of adverse comment in the press. The frustration and restlessness felt by many within the Senate had broken out on the floor. Senator Dodd of Connecticut blamed the failure to get much done on the Majority and Minority Leaders (though he later apologized). Senator Morse of Oregon said it was not the leadership; it was the fact legislation had not reached the floor from the committees. Senator Dirksen of Illinois said nothing was wrong at all. The Senate, he said, "is much like an old scow. It does not move fast; it does not move very far at one time; but it does not sink." Senator Russell of Georgia said, "I resent the Senate being constantly attacked about conditions over which it has no control."

As to why the Senate was in session in late November when the Reorganization Act of 1946 required us by law to adjourn no later than July 30 with our business finished, why we had not even had before us the President's tax and civil rights programs, why eight out of the twelve regular appropriations bills were not passed five months after the fiscal year had begun, I offered my own explanation:

> The reason why we are still in session in the middle of November, and the reason why, in all likelihood, we shall remain in session for the balance of 1963, is the control of these key committees by this small group of men, who seem determined to obstruct the program of the President of the United States. One might say that the ruling cliques in the Finance Committee, the Judiciary Committee, and the Appropriations Committee constitute the Senate establishment's nests of opposition to the program of the President. These men are conducting a sitdown strike against the people of the United States. In February I said this would happen. I say in November that it has happened.[4]

It is easier to pass a bill on the floor of the House than in the Senate; but it is a good deal harder to get it to the floor for passage. The centers of House Establishment power are four committees: Rules, Appropriations, Ways and Means, and Armed Services. The House leadership is also more powerful than its Senate counterpart.

The Rules Committee can, as a practical matter, prevent almost any legislation it desires to subvert from reaching the floor. Since 1910 the members of the Rules Committee have been elected by the House itself on nomination of the members of the Ways and Means Committee (for the Democrats) and the Committee on Committees (for the Republicans). The Speaker and the Minority Leader have a good deal to say about how vacancies in this important committee are filled. The nominations are approved largely *pro forma* by the party conferences. But once chosen, with rare exceptions, Representatives continue to serve on the Rules Committee for the balance of their tenure. Since membership is highly prized, Rules Committee members tend to be senior House members from one-party constituencies.

The House Rules Committee has been a problem for over a generation to those who favor majority rule. When a majority of the committee consists of supporters of the administration and of the House leadership, the Rules Committee functions as a helpful institution in assuring the orderly enactment of the party platform and in preventing measures opposed by the leadership from reaching the floor. It served this useful purpose during the earlier years of the New Freedom and the New Deal and also during the brief period in 1947-48 and 1953-54 when the Republicans controlled the House. But when the Rules Committee is controlled by a bipartisan coalition which opposes both the House leadership and the administration, it can hamstring effective action by either. The perverse power it exercises today is to veto floor consideration of legislation a majority would pass. The veto can be overruled, but it is difficult indeed to do so.

In January, 1961, the size of the Rules Committee was increased from twelve to fifteen in a famous battle demanded by President Kennedy, who knew his program would not even be fairly considered if the Establishment grip on the Rules Committee was not relaxed. Under the leadership of Speaker Sam Rayburn, the administration supporters won by the close vote of 217 to 212. Two more Democrats thought to be favorable to the legislative program of the Kennedy administration and an additional Republican were elected to the Rules Committee. The move was taken over the strong opposition of Chairman Smith, a number of influential Southern Democrats and all save 22 of the 170 Republicans.

The expulsion from the committee of Representative William Colmer of Mississippi, who had opposed the President in the 1960 election, was considered as an alternative to enlarging the committee but was rejected by the Speaker. Colmer was permitted to remain on the Rules Committee, where he has been a valiant ally of Judge Smith in creating roadblocks to administration legislation. Since all five Republicans on the committee are from the conservative wing of that party so far as welfare legislation is concerned, they frequently support Smith and Colmer and need only one more vote to swing the Committee 8-7 and thus prevent legislation reported favorably by a legislative committee from reaching the floor. This has been the case with federal aid to public schools. Congressman James J. Delaney, Democrat of New York, has voted with Smith, Colmer and the Republicans to keep these proposals from ever getting to the House floor after they have passed the Senate. This is not the case with respect to civil rights legislation, which is supported by Delaney and also commands some Republican Rules Committee support. It cannot be stymied indefinitely, though it can be delayed.

The fight to change the Rules Committee is an interesting example of the Establishment at work. Obviously, the clearest way for the leadership to make known its support for the administration was to remove Colmer from the committee. But that would have constituted a crime against the Establishment, which places far more emphasis on the prerogatives and traditions of the Congress as an institution than it does on a Presidential program. To remove Colmer would have meant tampering with seniority, invoking party discipline, acquiescing to the Democratic majority will, and risking a rupture with the Southern wing of the party. It was, therefore, rejected. Rayburn, instead, went along with the Establishment by using an alternative method. The price he exacted was some support from key members of the Establishment, which he got—particularly from Carl Vinson of Georgia, chairman of the Armed Services Committee. Thus, in order to avoid a frontal attack on the institution, which could be really dangerous, the Establishment allowed itself to suffer a temporary setback.

Two years later, when Homer Thornberry of Texas left the Rules Committee to become a federal judge, the battle was fought again—this time behind the scenes. There was an impasse in the House, with the new Speaker apparently giving in to the Establishment and the House Study Group liberals, about one hundred in number, ready to take to the barricades to support the Johnson administration. The problem was resolved by putting another relatively junior Texan, Congressman John Young, on the committee after, it is said, he promised to support the administration.

It is this kind of fight that permits journalists to laud the Establishment's parliamentary tactics and to condemn the liberals as ineffectual. What they overlook is that the Establishment has control of the machinery as long as the leaders hold the line for them against the administration supporters when the chips are down.

A powerful weapon of the Rules Committee which affects the Senate as well as the House—and sometimes is used—is to refuse to grant a rule to go to conference on a bill where the House and Senate versions are substantially different and the Senate version is closer to the administration's position. This the committee has power to do if only one Representative on the floor refuses unanimous consent to go to conference. The Senate, so to speak, legislates in the shadow of the House Rules Committee because it so often has to accept the House version of a bill whether it likes it or not if any legislation at all is to be passed.*

One way to get around the Rules Committee roadblock is to persuade a majority of the whole House, 218 members, to sign

* Except civil rights, where the reverse is true because of the filibuster.

a discharge petition. But many a timid member, fearing reprisal affecting his own privileges or immunities if he publicly defied the senior and powerful members of the Establishment, is reluctant to sign such a petition for a measure in which he has no deep personal interest but which he would be glad enough to vote for if it ever reached the floor. Here again the issue becomes one of the institution versus the program. Junior Representatives dependent upon the Establishment's largess for their district needs prefer not to disrupt the institution if they don't have to. Only two important pieces of legislation have been passed in recent times as a result of discharge petition procedure—the Fair Labor Standards Act of 1938 and the Federal Pay Act of 1960. Failure to get 218 signatures on a discharge petition on the civil rights bill in December, 1963 is a good example of the difficulty of using this weapon. A majority of the House was quite ready to vote for the legislation once it reached the floor, but not to sign the discharge petition.

Another way to overcome Rules Committee opposition is known as Calendar Wednesday. This rule, first adopted in 1909, permits legislative committees to call up their bills notwithstanding failure of the Rules Committee to grant a rule whenever the calendar of reported measures is called. However, the committees are called in alphabetical order and it is reasonably easy through dilatory tactics to prevent the bill of a committee far down on the alphabetical list from ever emerging on the floor. Nevertheless, in desperation the procedure has occasionally been used.

Representative Herman P. Eberharter of Pittsburgh summed the matter up succinctly in a letter he wrote to all House members in December, 1948:

> The committee often allows bills to come before the House only on its own terms. It frequently usurps the functions of the regular legislative committees of the House by holding hearings and reviewing the merits of bills that have already been carefully studied by the proper legislative committees. A reform of this undemocratic system is long overdue.

The reform occurred on January 3, 1949, when by a vote of 275 to 142 the House adopted the "twenty-one-day rule" under which the chairman of a legislative committee could call up for action a bill his committee had reported favorably at any time twenty-one calendar days after the favorable report if, in the meanwhile, the Rules Committee had failed to grant a rule. While the twenty-one-day rule was in effect, a number of important measures were brought to the floor and passed.* It rendered resort to the unpopular discharge petition unnecessary.

But the triumph of the supporters of the Truman administration was short-lived. At the opening of the Eighty-second Congress in 1951 the twenty-one-day rule was repealed. The Republicans had gained twenty-nine House seats in the 1950 election, and a large majority of them voted for repeal. The vote was 247 to 179. Thereafter the Establishment reasserted its control. The power of the Rules Committee to blockade bills has been in effect ever since.

Today the House Rules Committee is perhaps the single most powerful committee of the Congress. It exercises enormous power to flout democracy. The argument is sometimes made that the Rules Committee in its own way and its own good time does, after all, let a lot of administration-supported legislation get to the House floor for a vote. This is true. But a high price is often exacted for what, in a democratic legislature, should be done as a matter of course, not as a matter of bargaining with a ruling clique.

To the argument that the House Rules Committee bottles up a lot of legislation as a favor to many Congressmen who have to profess to be for it for political reasons but don't actually want to have to vote for it (the most typical example being the demand of the veterans' lobby for a $100-a-month bonus for World War

* Including anti-poll tax legislation, Hawaiian and Alaskan statehood, minimum wage and housing legislation. The indirect effect of the rule was to cause the Rules Committee to act favorably on other measures in order to save face and avoid the humiliation of action under the twenty-one-day rule.

I) it can be answered that it is time members of Congress demonstrated the courage of their convictions.

The House Appropriations Committee is very large—fifty members, thirty of them Democrats and twenty Republicans. Its chairman, Clarence Cannon of Missouri, its ranking Republican, Ben Jensen of Iowa, and most of its senior members are ultraconservative and antiadministration on fiscal matters. Among its subcommittee chairmen are John J. Rooney of New York, the scourge of adequate appropriations for the State Department, and Otto E. Passman of Louisiana, staunch antagonist of the foreign aid program. Passman's triumph over the Johnson administration was trumpeted around the world on December 16, 1963, the day before the new President went to New York to pledge his administration's support of the United Nations, funds for which Mr. Passman had just succeeded in cutting drastically.

Since the Appropriations Committee can make or break a run-of-the-mine Congressman by denying or granting appropriations for projects in his dictrict, its members, particularly the chairmen of its subcommittees, exercise great power which they do not hesitate to use. Michael J. Kirwan of Ohio, for example, is almost the czar of public works appropriations because of his chairmanship of the subcommittee on that subject. There are few in the House who are willing to antagonize him. The same is even more true of the venerable chairman, Cannon, whose wrath, it is said, is terrible to behold.

Under the Constitution revenue bills must originate in the House. There is no such requirement respecting appropriations bills, but the House Establishment insists on also initiating spending legislation. And throughout history the House has intimidated the Senate to such an extent that the upper chamber has never had the nerve to pass an appropriations bill first and see later what the House did about it.

The Senate Appropriations Committee does hold preliminary hearings at which administration witnesses and other interested persons are heard; but then matters are held in abeyance until the House acts, frequently months later. If the administration is dissatisfied with the amounts allowed by the House, as it usually is, it appeals for a restoration of the requested funds. The Senate is then apt to increase the House figure—sometimes to the amount requested by the administration—and go to conference.* Sometimes months pass before the conferees are able to agree.

In 1963 an open war broke out between the two Appropriations Committees as to where the conference committees should meet and who should preside over the meetings. The press billed the dispute as one between the two octogenarians, Carl Hayden of the Senate and Clarence Cannon of the House. Actually, these two men are on personally friendly terms. The trouble was far deeper. Many members of the House, despite Establishment relations with their Senate opposite members, would like to turn the Senate into a sort of House of Lords. Senate resentment at this desire is naturally fierce. Every so often the battle breaks out into the open.

Historically, the chairman of the Senate Appropriations Committee had always presided over the conferences, which had met on the Senate side of the Capitol. In 1963 the House conferees refused to go to conference unless the situations were reversed. A deadlock of several months ensued as the two Establishments glared at each other "eyeball to eyeball" with neither side "blinking." The whole appropriations process was stalled. Finally, the Senate, which was more interested in keeping the executive branch and the programs of the administration in funds, accepted a compromise on the place of meeting and the chairing of the conference without obtaining the concession it had requested—that the right of the Senate to initiate appropriations bills be recognized by the House. The conferences met in a neutral room and the chairmen took turns presiding. It was a typical Establishment minuet.

Appropriations bills should all be passed by July 1, which is the

* The Rules Committee has never refused to permit an appropriations bill to go to conference.

beginning of each fiscal year. The executive departments should know no later than then how much money they will have to operate with for the next twelve months. Such a procedure gives the committees and the Congress six months to pass the bills after the session begins.

The budget goes to Congress early in January of each year. It is difficult to understand why the appropriations bills cannot be passed by July 1, certainly by July 31, when, under the Legislative Reorganization Act of 1946, Congress is required to adjourn. To be sure, each bill is vastly complex, containing sometimes thousands of separate items. But the two committees are broken up into subcommittees which can work simultaneously.

Why did the appropriations process break down in 1963? Lethargy and indolence of committee members? The increasing complexity of the appropriating process as big government continues to grow bigger? The conflicting demands on the time of always busy Congressmen? Or are the economizers on both committees satisfied with things the way they are because it saves the government a lot of money?

At the end of each fiscal year on June 30 most appropriations for the year have either been spent or lapse. If the appropriations bill for a particular activity has not then been enacted, that activity, in theory, would have to cease. But Congress never goes quite that far. To prevent such catastrophes, both houses pass "continuing resolutions" at the very last moment, which authorize the executive agencies to continue spending in the new fiscal year at the same rate they spent in the year just closed.

One continuing resolution was passed at the end of June, 1963, when fiscal year 1963-64 opened. It authorized such spending for the months of July and August. As drowsy August drew to a drowsy close with the appropriations bills still undisposed of, another "continuing resolution" was adopted for the months of September and October. When the leaves changed from green to brilliant red and gold, another resolution was passed for November. The trees become bare, the snow flurries arrived. Congress (having just listened to President Johnson's call for "action now") interrupted its preparations for Thanksgiving long enough to authorize agencies to continue spending at the same rate until January 31, 1963. Those of us who tried to limit it to December 31 were beaten. The Appropriations Committee members said they could not complete their work by that date, but under the persistent prodding of President Johnson they did. Just before the new year the last bill was finally passed, almost six months late.

However, as our population has increased and with it the demand for services, as our military and space needs have risen, each year's appropriations have also increased. Each appropriations bill when finally passed is apt to be larger than its predecessor.

Thus, if spending is held to the same level as the year before for a six-months period from July through December, Congress has succeeded in saving the Treasury one-half of the difference between the total appropriations for fiscal 1963-64 and fiscal 1964-65 in those areas where the appropriations bill has not been passed by calendar year's end.

This result pleases the economizers, particularly the chairman of the House Appropriations Committee. By ignoring the responsibility placed on them by law, they are able to prevent, temporarily, the nation from meeting its increased responsibilities. They would not be able to do it if the law were obeyed and the appropriations bills brought to the floor. They haven't got the votes. But by utilizing the tactics of delay, linger, postpone and wait which the built-in rules and procedures of both houses make possible, the Establishment is able to cripple the program of the President and frustrate the will of a majority of the elected representatives of the people.

The administrative results are serious. Authorized expanded programs cannot move forward. Newly authorized programs cannot be started. Efficient executive advance planning is impossible. But the Establishment couldn't care less.

If the House Rules Committee reflects the essentially Confederate States aura of its chairman, Judge Smith, and the House Appropriations Committee exudes the crusty attitude of its border states chairman, Clarence Cannon, so does the powerful Ways and Means Committee reflect the urbane flexibility of its chairman, Wilbur Mills of Arkansas.

The Ways and Means Committee is not quite so receptive to Establishment influence as Rules or Appropriations. Membership on it is equally highly prized, but it is also more moderate, indeed more liberal, than its two counterparts. This is largely because the Democratic members who constitute the Democratic Committee on Committees are elected by the Democratic caucus, which is not controlled by the Establishment.

Nevertheless, the Ways and Means Committee, because of its responsibility for tax, trade and health care legislation, is where a great deal of the wheeling and dealing goes on. No committee is subjected to greater pressure from the lobbies, be they the powerful oil and gas lobby determined to protect the depletion allowance from erosion, or a tax lawyer bent on getting a special tax concession for his company or client. No committee through its filling of committee vacancies wields more power over the life of individual Congressmen.

The pressure is always on for tax privileges; to keep them, if you've got them; to get them, if you haven't. There are no lobbyists for the people save the President, and the administration's trumpet for tax reform has sounded an increasingly uncertain note as '61 and '62 have faded into '63 and '64 with no major tax reform bill passed by the Congress.*

Tax revision and reform have been badly needed by the country for many a long year. The Eisenhower administration, satisfied with the happy condition of the clients of the lobbies, was content with the last major tax bill of 1954 and somewhat fearful of what might come out of a committee controlled by the opposite political party.

Then, with President Kennedy, came the twin demands for accelerated depreciation for corporations and the Trade Expan-

* The bill finally enacted in winter 1964 contained some but not much tax reform.

sion Act. These two measures usurped the time and attention of the Ways and Means Committee during 1961 and 1962. Tax reform and over-all tax reduction were forced to "wait until next year." Then the lobbies went to work. Tax reform went down the drain. Tax reduction was weighted in favor of corporations and wealthy individuals. Months of 1963 went by with no very obvious evidence of urgency. Finally, in September, a bill emerged from committee, was granted a closed rule by the Rules Committee limiting amendments and debate and passed the House.

When one considers the composition of the Committee and the temper of the House, the bill was probably about as good as could be expected if one thinks of politics as the art of the possible. That the original administration proposals were far sounder than the bill which came out of the Ways and Means Committee and passed the House without amendment, few competent tax experts would deny. The compromise bill does contain one radical innovation: substantial tax reduction in a time of prosperity to induce a decrease in the unacceptable rate of unemployment and provide further incentives for business expansion.

Thus, unlike the Senate Finance Committee, it cannot be said that the House Ways and Means Committee lives in a vacuum removed from the disturbing fiscal theories of the modern world. It can act, if slowly and somewhat unsatisfactorily, when a majority of the body it represents is ready for action.

It must be concluded that there are no institutional changes in the operations or composition of the Ways and Means Committee which call for reform to permit the Congress to perform expeditiously its constitutional duties. The membership of the committee does not reflect current economic thinking. It does reflect the pressure of the lobbies. Many of its members are firmly anchored to the discredited economics of an earlier day. The traditions which control committee assignments leave much to be desired. But as time goes by, it seems likely the membership of the committee will adjust itself somewhat more rapidly to the fiscal needs of the nation.

There is the need to consider seriously whether the Congressional system is capable of dealing properly with fiscal legislation. Just as under the Hull Reciprocal Trade Treaties and the Trade Expansion Act of 1962 the Congress abandoned its efforts to write tariff bills, the question arises whether some flexibility similar to that given to the President by trade legislation should not also be given to him in connection with tax rates.

The complexity of tax legislation has to be seen to be appreciated. I am confident that not as many as ten Congressmen and Senators really understand the provisions of the tax legislation recently passed. Nor under present conditions, with their manifold other responsibilities, is it possible for them to do so.

The calendars in both the House and the Senate in the first session of the Eighty-eighth Congress in 1963 were kept up to date by prompt leadership scheduling and passage of bills favorably reported by legislative committees. The House Rules Committee delayed from time to time measures which the administration wanted passed and the House leadership supported. But whenever the leaders really wanted a rule badly enough to bargain for it, they eventually got it. Those administration bills passed by the Senate which were not called up on the floor of the House probably did not have the votes to pass there.

Perhaps some of this failure to summon sufficient support to pass the Area Redevelopment Amendments, the Youth Employment Opportunities Act, the Mass Transit Bill and several other measures is due to failure of the House leadership and the administration's Congressional liaison to whip enough Democrats into line. But there are limits to what can be done to overcome the resistance of a Representative who has either yielded to the pressure of a status quo lobby or is sincerely convinced that a majority of his constituents is opposed to a particular bill. And the conservative bipartisan coalition opposing the President is stronger in numbers in the House than in the Senate.

It is quite true that unlike the days of the New Freedom in 1913-14 and the New Deal in 1933 there was at first neither overwhelming popular support for President Kennedy's program nor an obvious economic or social crisis calling for prompt Congressional action for most of his legislative recommendations. Nevertheless, no one is really strongly against an appropriations bill, and the haggling over amounts between the Senate and the House is not a matter of either great public interest or of serious concern to most members. The proposed civil rights bill had a clear majority in both Houses. So did the tax reduction bill. Yet the Congress did not act on these measures in 1963.

To most observers there was more than lethargy and inefficient organization of both Houses behind the failure to enact a program and adjourn in midsummer.

As 1963 came to a close with the civil rights bill still stuck in the House and the tax bill still unreported from the Senate Finance Committee, a new explanation of the delay was receiving wide currency. This was that the Establishment in both Houses had determined by skillful use of delaying tactics to defeat the entire program of the President.

The prospect which confronted the Congress as it reconvened in January to consider the President's State of the Union message was an unpromising one. Every leap year we nominate and elect a President. We also nominate and elect Representatives to all 435 seats in the House and one-third of the 100 Senate seats. 1964 is no exception. Under our quaint customs we go about the process the hard way. There is a series of state primaries for both Republican and Democratic candidates. They begin in March and last until October.

Representatives are vitally interested in these primaries as well as in the general election in November—not only for themselves but because of their interest in the Presidential nominee of their party. Even for the sixty-six Senators not up for election there is important political business to be done back home. Most of them will be delegates to the party conventions which meet in July and August to nominate candidates for the Presidency and Vice Presidency.

Accordingly, this year, as in every Presidential election year, at least half the attention of every member of Congress is on politics back home. Hopefully, the other half is on his legislative responsibilities in Washington.

Throughout recent history no important legislation has been enacted in a Presidential year after the first national convention meets in July. Yet at the beginning of 1964 the following legislation would have to be passed unless the Democrats were to go to the country on a record of broken promises and inept Congressional leadership:

A Civil Rights Bill—passed by the House but facing a stubborn filibuster in the Senate.

A Tax Bill—finally passed in February.

A Health Care for the Aged Bill.

A Housing Bill (authorization for the present program has expired).

All legislation dealing with the "War on Poverty."

The various bills passed by the Senate and stalled in the House: Youth Employment Opportunities, Mass Transit, Domestic Peace Corps, Area Redevelopment, among others.

A new Foreign Aid Program.

Twelve regular and at least one supplemental Appropriations Bills.

As these words are written, the Congressional Establishment may well have succeeded in bringing Congressional action on most of these measures to a grinding halt. Whether, having done so, it will have laid the groundwork for the building of its own death chamber through Congressional reorganization and reform remains to be seen. Much will depend on the ability of President Johnson to overcome the Congressional obstacles which confront the program he inherited from President Kennedy. With his unquestioned ability to get things done it is possible that he can persuade, cajole and coerce the balky elephant and the stubborn donkey to pull together the creaking and rusty Congressional vehicle an acceptable distance down the road toward national well-being. But the odds are not promising as 1964 gets under way.

The techniques used by the Congressional Establishment are not enshrined in either the Constitution or law. In fact, they sometimes violate the law. The techniques arise from rules, customs, precedents and traditions which have developed largely through lethargy and indifference on the part of a majority in both houses, which has the power to change them if it has the will to do so.

VII

PROLOGUE TO REFORM

Relations between Congress and the President are unsatisfactory. The internal structure of Congress is obsolete. The record of Congress through much of American history is dismal. Many members of Congress are too preoccupied with getting re-elected, and too harried by their lesser chores, to perform with any distinction the high public service for which they are chosen.

Surely it is possible to improve the situation—to make Congress responsible, democratic, workable, constructive. It is, indeed. But there are obstacles to be overcome. There are also precedents to guide us through the maze of reform.

The first obstacle is the political time lag which is such an imposing part of Congressional tradition. Public realization that a continuing, affirmative, national legislative policy is necessary is a relatively new thing in American politics. It had its origin in Wilson's New Freedom and reappeared during the early New Deal. Yet it took World War II and the Cold War of the 1950s to convince the American people that positive national governmental action must replace political laissez faire. But Congress, because of its method of selection and its ancient customs, has not yet caught up with prevailing creative public opinion. The political stalemate described by Samuel Lubell in *The Future of*

American Politics and by James MacGregor Burns in *The Deadlock of Democracy* represents the facts of Congressional life today.

The customs, manners, rules and procedures of the Congress owe much to the American tradition of thinking in sectional and local social, economic and political terms. Americans, like most human beings, share a conviction that "The Lord helps those who help themselves." Until recently we were content to protect ourselves from alleged governmental restraint on our personal activities by Congressional devices designed to give minority interests (other than the Negro) a veto on the legislative process. The durability of these devices is also a tribute to the curious notion that to do nothing does not constitute a decision. The fear that the creation of a national legislature with the capacity to act might produce wrong decisions overlooks the fact that to do nothing in the modern world may itself represent a decision as disastrous as any affirmative action.

This strain of negativism runs deep. One may recall the interminable delays in enacting the constitutional amendments providing for the income tax, the direct election of Senators and women suffrage; and how long we waited for child labor legislation, unemployment compensation and a host of economic and social welfare measures passed a generation earlier in most other Western democracies.

While Congressional political lag has always existed—indeed, through failure to solve the slavery question it played its part in bringing on the Civil War—it did not become glaringly apparent until the Great Depression of the 1930s. Prior to that time the system worked tolerably well. Each section got its interests taken care of by logrolling. Our wealth made the price supportable. World affairs did not require decisive action by the Congress. The really vital interests of the nation were not adversely affected. The system operated through a national legislature so organized that sectional and economic interests were able to protect themselves from objectionable government policy during a period in which no vigorous government policy of any kind was required in the national interest.

A governmental system that is not capable of producing a coherent legislative program is not likely to appear deficient to a people imbued with a firm distaste for strong government and not confronted with crisis. It produced a government that did not interfere with the expanding economy, which was then the main interest of most influential Americans. Understandably, it was not then perceived that an arrangement which gave minority interests a stranglehold on national policy through control over Congressional procedures might, when crisis arrived, prove to be inoperable.

It is in the nature of minorities, as Joseph Chamberlain once said, "to devise some ingenious machinery by which [they] may be saved from the natural consequences of being outnumbered." Such ingenious machinery is the very nerve center of the present control of the Congress. It will not do to defend this machinery as a protection against "the tyranny of the majority," for it is nothing of the sort. It is a built-in defense for maintaining a status quo no longer tenable in the face of present conditions at home and abroad. And it violates every principle of popular rule on which free governments are based. It is the "tyranny of the minorities" we suffer from.

The central defect of the modern Congress is that it permits a minority determined on inaction to frustrate the will of the majority which desires to act. All the majority wants to do is to work the will of the people it represents. Minority obstructionism has merely reinforced that Congressional lag which gets us into trouble. We can reflect soberly today on the results of the bitterest Senate filibuster of the nineteenth century, which in 1890-91 defeated a bill, already passed by the House, to give the federal government supervision over Congressional elections. How much rancor and discord in our century would have been avoided had the majority in the Senate been able to pass this bill, aimed at eliminating Negro disqualification and intimidation in the South.

Those who delight in the fear of "majority tyranny" should seek election to a major governmental post under conditions of genuine political competition. They would soon learn how varied are the interests that must be conciliated if success is to be achieved at the polls. There is nothing monolithic and therefore no basis for "tyranny" in the majorities put together by Congressmen from two-party states and districts today. Potential tyranny is a characteristic of minorities like the John Birch Society or the Communists, not the mark of the representatives of a major party seeking the support of a national electorate.

It is the dynamics of democratic politics, not the erection of legal barriers to action, that make for moderation in our public life and provide the real protection from majority tyranny. In fact, while both major parties have extremists in their ranks, those extremists have never represented orthodoxy in the parties to which they belonged. Their very power emerged from their exploitation of devices aimed at protecting the minority. Huey Long and his one-man filibusters or Joe McCarthy arrogating to himself the investigatory power of the Senate and temporarily usurping executive prerogatives never seriously threatened to assume leadership of either party. There is an old saying in England that the House of Commons has more sense than anyone in it. The same thing can be said of any legislative body where a consensus is permitted to develop and take action. It is, therefore, a grave error not to establish procedures which permit the good sense of a majority to prevail.

Congressional preoccupation with legal checks on the majority is superimposed on functional checks implicit in the separation of powers, including the Presidential veto. Moreover, our strongly held respect for minorities gives them additional protection. It is the strength of that tradition which provides the moral support for the effort to integrate the Negro into American life. It is indeed ironic that this effort on behalf of our most disadvantaged minority is frustrated by devices ostensibly aimed at preventing "majority tyranny."

The obstructionist policies encouraged by those same devices are in the long run self-defeating. In 1925 Vice President Dawes advised the Senate that "under the inexorable laws of human nature and human reaction, the Senate rules, unless changed, could only lessen the effectiveness, prestige, and dignity of that body."[1] There can be no doubt that the Dawes warning was prophetic, if unheeded. A legislature which denies itself the power to act, particularly when the obstacles to action are so obvious and so publicly demeaning as the filibuster, merits only disrespect and the loss of popular esteem it has achieved.

Max Lerner's harsh description is a typical reaction:

> Congress has become a problem child of the American governmental family. It is noisy, volatile, vulnerable to pressure groups and lobbies, often parochial in its outlook, jealous of its prerogatives, insecure about its position, implacable in its vendettas, bewildered by its mounting tasks. It has lost its reputation for great debate, has become intractable to party leadership and discipline and incapable of disciplining itself, and in recent generations it has developed fewer examples of the great leadership it once possessed.[2]

Vesting the veto power in a minority goes far to destroy that spirit of desirable compromise which is one of the hallmarks of a democratic legislative assembly. A minority bent on inaction finds it unnecessary to compromise with a majority which is powerless to act. The Congress of the United States is, within very broad limits, favorably disposed to accommodate a wide spectrum of opinion. There is no compulsion to agree on moderate and reasonable action, however, when the rules offer hope that nothing at all need be agreed to. Defiance by the minority breeds in the end vindictiveness in the majority. Neither sentiment is congenial to useful action.

The risk of tyranny by the majority over the minority is today small indeed. Tocqueville's fears of democracy have proved groundless. It is a minority, not a majority, which imposes sterile uniformity. Today the Negro minority is tyrannized by a white minority. National democracy has had no fair chance to do justice.

Another obstacle to clear thinking about Congressional reorganization is the ancient and slightly dishonorable doctrine of "states' rights." We tend to forget that our venerated Constitution was a wise reaction to states' rights pressed to the verge of chaos under the Articles of Confederation. It was states' rights which nearly disrupted the union at the Hartford Convention in 1814; which took South Carolina down the primrose path of nullification in Jackson's first term; which, raised in defense of human slavery, played a major part in bringing on the Civil War; which has been the shield of the selfish men who have fought against social reform ever since; and which, today, is used as a major argument against that strengthening of the power of the legislative branch to act when its majority is ready for the action so necessary to national security and well-being.

As Henry Steele Commager has noted,

> For well over a century now, this pernicious doctrine [states' rights] has been invoked for two major purposes . . . to weaken government and to endanger freedom. A states' rights philosophy which is never inspired by generosity, never excited by a passion for freedom or for justice, never exalted by magnanimity but takes refuge in narrowness, selfishness and vindictiveness, exhausts its claim to tolerance.[3]

There is no greater nonsense circulated today than the theory that the states are the defenders of freedom and the national government its enemy. The fact is just the opposite. The growth of the power of the national government has secured an increase in individual freedom, social, economic and political. The effect of national power has been benign, not malign. It is a shame that the Congress has not sensed this basic political truth until long after it occurred to both the Supreme Court and the President. The use of states' rights as a rallying cry for those who desire to perpetuate an inept Congress unable to deal with pressing national problems is a cry to perpetuate plutocracy and greed and to protect those who are today violating civil rights and civil liberties with impunity. To rely upon the states for a solution of problems essentially national in their scope such as education, unemployment and social security is to insure that these problems will not be solved. Those who advocate states' rights are, therefore, in the vanguard of the opponents of Congressional reform. As long as they can keep the Congress negative their status quo philosophy is safe. It is state debt and state government employment which have risen almost astronomically in the postwar years, not the federal government's. Yet this enormous increase has not been sufficient to make appreciable inroads toward solution of the domestic problems which beset us. Letting the states do it is tantamount to letting the problems remain unsolved.

Closely related to the states' rights argument is the nightmare of "federal control" over individual liberties which haunts the dreams of our conservative friends. This is a sheer hallucination. I cannot think of one current program in which the "heavy hand of the federal government reaching out into our private lives" has actually been restrictive of our personal freedoms or detrimental to our economy—if, that is, one accepts the need for a justly organized society in a civilized world. The problem of protecting liberty against the demands of society is difficult and delicate, as John Stuart Mill made clear long ago. "Government, like dress," said Tom Paine, "is the badge of lost innocence." Sometimes the choice between liberty and order is difficult. In the great struggle for civil rights for all Americans, for example, it has been argued that equal access to public accommodations is an infringement on the liberty of the individual who owns or manages the facility. I would argue that the individual right of every American to the use of that facility is an *expansion* of basic liberty, not a *denial* of liberties. But the question is not easy.

The concern over minority rights and regional interests is understandable enough in view of our history. For the descendants of Southern planters, steerage immigrants, British convicts, African slaves and New England Puritans to live and work in peace and harmony, and pursue happiness together, is no easy thing. No other nation has had to attempt it. On the whole we have been successful, but we still have some miles to go on the road to the good society.

The motto carved on the New Senate Office Building is "The Senate is the Living Symbol of the Union of the States." That pretty well sums up the Congressional attitude. But time and history and world responsibility have made us a nation, and it is time that in our thinking and in our behavior we recognized contemporary fact. We must move toward national federalism, accepting the federal structure, but emphasizing the national.

There are many who persist in the mistaken view that the problems of Congress, like the poor, will always be with us. But the Congress has not always been as incapable of action as it is now, and majority rule has not always been so successfully thwarted. Like the tradition of Jim Crow in the South, which is not nearly so old as it is iniquitous, there is a tendency to accept as age-old and hallowed traditions the habits of a few decades. Most of the unfortunate traditions of Congress are not very old and not very hallowed. In a culture confronted with constant change it is surprising that so many still believe change in Congress is not possible.

Procedural reform in the Congress has a history at least as old as the practices which led to it. In the past hundred years, important procedural reforms have often been successfully accomplished as the need became clear.

How was it done before? There have been two classic instances of procedural reform in the House of Representatives. The rules and practices of the House grew like weeds from the First Congress until March of 1860, when a largely technical revision of the rules in the interest of clarity was adopted. Twenty years later the job was done again when the House approved a recodification recommended by a committee whose members included, among others, Samuel J. Randall of Pennsylvania, Alexander H. Stephens of Georgia, and James A. Garfield of Ohio, who shortly afterward was elected President. The committee's report consolidated into 44 rules what had formerly been 167, thus securing "accuracy in business, economy of time, order, uniformity and impartiality."[4] But the 1880 rules revision left untouched such dubious practices as riders on appropriations bills and the disappearing quorum—a technique of a minority under which members who were present refused to vote and thus invalidated the vote of the House for want of a quorum (in effect a filibuster).

All this history was preliminary to the first major reform of House procedures, "Reed's Rules" of 1890. Thomas Brackett Reed of Maine was a man of strong character and determined purpose. A large, stout, bald man with a walrus mustache typical of his day, and an acid tongue which withered opponents with invective and sarcasm, he believed that the duty of a legislature was to legislate. He became an expert on rules procedures and precedents.

In 1889, after twelve years in the House, he was elected Speaker. In those days the House, at the beginning of a new session, operated under general parliamentary procedure and, in due course and in leisurely fashion, eventually adopted rules which were generally, but not always, identical with those of the last preceding Congress. Shortly after the House met in 1889 the election case of Smith *vs.* Jackson was called up for consideration. Mr. Crisp of Georgia, a Democrat, raised the question of consideration. A roll call was ordered which resulted in 161 votes to take up the case, 2 opposed, with 163 not voting. The Democrats, who desired to stall, raised the question of no quorum.

Ever since the 1830s the practice had prevailed of all members of the minority party refusing to vote when they believed that not enough majority party members were present to make a quorum. Frequently, when the parties were fairly evenly divided, this tactic would be successful because some members from the majority party would fail to show up. Then a minority member would raise the question of "no quorum" and the presiding officer would rule the vote was invalid because a majority of the House had not voted. This despite the fact that enough members were present on the floor (though silent) to create a quorum had they responded when their names were called. Following this technique, a bill to admit California as a state in 1850 failed of passage on thirty-one roll calls in a single day. For this filibustering technique the House had no answer until Reed appeared on the scene.

When the suggestion of no quorum was made in the Smith *vs.* Jackson election case, Reed directed the clerk of the House to record the members on the floor who were present but not voting. He called off the names of forty-one of them, then announced that a quorum was present and that the resolution had been passed.

Bedlam broke out. The Democratic minority denounced the Speaker as a "scoundrel" and a "czar." "What becomes of the rights of the minority?" one member demanded. "The right of the minority," Reed replied mockingly, "is to draw its salaries and its function is to make a quorum."[5]

The near riot continued for three days. One key Democrat, with the parliamentary manual in his hand, addressed the Speaker:

> "I deny your right, Mr. Speaker, to count me present. . . ."
>
> "The Chair is making a statement of fact that the gentlemen from Kentucky is present," Reed retorted. "Does he deny it?"[6]

The doors of the House were customarily locked when a roll call was ordered. As Reed persisted on subsequent roll calls in directing members present and not voting to be recorded as present for the purposes of making a quorum, a rush for the doors would follow to get out before they were locked in and counted during the roll call. Congressman Constantine Buckley Kilgore of Texas carried, for the rest of his life, the nickname "Kicking Buck Kilgore" for having kicked down a locked door to the House to make his escape.

In the end the uproar subsided, Democrats acquiesced, the filibuster power departed for all time from the House, and Reed reigned supreme as Speaker. The following year, 1890, the Reed

Rules were adopted after full debate. They did more than destroy the practice of filibuster. They placed the Speaker in control of the House with almost dictatorial powers.

Reed acquired almost unlimited control over floor action. He would confer with William McKinley of Ohio, later to be President, Uncle Joe Cannon of Illinois, subsequently Speaker of the House, and one or two others on the Rules Committee, and then Reed would call in the minority leadership and say, "Gentlemen, we have decided to perpetrate the following outrage."[7]

Congressman Joseph Cannon became Speaker of the House in 1903. For seven years he ruled in the best Reed tradition. He was a genial man of strong conservative bent. He loved to play poker and drink whiskey. Senior Congressmen who shared the Speaker's political views and enjoyed similar habits formed a small oligarchy which under Cannon's direction ran the House. They had no program they were interested in enacting. They wanted to pass only such legislation as was absolutely essential, approve the appropriations bills and go home.

A number of insurgent Republicans and Democrats had been elected to the House during the Theodore Roosevelt years, however, and strong resentment against Cannon's dictatorial tactics built up. Cannon was using his power to defy members of his own party, the President included.

On March 16, 1910, a coalition led by liberal Republican George Norris of Nebraska, later to become Senator and the father of the TVA, initiated rule changes to cut the Speaker down to size. Cannon was removed from the Rules Committee, of which he had formerly been chairman.[8] Henceforth the Rules Committee was to consist of ten members, six from the majority party and four from the minority party, elected by the House itself, and it was to elect its own chairman. Cannon's power to appoint the standing committees of the House and their chairmen was turned over to the Ways and Means Committee.

It took a long debate and a continuous session lasting twenty-nine hours to accomplish these quite drastic reforms by a vote of

191-156 on March 19, 1910. The effect was to destroy a large part of the system of strong party government, party discipline and majority rule which the Republicans had erected under the leadership of Speakers Reed and Cannon. Insurgent Republicans, who had smarted under the Old Guard discipline, played a large part in the new reforms. As one of them, Congressman Nelson of Wisconsin, explained, "Members long chairmen of important committees . . . with records of faithful and efficient party service . . . have been ruthlessly removed, deposed, and humiliated before their constituents and the country because, forsooth, they would not cringe or crawl before the arbitrary power of the Speaker and his House machine. . . . We are fighting with our Democratic brethren for the common right of equal representation in this House, and for the right of way of progressive legislation in Congress."

Cannon continued as Speaker with substantially curtailed powers until the Democrats captured control of the House in November of 1910. When the Sixty-second Congress convened the following year, Champ Clark was elected Speaker. The Democratic majority then adopted its own rules, which retained all the curbs on the Speaker's power adopted the previous year. The day has come when it is obvious that these new rules are themselves insufficient. The trouble with these rules is that they continue the breach between the President and the House by making the Rules Committee and the chairmen of legislative committees immune to the pleas of the party leaders responsible for enactment of the President's program.

These two "revolutions" in the House were paralleled by an equally drastic revolution in the Senate in 1913.

After the election of 1912 the Senate of the Sixty-third Congress contained fifty-one Democrats, forty-four Republicans and one Progressive. As usual the ranks in both parties were split into liberals, or administration men, and conservatives. The Democratic National Convention which nominated Woodrow Wilson for

President at Baltimore in 1912 had adopted a liberal platform on which he ran under the slogan of "the New Freedom." Forty Democrats, ten Republicans and the one Progressive—the elder La Follette of Wisconsin—were in sympathy with the platform, whose principal planks dealt with child labor, women's suffrage, the tariff, monetary reform, antitrust legislation, strengthened Civil Service and pure food and health legislation.

Then, as now, conservatism in the Democratic party centered in the South and, through seniority, controlled the party chairmanships, where much power resided. With a liberal majority of only fifty-one to forty-nine it was obviously going to be impossible to push the New Freedom program through the Senate unless Wilson's men could be put in charge and be prepared to cooperate with the progressive Republicans.

Thirty Democrats met at the home on Massachusetts Avenue of the youthful Senator from Tennessee, Luke "Young Thunderbolt" Lea, on a Sunday late in February, shortly before the members of the newly elected Congress were to take their oaths of office on March 4, 1913. Lea had first been elected to the Senate in 1910.

It was obviously going to be a tight squeeze to organize the Senate for Wilson. The first objective, they decided, must be to elect a strong Majority Leader to preside over the caucus and manage the strategy of the legislative program. Senator Thomas Staples Martin of Virginia, a conservative, had been Caucus and hence Minority Leader for some time. While he was a man of pleasing personality and unfailing courtesy and was personally popular with his colleagues, it was felt necessary to replace him with a man who would support the President. The group decided on John Worth Kern of Indiana, who was not present at the meeting, being preoccupied with the trial of a lawsuit.

To say that Senator Martin was unhappy is to understate the case. But the Wilson men had the votes, and the Senator from Indiana was duly elected Caucus (Majority) Leader.

Kern was also serving his first term in the Senate. But he was a national figure, having been the Democratic candidate for Vice President in 1908. He was the oldest of the men committed to enact the New Freedom program into law. His mustache and Vandyke beard embellished his obvious dignity. He was a man of infinite tact and patience. Well liked by his colleagues, he had a reputation for sound common sense. He needed all these qualities, for never before, or for that matter since, had a Senator been called to the majority leadership after only two years of service.

His task was formidable. Three of the fifty-one Democrats were disaffected. Eight more were in the doubtful category. He would have to rally the remaining forty, hold as many of the doubters as possible, woo the ten liberal Republicans and the one Progressive to squeeze through with the necessary majorities on the floor. The rules of the Senate, then as now, were archaic and made for delay and inaction.

But with the staunch support of his colleagues he got the job done. The Steering Committee which he appointed was safely progressive but included two conservatives. Five of the nine members had served two years or less in the Senate. In assigning committee seats it set seniority aside without compunction when necessary to assure a majority for the President's program. Special committees controlled by liberals were created to deal with the Federal Reserve Bill and the constitutional amendment for women's suffrage. The reorganization of the Senate had been accomplished in a way paralleling the overturn of Cannonism in the House by the practical abolition of the seniority rule in making up committees.

"The Senate," said Kern, "will be Democratic not only in name but in practical results."[9]

The next step was the adoption of new rules which gave a majority of a committee authority to call meetings and dispose of pending business, a power hitherto vested in the chairman. They placed in the majority power to name subcommittees, to select conferees to meet with Representatives of the House and generally democratized Senate procedures. The result was to eliminate the power of a committee chairman to postpone action indefinitely on any bill which did not appeal to him. Committee chairmen became little more than presiding officers.

Yet these revolutionary changes were accomplished with a minimum of friction. Within a week the Democratic majority presented a solid front. Party discipline was maintained through the caucus.

The result is history. The Underwood Tariff, the Federal Reserve Act, the Federal Trade Commission Act, the Clayton Antitrust Act, the Seaman's Act, the Child Labor Law were among the major pieces of legislation adopted in a session lasting 567 days. The Congress met continuously from April 7, 1913, to October 24, 1914.* During that session and indeed for several years thereafter democracy with a small "d" and cooperation with the President of the United States combined to produce a legislative record in both houses worthy of a great nation.

There was another important Senatorial reform during Wilson's day. In 1917 a controversy arose over the President's request for legislation authorizing him to arm American merchant ships. They were being sunk with considerable regularity by German submarines imposing a blockade on Great Britain to starve her into submission. Popular opinion was outraged at the German action and strongly in support of the President.

There was at that time no way of terminating debate in the Senate in order to bring a bill to a vote. Twelve "peace" Senators were determined to hold off the vote on the President's bill by talking continuously until adjournment. And this they did, to the fury of the President, despite the fact that seventy-five Senators signed a declaration that they were prepared to vote for the bill if given an opportunity.

President Wilson denounced in words now famous "the little band of willful men" who had frustrated the national will. He described the Senate of the United States as "the only legislative

* There was no adjournment at the end of 1913.

body in the world which is unable to act when its majority is ready for action." Then he proceeded to arm the merchant ships anyway by executive action under his constitutional powers as Commander in Chief after Congress had adjourned.

But this was not good enough for Senator Thomas J. Walsh of Montana, who was later to become, shortly before his death, Franklin Roosevelt's first Attorney General. Walsh was determined not to permit the blot on the Senate's reputation to remain uncleansed. At the beginning of the Sixty-fifth Congress in April of 1917 he brought out of committee the first cloture rule in the Senate since the "motion for the previous question" had been abandoned in 1807. The seventy-five Senators who had been denied an opportunity to vote, most of whom continued to serve in the succeeding Congress, were in a mood for action. Walsh pressed to passage the most celebrated of all Senate rules, Rule XXII. It provided that two-thirds of the whole Senate could, by a vote taken without debate, on a petition filed by sixteen Senators, impose cloture and require a vote on any pending matter after each Senator had spoken for no more than an hour.

The Kern and Walsh reforms were the only occasions during more than one hundred and fifty years, from the founding of the Republic to the end of World War II, that the United States Senate bestirred itself sufficiently to make action possible when action was needed, and to render a Presidential program immune from sabotage by a small minority.

Vice President Charles G. Dawes made an earnest and logical, but wholly unsuccessful, effort to persuade the Senate to modernize its rules in 1925. The bipartisan Establishment of that day, which had moved back into power with the election of ex-Senator Warren G. Harding to the Presidency in 1920, laughed him into silence.

A generation later, after a depression, a Second World War and the emergence of the United States as the leader of the free world, there was another round of Congressional reform. A public demand arose for the modernization of Congressional rules, procedures, precedents and customs. It found two staunch supporters in Senator Robert M. La Follette, Jr., Wisconsin Progressive Republican, and Representative A. S. Mike Monroney, Oklahoma Democrat. With the blessing of the majority and minority leadership they steered through both houses in 1945 a concurrent resolution creating a joint Congressional committee of twelve (six from each House, evenly divided as to party) authorized to "make a full and complete study of the organization and operations of the Congress and to recommend improvements to enable it better to meet its obligations under the Constitution." Unfortunately, the charge to the committee excluded consideration of the rules, practices, procedures and floor action of either House. This exception eliminated the area where reform was most needed, but did leave the committee considerable scope in other directions. Members of the committee who signed the report and still serve in Congress are Senator Richard Russell of Georgia, Senator Everett Dirksen of Illinois, then a Representative, Senator Monroney, then a Representative, and Representative Claude Pepper of Florida, then a Senator.

As the committee stated in its practically unanimous report,*

> Our Committee was created in response to a widespread Congressional and public belief that a grave constitutional crisis exists in which the fate of representative government itself is at stake. The course of events has created a breach between government and the people. Behind our inherited Constitutional pattern, a new political order has arisen which constitutes a basic change in the Federal design.

Strong words, and true.

After an extended and comprehensive series of hearings the committee recommended a number of drastic reforms, many but not all of which were enacted into law in the Legislative Reorganization Act of 1946. The committee structure of both Houses was simplified. Unnecessary committees were abolished, overlapping

* Representative Thomas J. Lane of Massachusetts dissented from the otherwise unanimous recommendation that Congressional salaries should be raised.

jurisdiction was eliminated. The staffs of committees and individual Congressmen were strengthened. The Office of Legislative Counsel, which renders invaluable service in the drafting of bills, was enlarged. The power of committee chairmen to pickle bills was to some small extent curtailed. Lobbies were required to register and thus become visible.

But some of the most important recommendations of the committee were either defeated on the floor or not pressed to a record vote because of the bipartisan opposition of the Establishment of that day.

Thus the committee had referred to the "need for the formal expression within the Congress of the main policies of the majority and minority parties." Its recommendations called for some mechanism which could bring about more party accountability for pledges made in the national platforms of the major political parties.

The committee wanted each House to create at the beginning of each Congress a majority and minority policy committee made up of seven members, membership thereon to expire at the end of each Congress, since the policy committees were to be representative of the members of that particular Congress only. The two policy committees of the party holding the White House were to meet regularly with the President and his principal advisers to improve relationships between the executive and legislative branches. The group would be called the Joint Executive-Legislative Council and would be created and financed by statute. "By giving Congressional leaders a part in the formulation of policy, instead of calling upon them to enact programs prepared without their participation, better cooperation can be obtained."[2]

But that was as far as it got. The Establishment was not interested in responsible cooperation with the executive to enact the platform of the winning political party. The last thing it wanted was a move toward national party responsibility.

Another series of recommendations of the La Follette-Monroney Committee dealt with the more efficient use of Congressional time. "Prolonged sessions resulting from improper organization of the [Congressional] work load," said the committee report, ". . . are keeping members away from the people they represent for more than 10 to 11 months out of every year."

The committee recommended that Congress "provide for a regular recess period at the close of each fiscal year to insure the return of members to their constituents at definite intervals each year . . . their return is not required for 'fence building' or 'vacations' but is in fact the essence of representative democracy."

Congress acted on this recommendation. The Reorganization Act of 1946 requires that Congress shall go home on July 31 of each year, having passed all appropriations bills and other necessary legislation. Yet in the years I have served in the Senate we have never yet obeyed the law we passed to discipline ourselves. And, as every law student knows, you can't mandamus a legislature. Both the courts and the President are powerless to make us keep faith with ourselves.

A third recommendation of the La Follette-Monroney Committee dealt with fiscal control. It was proposed that the Congress, within sixty days of convening, should act on a joint resolution, recommended by joint action of the two Appropriations Committees, the Ways and Means Committee of the House and the Finance Committee of the Senate, fixing a maximum sum for appropriations for the next fiscal year. If this sum should be exceeded, all appropriations would be cut back pro-rata to bring them within the agreed total unless the Congress should by resolution authorize an increase in the national debt in the amount of the excess of appropriations over estimated revenues. This reform was enacted but never became meaningful. A number of other sound fiscal reforms were recommended by the committee. All were stricken from the bill when it came to the floor for action.

The matters discussed by the committee, but with respect to which no recommendations were made, are also of considerable interest. They included: (1) seniority of committee chairmen; (2) the powers of the House Rules Committee; (3) establishing a regular procedure for the questioning on the floor of the heads of executive departments; (4) limitation of debate in the Senate.

Most of the study committee's recommendations survived the scrutiny of the Senate Special Legislative Committee, chaired by Senator La Follette, which reported the bill to the floor. The language of this Legislative Committee Report is also prophetic:

> Devised to handle the simpler task of an earlier day, our legislative machinery and procedures are by common consent no longer competent to cope satisfactorily with the grave and complex problems of the post-war world. They must be modernized if we are to avoid an imminent breakdown of the legislative branch of the national government. . . . Democracy itself is in grave danger of disintegrating from internal dissentions under the terrific pressures of the post-war world.

So it is again today.

VIII

INTERNAL REFORMS FOR CONGRESS

The main objectives of internal Congressional reform are, specifically, four:

1. To change the party leadership structure so that within both parties and in both houses a majority will decide party policy and enforce party discipline against recalcitrant members.

2. To change the rules and procedures of both houses so that a majority *can* act when it is ready to act.

3. To substitute cooperation for competition in the relations between the two houses, and between the whole Congress and the President.

4. To establish and enforce high ethical standards for members of Congress.

Nothing less than such drastic treatment will restore the Congress to vigorous, working, democratic health. But I am neither so naïve nor so egotistical as to expect my colleagues to agree with me in the absence of a strong popular demand for Congressional reform. I do not think that the Congressional Establishment will respond to the arguments in this book, cast off lethargy and obstructionism and reform itself. A great deal of public prodding is needed.

In a series of brilliant speeches on the Senate floor, beginning in

February, 1959, Senator William Proxmire of Wisconsin laid down the specific requirements of reform.[1] He was speaking at a time when the Democratic Senatorial group had just been increased by the election of 1958 from forty-nine to sixty-four members. "The typical Democratic Senator has literally nothing to do with determining the legislative program and policies of his party," he said. He protested the total disappearance of the party caucus as an instrument of decision or even information. He concocted an epitaph:

> Here lies the Democratic caucus,
> Conceived by Senatorial responsibility
> And born with the Democratic Party—1800,
> Assassinated at the hand of Senatorial indifference—1953.
> She labored faithfully and well to make
> Senatorial leadership responsible to all the people.

We have made some progress since Senator Proxmire spoke. There have been several useful meetings of the conference since 1961.

The present Majority Leader, Senator Mansfield, has not only called formal Democratic Conference meetings far more frequently than in the recent past, but has adopted the practice of calling informal groups of Senators into his office just off the Senate chamber for coffee to hear what took place at important meetings of the leadership with the President, meetings which are held every Tuesday morning at breakfast. Sometimes at these coffee hours, major legislation about to be brought to the floor is discussed and the tactics which would best insure its passage are determined. All of this is most helpful in creating a sense of party unity, in keeping Senators up to date on the thinking of the President and in arriving at a consensus in support of legislation desired by the leadership and the President. But the meetings are still too desultory and haphazard.

My Republican friends tell me that the weekly luncheon meetings of their conference now help to achieve excellent results in coordinating the position of the minority party.

But while this is an improvement over the earlier procedure, it is not nearly enough. There should be regular meeting days for the Democratic Conference to formalize what is now a hit-or-miss performance. The initial object of these meetings should be to determine in general terms the legislative program for the coming session, based on the State of the Union, Budget and Economic messages of the President, and reports by the Democratic members of the Joint Economic Committee. The recommendations of the Policy Committee and of the leadership on these matters would naturally carry great weight with the conference.

Such formal action by the conference, based on written reports and a written agenda circulated in advance, would act as a curb on the tendency of the legislative committees to go their own way without much regard for party position or authority. What Woodrow Wilson said in 1885 is equally true in 1964:

> [The caucus is a vital] antidote to the committees, designed to supply the cohesive principle which the multiplicity and mutual independence of the committees so powerfully tend to destroy. The caucus is the drilling ground of the party. There its discipline is renewed and strengthened, its uniformity of step and gesture regained.[2]

The question of discipline is necessarily involved and the conference is the place to settle it. Hardly a Senator today would support the old practice of the binding caucus. "King Caucus" is dead in the Congress for the foreseeable future. Moreover, both parties are divided into liberal and conservative blocks so that substantial agreement would be impossible and revolt certain on all controversial measures if an attempt to bind were made.* Finally, the Establishment, even with its wings clipped, as I hope in due course they will be, will probably always be strong enough within the legislative committees to prevent dictation of policy by the conference.

* This situation should not, however, prevent votes being taken by the conference from time to time to enable the leadership to determine the strength which could be summoned for the passage of particular measures.

Nevertheless, there is a practical area where the conference should exercise discipline. No institution should countenance members who are consistently out of sympathy with its objectives and the Congressional Democratic Conference should be no exception. Senators and Representatives who are unwilling to support the Presidential candidate of their party in the campaign simply have no place in the Congressional conferences of their party after the election. Congressmen who are unwilling to support the platform planks of their party in the area of jurisdiction of a particular committee have no business serving as members of that party on that committee; and far less should they have the right through seniority to become or remain chairmen of such committees.

There is plenty of precedent for the exercise of such discipline. The action taken by the Democratic caucus in 1913 on the recommendation of its Steering Committee has already been related. After the election of 1924, the Republicans in the Senate, in the second session of the Sixty-eighth Congress, passed a resolution that Senators who had campaigned against President Calvin Coolidge that year "be not invited to future Republican conferences and be not named to fill any Republican vacancies on Senate Committees."[3]

Senator La Follette, who had run for the Presidency against Coolidge, and Senators Ladd, Brookhart and Frazier were expelled from the Republican conference. They were permitted to retain the committee assignments they had theretofore held, but placed at the bottom of the committee seniority list. Senator Ladd was demoted as chairman of the then important Committee on Public Lands and Surveys.

There are other precedents.[4] In 1859 Stephen A. Douglas of Illinois, then the only Democratic Senator from a non-slaveholding state holding the chairmanship of an important committee touching the public business of the government, was dropped from the chairmanship of the Committee on Territories, a position he had held ever since he entered the Senate. At the beginning of the opening session in 1866, the Republicans demoted Senators

Cowan of Pennsylvania, Dixon of Connecticut and Doolittle of Wisconsin as chairmen of their respective committees, because they had failed to support Republican party policy in voting to override President Andrew Johnson's veto of the Civil Rights Bill. In 1871 Charles Sumner of Massachusetts, at the instance of President Grant, was not only deposed as chairman of the Foreign Relations Committee, but left off the committee entirely. And in 1923 the Republicans became so embroiled in a factional row as to whether Senator Cummings of Iowa should be permitted to remain as chairman of the Interstate Commerce Committee and therefore permit the next ranking Republican on the committee, Senator La Follette of Wisconsin, to succeed him that, after a month of wrangling, the post went, on the thirty-second ballot, to Senator Smith of South Carolina, the ranking minority Democrat on the committee.

In our own day Senator Wayne Morse of Oregon was disciplined by the Republicans for political independence in 1953 by removal from membership on the Armed Services and Labor Committees. When he later joined the Democratic party, he was restored to the Labor Committee, but at the bottom of the list. Later he was placed on the Foreign Relations Committee.

In the House the Democratic party conference seems to be even less effective than in the Senate.[5] Note was taken earlier of the decade between 1910 and 1920 when "King Caucus" ruled the House through the Democratic caucus. But his rule was, in fact, ended when the Republicans won the House in 1918. When the Republicans took over the White House after the election of 1920, the "King" lost his throne, never to regain it in Democratic robes. The Republicans in the House today have, through the Republican Conference chaired by able Representative Gerry Ford of Michigan, created a modern and sensible vehicle for enabling the individual Representative to speak his piece and have his views considered before the party leadership and committees implement party policy. But there are two Republican parties in the House: one conservative, the other reactionary, with perhaps a handful of independent liberals. There are, accordingly, the same limitations on achieving any meaningful unity in the House Republican Conference as there would be in its Democratic counterpart if an equally effective vehicle existed in the latter party.

An attempt has been made by House Democrats to follow the example of the Republicans and democratize their party structure. After the death of Speaker Rayburn, Henry Reuss of Wisconsin pressed for the establishment of a Democratic Steering Committee. In March, 1962, the Democratic caucus adopted a resolution setting up such a committee. It consists of one member from each of the eighteen districts in which the nation is divided for party purposes —known as "whip" districts—plus the House leadership. But the committee has never met, and as of this writing there are no prospects for a meeting.

There are fewer examples in House history than in the Senate of demotion of committee chairmen and discipline of committee members. The most famous one resulted from the revolt of the Progressives of Wisconsin against the regular conservative Republican leadership in the early 1920s. It came to a head after the Presidential election of 1924 in which Senator Robert La Follette, a Bull Moose Republican, ran for the Presidency on a third ticket.

In the "lame duck" session of Congress held in December, 1924, after the election of President Calvin Coolidge that November, ten Representatives from Wisconsin who had supported Senator La Follette for the Presidency were deprived of committee posts to which they had previously been chosen as Republicans. One of them, John M. Nelson, was removed as chairman of the Committee on Elections and dropped from the committee. Another, Florian Lampert, was removed as chairman of the Committee on Patents, but allowed to remain on the committee on the bottom of the seniority list.[6] In 1949 Speaker Sam Rayburn caused John Rankin of Mississippi and Edward

Hébert of Louisiana to be removed from the House Un-American Activities Committee for "antics" which displeased him and, it might be added, most of the country as well.[7]

In each case in both houses these demotions caused enormous controversy. In many cases they have not received the praise of historians. Vengeance was perhaps a motive in some of them. But for an institution, like the Congress, which exalts precedent, the precedents are there. And in each instance the party leadership recommended the action taken by the caucus.

In order to achieve the needed reforms in the composition of the legislative committees in the Senate a new Democratic Steering Committee is needed. The present Democratic Steering Committee consists of fifteen members, four of whom, the Majority Leader, Whip, Secretary of Conference and President Pro Tempore of the Senate, serve ex officio but with full voting rights. The remaining eleven are named by the leader as vacancies occur.

There is no particular point in reducing the size of the committee. Moreover, it serves a useful purpose to have the leadership as members with the Majority Leader as chairman.

The requisites for a Steering Committee dedicated to democracy within the Senate Democratic membership are: (1) that it should serve for only two years, the duration of a single Congress; (2) that its members, other than the leadership, should not be eligible for re-election until two years after their initial terms have expired; (3) that members should be nominated by the leader, seeking such advice as he thinks desirable; (4) that they should be subject to confirmation or rejection by the conference, which should have the right by majority vote taken by secret ballot to make substitutions to the list submitted by the Majority Leader; and (5) that the eleven additional members thus selected should represent a fair cross section of the geographical and ideological representation of the party in the Senate.

Once such a Steering Committee is appointed and functioning it could be trusted (1) to fill committee vacancies with the best interests of the party and the program in mind and (2) to recommend to the Conference such disciplinary measures in terms of committee selection and seniority against recalcitrants as disagreeable necessity might require.

There is no serious problem on the Republican side of the Senate. Its conference now meets regularly and selects its committees for terms of two years on the basis of nominations by the chairman of the conference confirmed by the conference itself. The ideological and geographical representation on its Committee on Committees appears to meet the above recommendations. In short the Republican Senators democratized their conference a good many years ago.[8]

In the House there has been serious complaint about the way the Democratic Ways and Means Committee and the Republican Committee on Committees have functioned in filling committee vacancies. Nicholas Masters has pointed out the result of continuous service on the Ways and Means Committee:[9]

> For a key functioning unit of the Democratic party's legislative apparatus, so much continuity in the Committee-on-Committees makes it ill-designed for flexibility and responsiveness to electoral changes and public opinion trends. Rather, it is more analogous to a firmly entrenched bureaucracy, not completely immune but well insulated, and capable of considerable resistance to any pressures placed upon it.

As for the Republicans, Masters concludes that the system whereby each representative on the committee casts as many votes as there are Republicans in his delegation really places the effective power in the hands of a few senior members from a handful of the larger states. In the Eighty-sixth Congress members from seven states controlled 97 of the 153 committee votes. Masters' incontestable judgment is that "Both committees-on-committees are so constituted as to be virtually immune to immediate pressures brought about by electoral change. This is no accident."

Consideration should be given to taking the committee assignment function away from the Ways and Means Democrats, creating a new Democratic Committee or Committees and providing for its election every two years by the Democratic caucus or nomination of the leadership. The same procedure should apply to the Republicans.

A thorough overhauling and rebuilding of the Policy Committees of both parties in both houses is also a necessity. Here the recommendations of the La Follette-Monroney Committee of 1945 still have validity. The committee recommended that each party in both houses should select a Policy Committee of seven. The committees of the majority party in each House would meet with their opposite numbers in the other House to develop ways and means of enacting into law the platform of their party as adopted at the last national convention. If the President was the leader of the majority party in either or both houses, the Policy Committee or Committees would confer periodically with him or his nominees for the purpose of agreeing on tactics to carry his legislative program, based on the platform, into effect.

The Policy Committees of the minority party would confer to determine the position of their party with respect to the legislative program of the majority and on other matters of party political importance as they arose from time to time. They would confer with the President or his nominees on bipartisan matters such as defense and foreign affairs, and of course on any other issue at the request of the President.

The Senate adopted these recommendations of the La Follette-Monroney Committee, but the House threw them out of its bill. Because the session of 1946 was coming to an end, the Senate, instead of insisting on a conference, accepted the House bill, which became the Reorganization Act of 1946. Thereafter the Senate set up its own Policy Committee of seven by a rider attached to an appropriations bill, but it had no opposite number in the House to confer with, and it rarely, if ever, has met with the President.

The needed changes in present organization and operations of the Democratic Policy Committee in the Senate are:

1. To reconstitute the committee as recommended in 1946, i.e., as a committee of seven on which the leadership should serve as full members constituting a majority of the committee. It is desirable to strengthen the leadership and make the size of the meetings with the House Committee and with the President and his White House advisers manageable. The three members in addition to the leadership should be nominated by the leadership subject to confirmation by the conference. *All three of these Senators should be wholeheartedly committed to the platform of the party and the program of the President.* Unlike the Steering Committee, geography should play no part in this selection. The test of membership should be party loyalty and prestige in the Senate. While seniority would undoubtedly have a bearing on the choice, it should not be the determining factor.

2. The function of the Policy Committee would be to work with the House Committee and the President on the tactics and strategy of enacting the party platform into law.

3. Since continuity of policy is important and since the prestige of the Policy Committee should be sufficient to bring the chairman of the Legislative Committees into line behind the program, it would seem wiser to make membership on the committee indefinite in term, i.e., the members to serve like federal judges for as long as they behave themselves in office. Stated somewhat differently, they should serve at the pleasure of the conference, which, as in the case of the leadership, would probably mean until death, defeat, resignation or repudiation.

4. Since the leadership would be in the majority, such a Policy Committee could be trusted not to abuse the "traffic cop" functions now exercised by the present committee. This function should therefore be added to those recommended by the La Follette-Monroney Committee.

In the House it would seem advisable to an outsider for the Speaker to constitute formally a Policy Committee of seven, to consist of himself, the Majority Leader, the Whip, the chairman of the Rules Committee, the chairman of the Appropriations Committee, the chairman of the Ways and Means Committee and a seventh member, selected by him and approved by the conference, who was a member of great prestige in the House and a loyal supporter of the President. Of course, as long as any of these chairmen are unwilling to give wholehearted support to the party platform they should be passed over in favor of someone else who is.

As long as the Republican party in the Senate remains in the minority there seems no need to change its present arrangement of a Policy Committee of fifteen selected for a two-year period on nomination of the chairman of the conference ratified by the conference itself.

In the House the Policy Committee and the Republican Conference also appear to be serving well enough.

The effect of these changes would be to strengthen greatly the Presidential party in both Houses, to create an agency of high prestige with the mission of making party performance match party promise and to give party responsibility the lift it needs in the Congress to make that institution's behavior more acceptable to the American people.

The next major requirement of Congressional reform is a change in the rules, customs, procedures and floor action of the two houses with the end in view of making it easier for both bodies to act effectively when a majority is ready for action. The ultimate purpose of rules reform is to remove as many of these obstacles as is feasible while retaining adequate opportunity for careful consideration in committee and full debate on the floor of all bills under serious consideration.

In the House the problem seems simple. Floor action is expeditious and needs no significant change. "Reed's Rules" plus the reforms connected with the overthrow of Speaker Joseph Cannon in 1910 took care of that many years ago.

The problem in the House is to pry loose from the legislative committees and the Rules Committee bills which are part of the program of the President or whose passage is desired by a clear majority of the House. The presently available techniques to solve this problem have proved inadequate in practice.

Three methods of achieving the desired result which worked well in the past but were abandoned might be restored by changes in the House rules. The first would be to reinstate the twenty-one-day rule which resulted in the passage of much important legislation during its short lifetime in the Truman administration. The second would be to decrease the number of names on a discharge petition required to bring a bill from committee to the calendar from 218, or a majority of the whole House, to 150, which was the requirement from 1924 to 1935. The third would be to remove from the Rules Committee the power to determine whether a bill shall go to conference if one member of the House objects on the floor to a motion to appoint conferees, thus leaving the decision to the whole House.

Of course, even with restricted powers, it is essential to have the Rules Committee an ally and not an enemy of the leadership.[10] The best way to do this would seem to be to demote its chairman and any other members who are unwilling to commit themselves to the winning party's platform and candidate in 1964, as well as members of the minority party who are disloyal to their own national leader and platform. While demotion in the case of other committees should be confined to those who are unwilling to support the platform in the area of the committee's jurisdiction, the Rules Committee covers the waterfront, having authority to send to the floor or pickle *any* proposed legislation on *any* subject. This vast power should never be permitted to be exercised by a committee containing members disloyal to the platform of the party to which they ostensibly belong.

The result of these suggested changes would be to democratize committee action in the House and make the committees subject to the will of a majority of that body. Whether the majority of the House would be prepared to follow the platform of the majority party or of the President is quite a different story. The composition of the House might well be such that no such result would follow. But at least so far as internal operations are concerned the President and his party would fight under ground rules which are in the tradition of our American democracy rather than the outmoded result of control of the House by an ancient oligarchical and plutocratic minority unresponsive to the popular will.

Before discussing needed changes in Senate rules and methods of operation something should be said about the custom of seniority, a controversial subject in both houses and in the country at large.

There is an unwritten custom, sometimes violated in practice, that length of service in the House and Senate determines eligibility for appointment to committees, and that the majority senior member of a committee succeeds automatically to a vacancy in the chairmanship. The latter half of the custom is more scrupulously observed than the former. The few exceptions to it have already been noted. So far as the first part is concerned it was violated time after time in making Democratic committee assignments in the Senate in 1963;[11] it was also violated in making assignments to the Judiciary and Foreign Relations Committees in 1961. No doubt Senatorial history is full of other exceptions to the rule in filling vacancies below the level of the chairmanship. Nevertheless, seniority is usually followed in selecting committee members. In the House the Speaker, the Democratic members of the Ways and Means Committees and the Republican Committee on Committees give some weight to factors other than seniority in making initial assignments. This is because there are, with each new Congress, so many new Representatives with equal seniority to be fitted into committee vacancies.

Former members returning to the House after an earlier defeat or resignation are usually given priority in the choice of committee posts, but lose for all time their seniority on defeat or resignation.

The seniority rule has come in for much adverse public comment largely because it tends to give power to elderly conservative members of both houses, mostly from the South when the Democrats control the Congress, who are apt to use their power to defeat or delay the enactment of the program of their party and of the President.

It operates somewhat differently in the two houses.

In the Senate there is a custom that one Senator may not be chairman of more than one committee.

Seniority in the Senate carries down to the most minute detail. Thus among Senators elected at the same time seniority is based on the date of swearing in. Senator Jacob K. Javits of New York was serving as Attorney General of New York when elected to the Senate in November, 1956. For reasons of New York politics he did not wish to relinquish his Attorney General's office until after January 3, 1957, when the rest of us just elected were sworn in. He took the Senatorial oath on January 9, and for the rest of his service in the Senate he will rank below us. John Sherman Cooper of Kentucky and Strom Thurmond of South Carolina, who were also elected on November 6, 1956, assumed their seniority over the rest of us by being sworn in the day after election, even though the Senate was not then in session—a procedure they, but not we, were able to follow because there were no incumbents in their particular seats. Actually, they could have saved themselves the trouble because as former Senators they would have ranked ahead of the rest of us anyway.

Within our group seniority was established by prior public service. Thus Frank Lausche of Ohio and Herman Talmadge of Georgia shared top ranking because they had formerly been governors of their states. Next came John Carroll of Colorado and Thruston Morton of Kentucky, former Congressmen. That left Frank Church of Idaho, who had held no previous public office, and me, who had been Mayor of Philadelphia. We were near the bottom of the heap, just above Javits. The powers that be decreed that a mere mayor was not entitled to any seniority status and since in the alphabet "Ch" came ahead of "Cl" my very close friend from Idaho had priority. Two years later he got it when a vacancy occurred in the Foreign Relations Committee which we both sought.*

Over in the House the problem is different. While many members serve on more than one committee, hardly anyone who serves on the three key committees—Rules, Ways and Means and Appropriations—is permitted to serve on any other legislative committee; and in the few instances where this occurs the second committee is a relatively minor one such as House Administration. Thus once a member is appointed to a major committee he tends to dig his feet in and wait for death, defeat or resignation of his seniors to bring him out at the top of the list. In the Senate shifts from one committee to another are frequent. When I first came to the Senate I served on both the Post Office and Civil Service and the District of Columbia Committees. I abandoned the former for Rules and the latter for Labor and Public Welfare, retaining only Banking and Currency, a committee to which I was initially appointed.

Another factor affecting seniority is that Senators, with rare exceptions such as Presidents Kennedy and Johnson, have nowhere else to go, while many House members aspire to and often succeed in being elected to the Senate. Forty-one of the present one hundred Senators previously served in the House. Those who remain in the House can hope to improve their seniority position every two years when the whole House is elected, while in the Senate the six-year term slows down the workings of the system.

On the other hand, the relatively small numbers of doubtful districts in the House gives the Representatives from the secure seats a great advantage in terms of seniority. Every House chairman comes from a district safe for his party.

Thus it should be no surprise to discover how seniority has worked in the determination of important legislative committee chairmanships in both houses in terms of length of service and

* Possibly considerations other than seniority affected this choice.

geographical location. Here is a list of the chairmen of the more important House committees as of the end of 1963.

House

Committee	*Chairman*	*State*	*Date When Service Began*	*Age*
Agriculture	Harold D. Cooley	N.C.	1934	66
Appropriations	Clarence Cannon	Mo.	1923	84
Armed Services	Carl Vinson	Ga.	1914	80
Banking and Currency	Wright Patman	Texas	1929	70
Education and Labor	Adam Clayton Powell	N.Y.	1945	55
Foreign Affairs	Thomas E. Morgan	Pa.	1945	57
Government Operations	William J. Dawson	Ill.	1943	77
Interstate and Foreign Commerce	Oren Harris	Ark.	1941	60
Interior and Insular Affairs	Wayne N. Aspinall	Col.	1941	67
Judiciary	Emanuel Celler	N.Y.	1923	75
Public Works	Charles A. Buckley	N.Y.	1935	73
Rules	Howard W. Smith	Va.	1931	82
Science and Astronautics	Overton Brooks	La.	1937	61
Ways and Means	Wilbur D. Mills	Ark.	1939	54
Joint Committee on Atomic Energy*	Carl T. Durham	N.C.	1931	71

* Chairmanship rotates between House and Senate.

Note that Chairman Vinson has been re-elected twenty-five consecutive times, Chairmen Cannon and Celler twenty and Chairman Patman seventeen. In the Senate the three Senators with the longest service are Hayden, Russell and Byrd of Virginia. Hayden has been elected seven times, Russell and Byrd six.

When one considers how much the luck of the draw contributes to achieving a committee chairmanship, the geographical distribution in the House is not subject to serious criticism. While there is some overweighting from the South, it must be remembered that the next time the Republicans carry the House these Southern chairmen will be replaced by Northerners and Westerners. On grounds of ideology the story is different. In the area of their committees' jurisdiction four chairmen hold views not in accord with the platform of their party. In terms of age one notes three chairmen over eighty and five more who have seen three score years and ten go by.

The difficulty is not so much in the seniority system itself as in the failure to exercise party discipline in a manner which would require chairmen to conform to the platform of their party in the area of the committee's jurisdiction or resign and seek service on another committee.

Nor is there any apparent correlation between age and ideology. Representatives Celler and Patman, among the older chairmen, are as liberal as Representatives Smith and Cannon are conservative. And Chairman Cannon, while he delights in cutting the heart out of appropriations recommended by any administration, voted for both the civil rights and tax bills in 1963.

Nevertheless, a rule that would require chairmen to relinquish their positions as such on reaching age seventy or seventy-five while still remaining as members of the committee, as Senator Theodore Francis Green did voluntarily on the Senate Foreign Relations Committee a few years ago, would avoid the embarrassment of the public display of a slowing down of mental agility and energy which are recognized by all save the elderly chairman himself—and which slow down and sometimes prevent the effective conduct of committee business. There would be a few cases where such a rule would deprive the committee of a useful chairman, but there would be many more where the result would be wholly salutary. Such a rule should apply both to the House and to the Senate.

On the following page is the list of Senate chairmen of important committees as of the end of 1963.

The geographical distribution of chairmanships in the Senate resulting from the operation of the seniority rule favors the South at the expense of the Northeastern and Middle Western states. Eight chairmanships are held by Southern Senators, only one from the Middle West and one from the Northeast. Two are held in the far West, two in the Southwest. The luck of the seniority draw has been unkind to Paul Douglas and Hubert Humphrey, neither of whom chair a committee but both of whom have more seniority than three of their colleagues who came later to the Senate but are now chairmen of important committees.

Senate

Committee	*Chairman*	*State*	*Date When Service Began*	*Age*
Aeronautical and Space Sciences	Clinton P. Anderson	N.M.	1948	68
Agriculture and Forestry	Allen J. Ellender	La.	1937	74
Appropriations	Carl Hayden	Ariz.	1927	86
Armed Services	Richard B. Russell	Ga.	1933	66
Banking and Currency	A. Willis Robertson	Va.	1946	77
Finance	Harry Flood Byrd	Va.	1933	77
Foreign Relations	J. William Fulbright	Ark.	1945	58
Government Operations	John L. McClellan	Ark.	1943	67
Interior and Insular Affairs	Henry M. Jackson	Wash.	1953	51
Interstate and Foreign Commerce	Warren G. Magnuson	Wash.	1944	58
Judiciary	James O. Eastland	Miss.	1943	59
Labor and Public Welfare	Lister Hill	Ala.	1938	69
Public Works	Pat McNamara	Mich.	1955	69
Joint Committee on Atomic Energy*	John O. Pastore	R.I.	1950	56

* Chairmanship rotates between House and Senate.

In terms of ideology there is no discernible preponderance of conservatives. McNamara, Pastore, Magnuson and, until recently, Jackson have been as liberal as Russell, Byrd, Eastland and McClellan have been conservative. Of course, if the Republicans come in, which cannot conceivably be before 1967, the South will lose its geographical preponderance. But the ideology of the ranking Republicans is more conservative than their Democratic opposite numbers.

Five Democratic Senate committee chairmen are in opposition to the platform of their party in the area of the committee's jurisdiction. As a result the seniority system in the Senate was a factor in watering down or delaying action on important legislative recommendations of the Kennedy administration in the field of civil rights, tax reduction and reform, and agriculture. It has also given the executive a continuous headache in the conduct of critical investigations by the Government Operations Committee. The opposition to the Test Ban Treaty and other efforts to ease Cold War tensions, emanating from the Preparedness Subcommittee of the Senate Armed Services Committee, is at least to some extent attributable to seniority.

Yet the point should not be overemphasized. Committee chairmen in the Senate have less actual power than their opposite numbers in the House. Armed Services, Judiciary and Finance are the only three committees where the will of the chairman prevails without much question; and in all three cases it is the other members of the committee, not the chairman's own power, which give them the authority to work their will.

Seniority is a convenient method of eliminating internal politics in both Houses. It is, in a sense, a lazy man's way of avoiding a struggle and a decision. It makes it possible for the most senior Congressman around to get what he wants without a struggle. But it also gives other Congressmen an excuse not to start a fight. The constituents pleading for action to get a committee off dead center can always be told, "What can I do?"

That invariable following of the seniority rule can do great damage to the legislative process is clear beyond doubt. History is full of instances where incompetent or senile men have obstructed the national interest through their positions as committee chairmen attained through seniority. Even worse are the instances, several of which presently exist, where extremely capable men have used their power as committee chairmen, acquired through seniority, to obstruct and often to defeat the programs of their own party and the President that party sent to the White House.

The remedy is not to eliminate seniority, but rather to curb and regulate it. Primarily this could be done by the exercise of party discipline as recommended earlier in this chapter. Another effective step would be always to fill committee vacancies, regardless of seniority, with men known to be in sympathy with party policy in the area of the committee's jurisdiction. This, of course, requires a Steering Committee or Committee on Committees responsive to a party conference prepared to support party programs.

A third reform to curb the evil effects of seniority would be to provide by rule that the chairmen of all standing committees should be chosen at the beginning of each Congress by secret ballot of the committee members of the majority party. Nine times out of ten the choice would be the senior Senator or Representative. But in the tenth case a recalcitrant chairman would be deposed or a prospective recalcitrant candidate for the chairmanship relying on seniority defeated. And in the other nine cases the chairman chosen because of seniority would bend over backward to be fair, to assure his continued tenure against the threat of demotion by his colleagues.

Finally, the evil effects of seniority or indeed of arbitrary action by chairmen could be curbed by enacting by rule a "Committee Bill of Rights." Some committees presently have rules of procedure which are in accord with normal parliamentary practice. Others do not. It would help very much in the latter cases to provide by rule that a majority of the members of a committee could convene meetings, fix the agenda, call up bills for consideration, regulate the conduct of hearings and terminate debate within the committee after a reasonable time. Ordinarily these matters are left to the chairman, and properly so. But the power of the majority to act if the chairman fails to do so should be clearly established.

Because these procedures were followed in the Senate Committee on Interstate and Foreign Commerce, the Public Accommodations title of President Kennedy's Civil Rights Bill was promptly considered and favorably reported in the fall of 1963. Because they were not, much of the rest of the bill was never reported by the Senate Judiciary Committee.

In the House the absence of effective committee procedures

enables the chairman of the Interior Committee to pickle indefinitely the Senate-passed Wilderness Bill, and the chairman of the Rules Committee to delay for months major legislation already approved by the appropriate standing committee.

The seniority system, then, is a serious obstacle to effective Congressional performance of duty. But the remedies for the evil are close at hand. All that is needed is to put them into effect and thus bring the system under control. There is no need to throw the baby out with the bath water. Properly regulated, the seniority system has its uses, principally in minimizing internal conflict between members of Congress.

One serious Senate problem results from the work placed on Senators through multiplication of committee assignments and floor responsibility. The committee responsibilities of that very senior Senator, Richard B. Russell of Georgia, illustrate the problem.

Senator Russell, who came to the Senate in 1933 and is the second most senior Senator, is the Commander in Chief of the Senate Establishment. As such his duties begin before each Congress convenes and continue throughout each two-year session. He regularly floor manages the opening session fight against changing the filibuster Rule XXII. He masterminds the meetings of the Democratic Steering Committee. He takes an active role in the work of the Policy Committee. He is chairman of the Armed Services Committee with its enormous responsibility for the defense program. He is a member of the Appropriations Committee and chairman of its Subcommittee on Defense, which passes on the Defense budget. He is senior member although not chairman of the Committee on Aeronautical and Space Sciences, which, among other things, deals with the legislative aspects of landing a man on the moon. He is senior member although again not chairman of the Joint Committee on Atomic Energy. He is a member of President Johnson's commission to investigate the assassination of President Kennedy. He is the senior ex officio member of the Boards of Visitors to the Military, Naval and Air Force Academies.

Senator Russell is unquestionably the most heavily overworked Senator. But others are not far behind. Senator Carl Curtis of Nebraska, Republican, serves on the Space, Finance, Rules, Government Operations and Joint Atomic Energy Committees. Throughout 1963 he was preoccupied with the trip to the moon, the tax bill, TFX, Joe Valachi, Billy Sol Estes, Bobby Baker and the peaceful uses of atomic energy.

Nine Senators serve on four legislative committees. A total of twenty-one serve on three major committees or more. And this does not include the subcommittees within committees, where the workload is often as great as it used to be on a major committee fifty years ago.

One morning late in November, 1963, I had four committee meetings at ten o'clock. One was a hearing before the Subcommittee of the Labor Committee on Manpower and Employment, of which I am chairman, where witnesses from the Defense Department were to testify on the impact of defense contracts on employment and unemployment. Another was a hearing at which Senator Fulbright and Secretary of the Treasury Dillon were to appear in opposition to the Mundt bill prohibiting the Export-Import Bank from insuring credits extended by banks to grain dealers selling wheat to Russia. While this hearing was before the full Committee on Banking and Currency, it ordinarily would have been held before the Subcommittee on International Finance, of which I am chairman. Since Senator Robertson, the chairman of the full Committee, favored the Mundt bill and I opposed it, and the vote on the bill in the committee was sure to be close, I felt it important to hear all the testimony and interrogate the witnesses.*

The third meeting was an executive session of the Rules Committee on the Bobby Baker case, where important questions of

* The vote was 8-7 against the bill, which was reported to the Senate with a recommendation that it not pass and was defeated by a vote of 55-37.

procedure were to be decided. The fourth was a meeting of the Special Committee on Problems of the Aging.

In the end I persuaded Senator Randolph to chair the Employment hearings, and I read later the prepared statements of the witnesses. I notified the Aging Committee staff that I could not be present, and spent the morning running back and forth between the fifth floor of the New Senate Office Building and the third floor of the Old Senate Office Building, picking up as much about wheat sales to Russia and Bobby Baker's fabulous career as I could.

Enough has been said to make the point that the present committee assignment load on Senators, even as far down the seniority list as I—and I am No. 50 as these words are written—is heavier than it ought to be. On senior Senators it is much too heavy to permit effective service.

The remedy is simple. No Senator should be permitted to serve on more than two legislative committees. The present rule that no Senator should serve as chairman of more than one committee should be extended to subcommittees—and particularly to subcommittees of the Appropriations Committee. Where necessary the size of the committees and subcommittees should be reduced to make these changes feasible.

To illustrate: Senator Russell would have to give up two of his four committees, keeping, presumably, Armed Services and Appropriations, but relinquishing his chairmanship of the Subcommittee on Appropriations on Defense. He would retain his position on the Steering Committee as a representative of the Southern philosophy. He would resign from the Policy Committee because he only sporadically supports the program of the President. He would continue to serve as a member of the Board of Visitors of the three service academies. And, of course, he would remain the Commander in Chief of the Establishment.

I would have to relinquish one of my three legislative committees (Rules, Banking or Labor) and one of my two Subcommittee chairmanships (Employment and International Finance).

If the size of committees and subcommittees were cut, I would probably lose my position on the Subcommittees on Education (under Labor), Housing, and Production and Stabilization (under Banking). But in return I would have a manageable workload and could dig much deeper into the areas of legislative responsibility I retained.

The end result would be substantially to improve both the speed and the thoroughness with which committee work is accomplished.

On July 1, 1960, I submitted to my Senate colleagues ten proposed changes in the rules of the Senate, all intended to make for more efficient action on the floor itself. These proposals have since been revised, refined and added to. Some are far more important than others. All of them would help, in varying degrees, in eliminating Congressional lag. Several of them have already been discussed. I list the others in the ascending order of their importance:

First: The requirement that the Journal of the preceding day's session must be read the following day unless unanimous consent to dispense with the reading is obtained should be eliminated. It is utilized only for purposes of delay and is an anachronism carried over from the days when the Journal was kept in longhand.

Second: The morning period reserved for minor business is cumbersome, obsolete, makes for delay and should be changed to permit the more expeditious conduct of minor business, thus leaving perhaps an extra hour a day for legislation. Known as the "morning hour," it usually lasts much longer.

Third: A useful reform would be to prohibit any Senator from holding the floor for more than two hours, except when floor managing a bill or by unanimous consent. We have no time or need in the modern world for marathon speeches.

A few months after I came to the Senate and, as a junior, was frequently called upon to preside, I was a somewhat unwilling participant when Senator Strom Thurmond broke the Morse record by holding the floor for twenty-four hours and eighteen minutes. I had been dining well at my brother-in-law's house when shortly before midnight on August 28, 1957, I got a call from Bobby Baker. "Please come down and help us out," he said. "Senator Church has been in the chair since six o'clock and is tired out." I leaped into my car, dropped my wife at home and repaired to the Senate in my dinner coat and black tie. The grateful Senator from Idaho turned over the Vice President's chair to me and went off to a well-deserved rest.

There on his feet in the back row was the junior Senator from South Carolina, looking fresh as a daisy, reading excerpts from the laws of each of the forty-eight states dealing with civil rights. He spoke in a low but audible voice. He had been at it since a few minutes before nine o'clock that evening. He was engaging in a filibuster against what shortly thereafter became the Civil Rights Act of 1957. About three A.M. Barry Goldwater wandered in and asked Strom to yield to him. Strom asked unanimous consent that he might yield briefly to the distinguished Senator from Arizona without yielding his right to the floor. I could have objected from the chair under the rules, but did not do so. Instead, I inquired of the practically empty chamber, "Is there objection?" And then: "Hearing none, it is so ordered." Strom went to the gentlemen's room. Barry spoke for a few minutes on a subject that now escapes me. In short order Strom returned and resumed his discussion of the civil rights laws of the different states.

I had a weary page who had been left on duty bring me a copy of the Washington *Post*. My alert gaiety had worn off and I was sleepy. I leaned back in the overstuffed swivel chair of the Vice President, spread a double page of the newspaper over my eyes to keep out the glare of the lights from overhead and went to sleep.

Around seven o'clock in the morning I awoke, feeling quite seedy, and began to complain about my long ordeal. Strom was still going strong. Bobby Baker had spent the night on a sofa in the Democratic Senate cloakroom. A page roused him. He sent out for reinforcements. At eight-fifteen Dick Neuberger of

Oregon arrived, fresh from a good night's sleep, and took over as acting President Pro Tempore of the Senate—the Vice President and the President Pro Tempore being, in the arresting words of the *Congressional Record*, "unavoidably absent." Strom talked on for over twelve more hours.

Obviously none of this makes the slightest sense and should not be tolerated in a supposedly mature legislative body. In fact, it is not tolerated in any other legislative body in the civilized world.

While the suggested change in the Senate rules would not often be invoked, it would nevertheless be a handy weapon to have around when the wind on Capitol Hill gets particularly gusty.

In this connection I also suggest that Rule XIX should be amended by adding at the end thereof the following sentence: "Upon the request of any Senator who has been recognized, his remarks on any subject may be delivered in writing, and if so delivered, shall be printed in the *Congressional Record* in the same manner as if those remarks had been delivered orally."

At present a Senator who asks leave to have a statement he does not read printed in the *Record* is always granted permission, but the remarks are printed in that miserable fine print reserved by the dowdy old *Congressional Record* for insertions of the deathless prose of nonmembers.

Many Senators get around this procedure by getting the floor, reading the first and last paragraph of, say, a thirty-page speech, telling the Senate reporters to print it in full and retiring from the chamber to attend to other business. But some Senators are either unwilling to engage in such subterfuge or enjoy reading at length to a rapidly emptying chamber and a gallery whose occupants must wonder how the Senate got its reputation as "the greatest deliberative body in the world."

Fourth: A motion to take up a bill on the calendar made by the Majority Leaders should be determined by vote without debate. At present such a motion is subject to unlimited debate, thus giving the opponents of the bill two chances to filibuster instead of only one, i.e., (1) when the motion to take up is made the pending business and (2) after the motion is finally approved and unlimited debate begins on the bill and amendments.

Fifth: The Senate should adopt a rule requiring debate to be germane when legislation which the leadership wishes to expedite has been made the pending business. No other legislative body in the world, so far as I have been able to discover, operates without a rule of germaneness. The principle is well laid down in Jefferson's Manual and was originally followed in the Senate: "No one is to speak impertinently or *beside the question*, superfluously or tediously." Some years ago the Parliamentarian ruled Jefferson need no longer be followed. No one can prevent a Senator from being tedious, but it should be possible to require him to stick to the subject.

In 1961 my staff made a study which disclosed that nongermane speeches occupy about one-third of the *Congressional Record*, excluding insertions of printed matter.

Early in 1964 the Senate adopted a rule requiring debate to be germane for three hours each day. It rejected an amendment I proposed which would have permitted the floor manager of a bill or the Majority Leader to require all debate to be germane until the pending business was disposed of. Several Senators, particularly Senator Dirksen, who greeted the possibility of the Senate's adopting a rule of germaneness with hoots of derision, have been trying to discredit the new rule by various tongue-in-cheek parliamentary objections. It is too soon to tell whether this effort at sabotage will be successful. Experience is building up, however, to indicate a more flexible rule would work better.

Sixth: Section 134 (c) of the Legislative Reorganization Act of 1946 should be amended to permit committees of the Senate to sit while the Senate is in session unless on motion decided without debate the Senate decides otherwise.

For many a long year it has been impossible to secure attendance on the floor of the Senate while discussion of pending legislation is taking place. Quorum calls are quite ineffective for this purpose. On Tuesday, November 26, 1963, I was prepared to call up an amendment to a "continuing resolution" proposed by the Appropriations Committee permitting government departments to continue spending until January 31, 1964, at the rate appropriated for the preceding year. Some such continuing resolution was necessary since at that time only four of the twelve regular appropriations bills had been passed. My amendment would have changed the date to December 31, 1963. Hopefully this would have expedited action on the appropriations bills.

We had just returned to the Senate from the House, where President Johnson had spoken to a joint session urging the Congress to complete promptly its legislative duties. "This is no time for delay. It is a time for action," he said. I was anxious to get as many Senators as possible to the floor to hear my argument. Since I was going to ask for a roll call vote I needed at least eleven Senators on the floor to join in my request for the "ayes and nays."

The continuing resolution was called up at around one o'clock, when most Senators were eating lunch. To prevent immediate passage of the resolution by voice vote I had to call up my amendment right away. There were half a dozen Senators on the floor. I suggested the absence of a quorum. The clerk called the roll. The bells rang twice in the Senate side of the Capitol and in the two Senate Office Buildings where committee rooms and Senators' offices are located. A few Senators drifted into the chamber, answered their names and departed.

Mike Mansfield said to me, "Joe, do you want a 'live' quorum?"

I said, "Yes." With a look of only mild pain he departed without asking that the quorum call be suspended, knowing that if he did so I would object to his unanimous consent request.

The clerk having completed calling the roll, a quorum not being present, Danny Inouye, Senator from Hawaii, who was in the chair, directed Ted Mansure, the clerk, to "call the roll of the absentees." The bells rang three times, more Senators filed in, answered to their names and departed.

When Mansure got down to the S's the second time around—"Mr. Saltonstall, Mr. Scott, Mr. Simpson, Mr. Smathers"—he increased his pace. I knew then that fifty-one Senators had answered to their names and that a quorum was technically present. "Mr. Young of North Dakota, Mr. Young of Ohio," said Mansure and, turning to Senator Inouye, "A quorum is present."

There were only seven Senators in the chamber, four less than the number necessary to get the "ayes and nays."

"A quorum is present," repeated Inouye. I was on my feet. "Mr. President, the Senator from Pennsylvania takes judicial notice of the fact that a quorum is not present and asks the clerk to observe that there are only seven Senators present in the chamber," I said.

Danny consulted Floyd Riddick, the assistant Parliamentarian. Then he announced, "The record shows that a quorum responded."

I was in a quandary. Under the rules I could not ask for another quorum call until the Senate "transacted business." I searched my mind for a quick way out and began to talk rather aimlessly, hoping some bright idea would come to me.

Relief came from an unexpected quarter. Everett Dirksen broke in.

"Mr. President, is it the transaction of business to address a parliamentary inquiry to the chair?" he said.

Danny conferred with Riddick briefly and then told him that it was not.

"Is it the transaction of business to ask unanimous consent to insert a matter in the *Record*?" Dirksen said.

Danny turned to Riddick again. Then he announced that it would be if the request was granted.

Dirksen asked me to yield, which I was glad to do. He then got unanimous consent to make an insertion in the *Record* and turned to me.

"Go ahead, Joe, get your quorum call," he said, "but call it off when you get enough Senators here to give you the ayes and nays."

I was happy to comply. Sixteen Senators showed up a few minutes later, I got the ayes and nays ordered, and we went ahead with a two-hour debate on my amendment. It failed to pass 20-63.

This incident is typical. Except just before a roll-call vote which has been announced in advance, Senators will not come to the floor.

In an attempt to remedy this situation the La Follette-Monroney Act of 1946 provided in section 134 (c): "No standing committee of the Senate or the House, except the Committee on Rules of the House, shall sit, without special leave, while the Senate or the House, as the case may be, is in session." The Rules Committee often has to sit while the House is in session to regulate procedure on pending bills, hence the exception.

The attempted cure for absenteeism has turned out to be worse than the disease. What has actually happened has had a serious and unanticipated effect on the conduct of committee business. The proponents of the change thought that "special leave," as used in the act, could be obtained on a motion decided without debate. But some years ago the Parliamentarian ruled that such a motion-barring unanimous consent (1) could be made only during the morning hour and (2) was debatable.

The result has been that committees may meet while the Senate is in session only by unanimous consent, which is often refused, particularly during a filibuster. Any Senator wishing to prevent a committee from meeting on a particular day while the Senate is in session can get the floor and filibuster until the time during which the committee desired to meet has expired. It is thus useless to persist in seeking leave to meet if one Senator objects.

During part of the summer and fall of 1963, in anticipation of civil rights action, Senator Olin D. Johnston of South Carolina was under instructions from the Southern bloc to object to any committee meeting while the Senate was in session. The Senator is a kindly and accommodating man. As the fall wore on and it became clear that the House Establishment would stall the Civil Rights Bill in that body until the end of the year and that the Senate leadership had decided on the strategy of waiting for the House bill before initiating Senate floor action, Johnston relented and withheld his objection wherever he was persuaded that no damage to the Southern cause was directly involved. However, during consideration of the tax bill early in 1964 Senator Dirksen prevented most committees from sitting. And, as this is written, most Senators believe that the Southerners will prevent all committees from sitting while the civil rights filibuster continues.

Significantly, the Appropriations Committee obtains unanimous consent at the beginning of each session to sit at any time during that session whether or not the Senate is in session. The alleged reason for this exception is that the committee meets in the Capitol near the floor and can respond promptly to quorum calls and votes, while other committees meet across the park in the Senate Office Buildings and take five or ten minutes to get to the floor after the bells ring. The real reason is that the appropriations bills would *never* get out of committee if meetings could not be held while the Senate is in session.

This unanimous consent has heretofore been given because of the enormous prestige of the Appropriations Committee and its chairman, Carl Hayden. It would be a brash Senator who denied such consent.* Thus more than a quarter of the Senate, serving on one committee, has a special privilege to meet not accorded to the other three-quarters. It is also significant that the committees denied the privilege of sitting include both those a majority of whose members are anxious to move forward with the program of the President (and therefore often want to meet) and those, like Finance and Judiciary, where the chairmen are

* I did so at the beginning of the second session of the Eighty-eighth Congress in January, 1964.

only too anxious to delay the President's program (and therefore don't want to meet).

The best way out of this dilemma is to permit committees to sit while the Senate is in session on approval of a nondebatable motion, except when the germaneness rule is in effect. The exception would make it possible for Senators to be on the floor whenever the leadership or the floor manager of the pending measure really wanted them there.*

There is no feasible way to make the Judiciary or Finance Committee meet while the Senate is in session if their chairmen don't want to meet unless a majority of the committee is prepared to overrule the chairman and a committee "Bill of Rights" has been adopted.

Seventh: Rule XXIV of the Senate should be amended by adding a new paragraph reading: "A majority of the Senate members of a committee or conference shall have indicated by their votes their sympathy with the bill as passed and their concurrence in the prevailing opinion of the Senate on matters of disagreement with the House of Representatives which occasion the appointment of the committee."

This sound, democratic principle, which is recognized in Jefferson's Manual, Cleaves' Manual, and the Watkins and Riddick book on Senate procedure, has been violated on a number of important occasions in recent years. Thus the Senate has been represented on particular bills, as it was in 1959 on the question of extending the temporary unemployment compensation law, by Senators who voted against the Senate position and in favor of the House position on the bill as a whole or particular provisions of it.

Under the existing situation, if a Senator wishes to protest that the practices as stated in the manuals are not being adhered to, he must publicly challenge one or more of the conferees.

* An amendment to the Reorganization Act to this effect proposed by me was defeated by a vote of 43-36 on January 30, 1964. The Senate did, however, approve Senator Church's resolution which allows committees to sit while the Senate is in session during the transaction of morning business.

This has been done successfully on several occasions, but for obvious reasons it has usually created personal ill will, which might be avoided if a Senate rule incorporated the principle and it could be invoked by a point of order.

The need for the change at present is largely, but not entirely, confined to instances where the Senate overrules its Finance Committee on a tax bill. In these instances the senior members of the Committee, who would normally be the conferees, would in all likelihood have voted with the minority on the floor.

Eighth: Perhaps the most important needed change in Senate rules is the liberalization of Rule XXII, which presently provides for terminating debate, only on the affirmative vote of two-thirds of the Senators present.

The latest effort to decrease the number of Senators required to bring debate to an end from two-thirds to three-fifths, advocated by Senator Anderson, or to a simple majority, urged by Senator Humphrey, failed in February, 1963, although fifty-six Senators were on record in support of the Anderson resolution. Both resolutions remain on the calendar, but it seems certain they will not be called up again during the Eighty-eighth Congress.

The failure of the House to have a procedure for terminating debate rendered that body powerless to act when action was required in the national interest before "Reed's Rules" put an end to House filibusters in 1890. More than seventy years of experience under that procedure have amply demonstrated its usefulness. Failure to curb filibusters in the Senate, on the other hand, has blocked the consideration of many bills favored by a majority. Even when there is no actual filibuster, the threat of one hangs over proposed legislation, requiring it to be watered down to suit the South and frequently resulting in failure to make a serious effort to pass it at all. The Senate is constantly legislating in the shadow both of the conservative House Rules Committee and of its own custom of unlimited debate which can be terminated only under the clumsy provisions of Rule XXII by a vote of two-thirds of those present. Surely the time has come to make a change.

Rule XXII is indeed a clumsy vehicle for achieving the desired end. It requires sixteen Senators to sign and file a cloture petition asking that a vote be had forty-eight hours later on whether or not to limit further debate on the *pending business*. When the vote is taken, two-thirds of those Senators present and voting are required to vote in the affirmative to limit debate. If they do so, each Senator is permitted to speak thereafter for one hour, although the time is not transferable. Assuming a close vote in favor of cloture, there might still be thirty additional hours of debate on the pending business before it could be brought to a vote. Toward the end of a session to permit thirty hours of debate on one bill is not feasible. Thus it is practically impossible to pass any legislation to which the South, or any other small group of determined Senators, seriously objects unless it is done early in the session.

But the *pending business* is often only a preliminary motion to take up a bill. So the whole cloture procedure, if successful, has to be invoked all over again. What then happens to amendments which have been filed to the bill when it is brought up? The one-hour-per-Senator rule would seem to apply to them if they were not called up before the second cloture vote. If there were a dozen or more amendments, they could not all be discussed adequately.

If, however, an amendment were called up before the second cloture petition was filed, the cloture voted might apply only to the amendment and accordingly the process would have to be repeated for the third time.

In view of these complications whose ramifications are almost infinite, each of which requires complex parliamentary rulings based on musty and frequently irrelevant precedents, or no precedents at all, I believe it would be wiser to abandon Rule XXII in its present form and reinstate the right to move the previous question as it once existed in the Senate and as it presently exists in the House and in most state legislatures.

This could be done by adding an amendment to Senate Rule XXII which would permit debate to be terminated, on the motion of any Senator, whenever any measure had received consideration for a total of not less than fifteen hours, during a total of not less than three calendar days.* Such a motion would be submitted directly to the Senate by the presiding officer and decided without debate by "yea and nay" vote. The previous question could then be moved and ordered with respect to one or more pending measures, motions or matters, including separate amendments, and the Senate could proceed to final passage of the bill or resolution in question. One hour of debate, equally divided between opponents and proponents, should be allowed thereafter on any preliminary motion or amendment relating to the bill, and four hours of debate, divided in the same manner, allowed on the final passage of the bill itself.

The United States Senate from 1789 to 1806 recognized in its rules the motion for the previous question. It is called for in Jefferson's Manual. Extensive research by the eminent American historian, Irving Brant, supplemented by research of Senator Paul Douglas and his staff, has shown that the motion was used on four occasions during those early years. On two of those occasions the motion was made for the purpose of closing debate and bringing a vote on the pending business. On one of those two occasions, that actually happened, and on the other occasion the motion, though not voted upon, achieved the same result.

The motion has been used frequently since 1811 in the House of Representatives for the purpose of ending debate and is specifically incorporated in House Rule XVII. The same procedure is permitted in practically all state legislatures of the country.

* The number of hours is relatively immaterial. It might be more or less than fifteen. The foreign aid authorization bill took eighty-three hours of actual debate in the fall of 1963 and was the pending business for twenty days.

Thomas Jefferson pointed out that this kind of procedure was used in the British Parliament as long ago as 1604. Certainly it cannot be considered a practice alien to sound Anglo-Saxon parliamentary procedure.

Vital Senatorial business cannot be handled at the same leisurely pace that has characterized Senate deliberations in the past. Full and fair debate is desirable, even essential, to democratic processes. Unlimited debate is an abnegation of those processes. Fifteen hours of germane debate on a given issue would provide ample opportunity for the Senate to determine whether it has exhausted the possibilities of productive discussion. If not, a majority vote against the previous question motion would permit additional debate. If a majority wished to come to a vote on the pending business, and the motion were approved, there would still be an opportunity for one hour of additional debate on each amendment covered by the motion and four hours of additional debate on the passage of the bill or resolution.

There are a number of reform proposals applicable to both House and Senate.

The first of these is to install electric voting machines in both houses, as has been done in many state and foreign legislatures. I have inspected the devices in the Swedish Riksdag in Stockholm. Without leaving his seat the member votes by pressing a button on his desk. His vote is immediately indicated by the flashing of a light on the desk of the presiding officer. A simple counter records the total "ayes and nays" and also how each member voted. The result is announced almost immediately. Each member can verify his vote and protest if he has been erroneously recorded. The whole process takes approximately two minutes.

In the Senate a roll-call vote takes at least fifteen to twenty minutes, in the House about four times as long. On a busy day on the floor there may be as many as ten roll calls. The time saved by the machine could be as much as two or three hours a day. There are already lights and buzzers in Senate and House offices. It would be an easy matter to provide a warning signal of a few minutes to bring members to the floor in ample time for a vote.

And while the electricians are in the Senate chamber they might as well install some microphones, as has already been done in the committee rooms, so that soft-spoken Senators could be heard as well by their colleagues as leather-lunged Senators.

Another proposal which would save a great deal of time without doing violence to the bicameral concept of the legislative branch would be to schedule joint hearings of House and Senate committees on legislation pending in both houses whose passage is desired by the administration and the leadership. This procedure would eliminate one appearance before the Congress of hard-pressed and overworked administration witnesses. It would be particularly helpful on appropriations bills, where the testimony is, or could be, largely identical. Having heard the evidence and questioned the witnesses together, the two subcommittees of the Appropriations Committees could retire to mark up the bill separately and report it, through their parent committees, to the floor of their particular chambers.

There is, moreover, no valid reason, other than false pride on the part of the House, why the Senate should not act first on half of the appropriations bills. This, too, would expedite significantly the processing of the bills. While it would eliminate the appeal process before the Senate subcommittees for restitution of amounts deemed necessary but cut by the House, this requirement could probably be met in advance at the joint hearing. If not, it could be dealt with informally by the chairman of the Senate subcommittee, or vice versa, if the House made the cut, before the bill went to conference.

The same principle could be well applied to much other legislation, particularly tax bills. Many weeks would have been saved if joint hearings had been arranged on the tax reduction and reform bills of 1963. And there are many other legislative areas where the same procedure would be useful and timesaving.

This suggestion is made because it does not seem feasible in the present climate in both houses to eliminate separate House and Senate standing committees and deal with all legislation on a joint committee basis, as has been done so successfully for almost twenty years by the Joint Committee on Atomic Energy.

Another new procedure would again require a good deal of self-discipline, but would pay off many times over in terms of a more effective performance of the legislative function. That would be for the leadership on both sides of the aisle in both houses, in consultation with the President, after the State of the Union and budget messages had come down, to prepare a careful schedule of floor business for the coming session. If the two Democratic Policy Committees advocated here were set up and functioning, they could help enormously in this task. It would also require the active cooperation of the chairmen of all legislative committees, which under present circumstances, in the absence of any loyalty to their party and their President, might in some cases be difficult indeed to get.

The suggestion includes a week-by-week legislative calendar for both houses. The first step would be a firm decision as to when each House was going to eschew conducting legislative business in order to go home to mend fences or somewhere else for a vacation. Customarily this means the middle two weeks in February (Lincoln's and Washington's Birthdays), ten days over Easter, five over Memorial Day and a week over the Fourth of July.

Next would come a decision as to approximately when each of the regular and supplemental appropriations bills could be brought to the floor of each House, passed, sent to conference, brought back from conference for approval of the conference report and sent on to the President for signature. This would require careful organizing by the executive agencies as well as by the legislative planners and the chairmen of the two Appropriations Committees. The deadline imposed for the last appropriations bill to be passed should be July 1, the beginning of the fiscal year.

The final step would be to schedule with the chairmen of the relevant committees the time for reporting and taking floor action on other high-priority measures desired by the President, or, if the bills result from legislative initiative, by the legislative leaders and committee chairmen.

This Congressional legislative schedule should be revised weekly to meet constantly changing legislative conditions. It should be given wide publicity so that the public would be aware of what has gone wrong and who is responsible whenever a major change in the schedule has to be made.

In this connection Senator Warren G. Magnuson of Washington has for ten years introduced a bill (which I have cosponsored) to split each session of Congress into two parts. The first would run from January through July and would deal entirely with legislative matters, with priority given to recommendations contained in the various messages sent down to Congress by the President. The second session would deal solely with fiscal matters and would convene immediately after election in even-numbered years and around October 1 in odd-numbered years when no members of Congress were up for election. Of course the Ways and Means Committee, the Finance Committee and the two Appropriations Committees would proceed with their hearings and the initial marking up of their bills during the first session so that they would be ready to go to the floor as soon as the fiscal session convened in the fall. This proposal would call for a change in the fiscal year to make it accord with the calendar year.

It would be useful if, in anticipation of the proposed fiscal session, the Joint Economic Committee made an annual study in some depth of the President's budget and made recommendations as to where it believes cuts or additions should be made and what, if any, changes in tax legislation should be considered by the two Congressional committees responsible for taxation.* By the time the second session convened all the authorizing legislation would have been enacted and it would be possible to tell to what extent appropriations should be cut or increased from the budget figure.

The single most desirable change in the present attitude of both houses, a change which would do more than any other to bring the President and the Congress together on a program for the country, would be passage of a concurrent resolution committing both houses to bring to a vote on its merits any legislative proposal on which the President requests prompt action within six months of the date his proposed legislation is sent down to Capitol Hill. In this way the original intention of the framers of the Constitution could be resuscitated. The Executive would report annually on the State of the Union and how he had performed his duty to see that the laws should be faithfully executed as provided in Article II of the Constitution. He would make his recommendations for needed legislation to the Congress; send down his budget; and the legislative arm would promptly act on those recommendations—accepting some, modifying others, rejecting still others. It would then pass and send to the President for veto or approval such other laws as in its wisdom, exercising its extensive powers under Article I of the Constitution, it thought should be enacted and go home by the middle of the summer—unless the two-session plan suggested above were in effect. So might the public business be expeditiously dispatched.

Until the Congress accepts this obligation there is little hope that our tripartite system of checks and balances with all its frustrations, with all its roadblocks to needed action, with all its futilities and with all its callous disregard of the public interest can measure up to the responsibilities placed on it in the modern world.

* For some years the Senate has proposed and the House rejected creation of a joint committee on the budget. Since there seems to be little likelihood of the House changing its mind, giving the over-all fiscal task to the Joint Economic Committee, which is already in existence, is suggested.

The mechanics could be simple enough. Any committee member, citing the concurrent resolution, would be authorized to move within the committee to report out favorably the bill submitted by the President. When the bill reached the floor, the Majority Leader would promptly motion it up. If a committee failed to act, a discharge motion or petition could be filed to bring the bill to the floor. The resolution would provide that these motions to report and take up would by-pass any reference to the House Rules Committee and would not be subject to Senate filibuster. The motion for the previous question would terminate debate in both houses.

Walter Lippmann has made a similar suggestion. "To make our system work, it is essential that the initiative of the President be respected by Congress, and when he says a measure is of great national importance, his proposals should be accorded enough priority to bring them to a vote and a decision within a reasonable time—say three months."[12]

There remains the much discussed question of ethics and conflict of interest of members of Congress and their employees. For years the Congress has been under heavy criticism for hypocrisy. It is said that we insist on the most rigorous standards of integrity for members of the executive departments, particularly those whose nominations to office by the President are subject to confirmation by the Senate. Thus Charles Wilson, Secretary of Defense in the Eisenhower administration, was required to divest himself of all his General Motors stock before he could be confirmed as Secretary of Defense because General Motors held many large defense contracts and its former president might be tempted to favor its bid on still other contracts if he kept the stock while awarding the contracts as Secretary of Defense.

On the other hand, George Humphrey, President Eisenhower's Secretary of the Treasury, was not required to dispose of his holdings before his appointment was confirmed. But the report of the majority of the special committee, chaired by Senator Stuart Symington, which investigated stockpiling alleges that Mr. Humphrey had made an additional fortune by ordering the purchase and stockpiling of supposedly critical materials from companies in which he had a substantial personal financial interest.

One could go on indefinitely mentioning everyone from Under Secretary of Defense Gilpatric to Billy Sol Estes. And in doing so one might well conclude that after all the tumult and shouting no one in the executive branch was guilty of the slightest impropriety so far as his relations with the government are concerned.

The point is that Congress is suspicious of the ethics and standards of members of the executive branch and often seems careless of its own. Public suspicion of Congressional integrity, always smoldering, was fanned into flame in the fall of 1963 by the revelation of the financial transactions of Bobby Baker, secretary to the Senate majority, and of Representative John Byrnes of Wisconsin. Both appear to have been put in the way of making a quick and substantial profit in the stock of a Wisconsin mortgage company in return for favors they were thought to be able to perform by reason of their official positions.

The fact that a few members of the Senate, including Senators Hugh Scott of Pennsylvania, Steve Young of Ohio, William Proxmire of Wisconsin, Wayne Morse of Oregon, the Majority Leader, Senator Mike Mansfield of Montana, and I, have made a public disclosure of our financial holdings has been held up as an argument in favor of passage of "disclosure of possible conflict of interest" bills, one introduced by Senator Clifford Case of New Jersey and cosponsored by Senator Maurine Neuberger of Oregon and me, the other sponsored by Senator Morse.

These bills not only call for public disclosure of the financial holdings of all members of Congress, but also require such members and all executive departments to keep a written record, open to public inspection, of all requests for action, whether written or oral, made by any member of Congress to any executive office or regulatory commission.

This proposed legislation aroused the ire of Senator Dirksen in mid-November, 1963. It would make of him, he said, "a second-class citizen" into whose private affairs every Peeping Tom could probe. He distinguished members of the executive establishment from members of Congress on the ground that the former did not have to meet the scrutiny of the voters through the electoral process. He did not divulge how the voters were to know whether a particular Congressional candidate would, upon election, be subject to the pull of conflicting interests if the candidate, prior to election, did not choose to make his holdings public.

For myself, Senator Dirksen's arguments are quite unconvincing. I do not believe that one can legislate public or private morality or supply a workable code of ethics to anyone in public life who does not have his own code to start with. But I am strongly of the view that nothing is quite so good for the soul as confession. A public airing of private financial holdings of members of Congress and a public record of contacts with the executive branch by Congressmen on behalf of themselves, their friends or constituents would, in my judgment, provide a salutary check on action which if kept secret might well conceal a violation of reasonable standards of decency.

I believe the Case bill or something very much like it should be passed.

Such are my personal recommendations for turning the Congress into an effective working partner with the executive and judicial branches of our federal government. But to convert such a program into reality a very large part of Congress will have to take a serious interest in reform. To rally support and achieve solid results, Senate Concurrent Resolution 1 was introduced early in January, 1963, by thirty Senators. Senator Clifford Case and I were the principal sponsors. Modeled on the La Follette-Monroney resolution of 1945, it called for the creation of a joint Congressional committee of seven members from each House to make an over-all study of needed Congressional reorganization and to report back its recommendations to the Congress within a year of its passage.

A hearing was held on the resolution before the Subcommittee on Standing Senate Rules of the Committee on Rules and Administration on June 27 and 28, 1963. The subcommittee consists of Senators Hayden, Cannon and Cooper, none of whom has much zest for Congressional reorganization. However, the subcommittee reported the resolution favorably to the full committee, but with an amendment which removed from the consideration of the Joint Committee "the rules, practices, procedures, and floor action" of either House. Feeling that this amendment deprived the resolution of much of its usefulness, I moved to restore the resolution to its original form, but was defeated in the full committee by a vote of six to three. Senator Case and I, joined by Senator Kenneth Keating of New York, notified the Senate we would move the same restoring amendment on the floor.

The resolution as amended was attempted to be motioned up by the Majority Leader December 3, 1963. Senator Russell immediately refused unanimous consent to approval of Senator Mansfield's motion. Privately I was given to understand that if Senator Case and I withdrew our amendment the Establishment would not oppose the resolution in the form reported by the Rules Committee. We refused, charging the Southerners with instituting a two-word filibuster: "I object." In the limited time available we were unable to bring the motion to take up to a vote. Because of a technical quirk in Senate procedure the motion was automatically displaced when the Senate adjourned for the weekend on Friday, December 5. Thus without actually speaking for more than an hour the Southern members of the Establishment were able to prevent a vote on even a motion to take up a resolution, to say nothing of the merits of the resolution itself.

What the future holds for the resolution is at present obscure. If it is passed in its original or its amended form, there is grave doubt as to whether the House would take similar action. Nevertheless, the need for such a study is obvious, and I have no doubt some sort of study will be authorized, if not immediately, then in the foreseeable future.

If the road through a concurrent resolution proves to be blocked, its sponsors may press for a special *ad hoc* Senate committee to make a separate study of what needs to be done on the Senate side, with authority to consult with any body with like authority in the House, possibly the Subcommittee on Organization and Procedures of the House Government Operations Committee.

One way or another the massive job of Congressional reorganization and reform must get under way before it is too late and Congressional government breaks down under the strain of modern pressures for action.

IX

EXTERNAL REFORMS FOR CONGRESS

Acceptance of the reforms I have proposed would go a long way toward making it possible for the Congress to act responsibly when a majority in the Congress is ready to act. These reforms are, of course, institutional; they are internal. The Congress itself has the power, if not yet the will, to make them.

There remains, however, the problem of assuring that the Congress truly represents the majority will of the American people as expressed in national elections. There is reason to believe that today it does not. And it is very important that it should, primarily because the success of our form of government requires it, and also because the internal reform of the Congress is to some extent dependent on the proper working of our political processes.

The relationship between the political system and the organization, rules, customs and procedures of Congress is reciprocal. A change in one will very likely in the long run produce changes in the other. Just as the performance of the modern President reflects the composition of the Electoral College, so today's Congressional performance reflects the process by which its members are elected.

If, for example, there were more two-party districts in the House, particularly in the South, seniority would be less important and legislation for which a majority would vote could more easily be brought to the floor for action. If the filibuster rule could be changed in the Senate, additional voting rights legislation could be passed and enforced which in a few years would revolutionize politics in the South and bring the one-party system in that region to an end.

It is obvious, then, that external reform in the political process itself is important in achieving majority rule both in the Congress and in the country. Right now the problem is not, as textbook writers warn us, that our political system occasionally permits a President of one party and a Congress of the other. Our problem is, rather, that the political process results in a continuing and nearly irreconcilable clash between any Congress and any President, regardless of the nominal partisan composition of the Congress.

The cause for the clash is that while both are the products of political processes, by which they were nominated and elected, those processes are different and have different results.

The political forces which select the modern President are such that for the last thirty years he has been oriented in an urban, industrial, international, activist, pro-civil rights and at least moderately liberal direction. A substantial number of the members of Congress in both parties are the product of political forces which give them a rural, pro-business, anti-labor, isolationist, conservative perspective with an attitude toward civil rights which ranges from passive unconcern to outright hostility. These differences represent genuine cleavage over the content of public policy. The hostility between the Presidential and Congressional attitudes deepens as problems central to the cleavage, i.e., the state of the economy, disarmament or civil rights, press for solution.

The political system thus normally produces a President, chosen through a process in which national considerations predominate, whose program as set forth in his party's platform is then submitted to a Congress chosen through a process profoundly local—one in which parochial considerations predominate. Presidents thus achieve, or fail to achieve, legislative success to the extent that they can extract support from a balky and often hostile Congress. Congressional opposition suddenly appears from quarters which were mute and almost invisible during the campaign. Within his own party the President faces opposition to the very principles his party espouses and proclaims in the platform.

At the national level the parties simply fail to perform the function of permeating a government divided constitutionally into separate branches with a common philosophy of governmental action. The division within each party is such that the President lacks an effective majority within his party, even though it is the majority party in Congress, to secure the adoption of the Presidential program. President Eisenhower needed and got Democratic support for his program when the Republicans controlled the Congress; Presidents Kennedy and Johnson needed and, alas, less often got enough Republican support for their programs to enact them. The combined liberal wings of the two parties hold a precarious majority over the conservative bipartisan coalition on many issues, but by no means on all the important ones. And since the coalition is, generally speaking, opposed to all significant action and perfectly content with the status quo, no President elected by the nation, regardless of his party, is likely to receive support from it for the positive program on which he based his campaign for election.

A Congress which defeats the President's program does not enact one of its own. Congress does not have and, because of internal contradictions, cannot produce its own program. The same party divisions which prevent the President's party from uniting in support of his program prevent it or the opposition from uniting in support of an alternative.

In theory, of course, the elements in each party which share the Presidential outlook could unite across party lines. They do so on many issues before the Congress; but the alliance is temporary and on the whole less successful than the "Congressional party" alliance between the conservative Republicans and Southern Democrats. The forces operating against any permanent working arrangement are immense and arise principally from the complex political structure within each party which intermingles local, state and national politics. The success of the conservative coalition, now in my judgment breaking up, has depended upon its age and upon holding a significant number of one-party districts with the seniority attendant thereto, thus enabling it to hold leadership positions and to capitalize on those rules and procedures of both houses which make for inaction. The Presidential Congressional coalition, while it, too, relies on many Representatives from one-party districts, is built on sand because too many of its members have little assurance of tenure and less of seniority. Too many of them come from doubtful districts and states. Moreover, the Northern Democrats from big-city, one-party districts are all too apt to leave the House after a few terms to accept snug harbor in judgeships. A career in the House is not so alluring a way of life north and west of the Mason-Dixon line as it is below it.

Our two-party politics, like our private enterprise system, is supposed to have competition as its foundation. In too many cases our politics is simply not competitive in any meaningful way. The element of competitiveness should be increased wherever possible. As we have seen, a large proportion of the states now enjoy substantial two-party competition in statewide elections. This means a large majority of Senators have to win a contested election to gain their seats. That degree of competitiveness is absent in most House and state legislative districts. Since the state legislatures are the key to reapportionment, they occupy a position of importance in the political process.

That is why the decisions of the United States Supreme Court in recent apportionment cases, in which it renounced its long-imposed self-denying ordinance against judicial intervention into legislative apportionment, are so important.* Already the response by state legislatures and lower federal courts to the decisions marks a major breakthrough. At last there is a judicial weapon with which to remedy a long-standing legislative abuse of constitutional power. It seems not too much to hope that the courts will soon require all Congressional and state legislative districts will be compact, contiguous and generally equal in population within a decade. **

Reapportionment of the state legislatures has an enormous potential for affecting our politics. Congressional reapportionment does not have a marked impact on state politics, but reapportionment of the state legislatures would drastically affect both state politics and Congressional apportionment and thus, indirectly, national politics. This is because present systems of apportionment, by denying a sufficient voice to metropolitan areas, impose a brake on the dynamics of competitive politics. District lines drawn so as to make hopeless the minority party cause keep that party moribund. The depressed state of the minority party then causes it to fail to make its influence felt in Congressional elections as well, thus contributing to the multiplicity of one-party districts in the composition of the Congress.

An illustration indicates how state legislative districting over-depresses the competitive potential of the system. Many of the states employ the multi-member district system of representation, by which two or more state legislators are elected at large from an entire district. In an area entitled, let us say, to three representatives in which the majority party enjoys a two-to-one advantage, the cause of the minority party is hopeless. Frequently the elec-

* In particular Baker *v.* Carr, 369 U.S. 186 (1961), and Grey *v.* Sanders, 373 U.S. 368 (1963), Wesberry *v.* Sanders, 32 U.S. Law Week 4142, Feb. 17, 1964.

** Its importance is recognized by the opponents of fair representation as well, for they speedily prepared a constitutional amendment for submission to the state legislatures that would reverse the Court's decision. It would appear, however, that this proposed amendment has little chance of adoption.

tion goes to the majority by default. If that same area were divided into three separate districts, the minority party might have a fighting chance in one and, therefore, an incentive to organize, to work and to seek out an attractive candidate. Until that happens the minority will continue to languish, the majority party to grow slack. The latter will nominate mediocre candidates all too often beholden to the local organization and, because of its support, assured of election.

Politics is sometimes defined as the struggle for power. Too often, however, our concern with power blinds us to the importance of insuring that it be won by a struggle and that a struggle to retain it be in due course assured. This conception of electoral competition is crucial in a free society. Democratic politics, then, ought ideally to involve an intraparty struggle for nomination and an interparty struggle for election. Only the parties, because of their continuity, can contribute the accountability and permanence that make the struggle meaningful.

Competitive politics is altogether different from the politics practiced in areas where one party's victory is assured. Essentially, one-party politics is issueless politics. If the incumbent is renominated without a real contest and the general election is a formality, there is no need to campaign or to discuss issues. The dominant party candidate wins in a walk and holds his seat until he dies, quits or is removed because he "bucked the organization." He is never defeated for re-election. The adroit use of patronage and political favoritism, discouragement of citizen participation and, above all, the downgrading of issues—this is the stuff of which one-party politics is made. The only exceptions are: (1) when "the old man" dies or quits and the seat is up for grabs or (2) an incumbent from a Northern boss-controlled district is jettisoned if he shows undue independence of the party machine or is promoted to a judgeship after a few terms in reward for faithful service. In either case seniority is lost.

The drive of competitive politics is altogether different. Here the emphasis is on the exploitation of issues and the ability and character of the candidates. Both parties are compelled to broaden their base, develop programs and nominate better candidates. Often the need for success is such that candidates with some independence of mind are chosen, sometimes after a contested primary.

There is another curious aspect of one-party politics. Frequently the ablest candidates of the minority run in districts where they have no chance of winning, while the weakest candidates run where victory is assured. This is because only dedicated, policy-oriented candidates will lead a hopeless cause.

One concludes that fair reapportionment enforced by the courts can be a useful but not an invincible weapon in the task of external Congressional reform. Party competition is accelerated when elections hinge on issues which cut across, and thereby erode, sectional strength. So long as members of Congress can get elected on issues of purely local concern they remain isolated from the forces which determine the direction of national policy. They thereby insulate themselves from the program of their party's national leadership. This has its most disastrous consequences when a President elected on national issues seeks to rally support from members of Congress whose own election bore little relation to those issues. The limitations on what fair reapportionment can do were pointed out earlier. There is no assurance that compact contiguous districts of equal population will not turn out to be one-party districts.

The creation of effective Congressional support for Presidential programs thus depends in large measure on assuring that electoral success for both the President and a Congressional majority reflects a common identification of issues. There are signs that we are moving in this direction, but much remains to be done to accelerate it. A further strengthening of the parties at the national level is essential to this end.

The policy differences between the Presidential forces within each party and those centered in the Congressional party are faithfully reflected in the internal structure of each party. The National Committees concern themselves with the election of a President and very little else. The Senatorial and Congressional Campaign Committees concern themselves primarily with the election of members of Congress.

The National Committee of the party which controls the White House will be the creature of the President and the National Chairman will be the President's agent in party affairs. The National Committee will therefore faithfully reflect the views of the White House on issues. Insofar as it operates in the realm of policy at all—and it rarely does—it will merely reflect Presidential policy. Actually, it is primarily concerned with patronage and fund-raising.

The party out of power faces a more difficult problem. To prevent the national image of the party from being fixed exclusively by the Establishment-oriented Congressional leadership, which would win few new friends or favorably influence few voters in those two-party states where success is required to win the Presidency, the national forces within the party must find some other vehicle or body as spokesman for the national party point of view.

When President Eisenhower was in office, the Democratic Advisory Council to the Democratic National Committee was created for this purpose. Though the Democratic Congressional leaders boycotted it, such important leaders as President Truman, Adlai Stevenson, Eleanor Roosevelt, Averell Harriman, Senator Humphrey, Governor G. Mennen Williams and Senator John F. Kennedy used it to articulate national Democratic party policy. Out of office General Eisenhower has become the principal driving force behind the All Republican Conference—as of this writing not nearly so successful as the Democratic Advisory Council. But the Republican Congressional leadership is grumbling and grudging about it just the same. Senator Goldwater declined to attend the organization meeting, announcing instead his "dismay" at learning of an intention to set up a citizens committee "to duplicate what the National Committee is doing."

What all this adds up to is that the two political parties display the worst features of both federalism and the separation of powers. Within government we have developed a number of effective techniques for national-state cooperation; within the political structure we have been much less inventive. Every schoolboy knows that under our system of government a law must have the concurrence of both the executive and legislative branches, yet we have no formally established party organ with any continuing capacity to unite elements of both branches of government.

Realistically, the expectations of Presidential policy leadership that have been developed in American government are such that that office will continue to dwarf any party organ developed to formulate policy. Nevertheless, the persistence with which the party not controlling the White House has been compelled to develop, in spite of strong opposition within the party, a party agency that can reflect a national policy attitude demonstrates that such an agency responds to a deeply felt need within the parties. A Party Council of perhaps fifty members comprised of a few National Committeemen, the Congressional leaders, state governors from doubtful states and party "eggheads" could serve the useful purpose of coordinating party efforts and defining issues for the next national election. It should include the President and Vice President and, for the party out of power, the defeated candidates for these offices.*

Such a Party Council could function as the Executive Committee on Policy for the National Convention during the period between Presidential elections, with the task of preliminary formulation of national party policy and continuing interpretation of the platform adopted by the last National Convention. As

* A detailed proposal to this general effect was made some time ago by the Committee on Political Parties of the American Political Science Association. See pp. 39-44 of their report, *Toward a More Responsible Two-Party System* (New York, 1950).

such it would make clear when elements within the party departed from the party consensus. Once established, it would in time develop appropriate techniques for dealing with unorthodoxy within the party. There has long been a need to deny party Congressional rewards such as the chairmanship of committees to those, like Senator Byrd of Virginia, who consistently refuse to support either the party's Presidental candidate or its platform. The initial task of the Party Council, however, would be the development of a party policy consensus through an agency so composed as to transcend the limitations of federalism and the separation of powers.

A Party Council, by the achievement of such a party consensus, could make two contributions to government. It would make more difficult the hypocrisy with which candidates for Congress ally themselves with the personality of the Presidential nominees while remaining indifferent, or hostile, to their programs.* And it would raise the level of public debate between elections by creating a drive within the minority party to formulate positive policy alternatives to those of the party with the Presidency.

Of course, it is neither wise nor possible to create two monolithic parties, highly centralized and with iron discipline. The diversity of the country, our political tradition and, to a considerable extent, our governmental institutions all combine to make this undesirable. But it should be possible to move from political organizational anarchy toward order without being accused of urging national party dictatorship. We are surely capable of avoiding the extreme of excessive decentralization under which both parties now suffer. When the right wing of the Democratic party overlaps the right wing of the Republican party, it creates a situation which makes party platforms hypo-

* The Republican program in the House of Representatives is in the hands of a Minority Leader whose attitude to the most recent Republican party platform is a matter of public record. "We will take it out and read it from time to time," Mr. Halleck has volunteered. "But the congressional people generally have very little to do with writing party platforms." Quoted in Burns, *The Deadlock of Democracy*, p. 255.

critical, political campaigns a sham and governmental responsibility nonexistent. Surely these are ills sufficiently great to suggest the need for political reform.

The subject of money in politics has received much deserved attention in recent years.[1] There is general agreement that some method must be found for securing mass financial support for political candidates. The pernicious consequences of reliance on a few wealthy contributors for large donations is obvious. The cost of conducting a modern campaign is huge, in fact too big to be sustained by a few well-heeled contributors. Moreover, there has been a shrinkage, in many ways healthy, of the traditional sources of party support. The reduction in political patronage and the nonpolitical requirements of bidding for government contracts have sharply decreased both the number and size of political donations offered more as a hostage to fortune than as a contribution to civic rectitude. It is no longer possible to say, as did Governor Gifford Pinchot of Pennsylvania about the election of his rival William S. Vare to the United States Senate in 1926, that his election "was partly bought and partly stolen."

In November of 1961 President Kennedy appointed a Commission on Campaign Costs. Chaired by Alexander Heard, the leading academic authority on party finance, seven of its nine members had had considerable experience with political fund-raising, and the ninth member, the late V. O. Key, Jr, of Harvard, had long been a commentator on the subject. In April, 1962, the Commission issued its report.[2]

It recommended that for an experimental period of two Presidential campaigns political contributors should be given a credit against their federal income tax of 50 percent of their contribution up to a maximum of $10 or alternatively to claim up to $1,000 in contributions as a deductible item.

The only contributions eligible for these benefits would be those made to the national committees or a state organization designated by the national committee.

These recommendations, if implemented, would go far toward transferring the support of politics to the ordinary citizen. They might well eliminate the need for larger contributions. The Senate Finance Committee made a modest start in late 1963 by adopting an amendment to the pending tax reduction bill which would allow a tax deduction of $50 for individuals for political contributions but it was dropped in the final version of the bill. Yet a deduction unlike a credit, is useful only to those of sufficient means to file a detailed tax return instead of taking standard tax deductions.

Perhaps even more important than the technical means of achieving mass financial support for the parties is the Commission's recommendation that the money be disbursed through the National Committees and state committees designated by them. Obviously this would place a disciplinary weapon of the first importance in the hands of the national party agencies. It would create a powerful centralizing force in American politics to counter the decentralizing forces present elsewhere. It would substitute national for parochial direction of the parties' financial efforts and concern.

And it would elevate politics in the national scale of values. Too often the political process seems a mystery which the average citizen cannot comprehend and with which he feels no sense of involvement. The curtain of secrecy which envelops the process of party finance contributes to this feeling. Nor do grand jury investigations into the corrupting influence of money on politics heighten the voter's approval of the role of politics in a democratic society. Yet in spite of the huge sums of money spent on electioneering each year in the United States the total cost is only about a dollar per citizen even in a Presidential year. Unless the burden of support can be broadened, leadership is faced with the strong temptation to accept funds that come from sources that are demeaning when they are not actually illegal.

None of this can be done without a heightened concern for policy, particularly national policy, on the part of the parties. People will contribute their money voluntarily to a cause, as the results of thousands of volunteer civic and welfare organizations attest. But except for those who seek jobs or favors they are not entitled to, or who are "maced" by unscrupulous political leaders and hold jobs without Civil Service protection, they will not willingly contribute in order to maintain an amoral political machine in power.

There are heartening signs that forces are at work in both parties which are leading in the right direction. Both parties, for example, now have membership programs at the national level with annual dues of $10. Each year there is a "Dollars for Democrats" campaign in which $1 contributions are solicited on a house-to-house canvass basis. Success has been modest, but the recognition of the concept augurs well for the future.

There has been much discussion recently of changing the constitutional rules which govern the election of Presidents by the somewhat awkward method of an Electoral College. Under the present system the populous states are pivotal and the large urban and suburban areas within them, with their ethnic minorities and mass pressure groups, partially offset by middle-class "white collar" suburbanites, are crucial to victory. President Kennedy, for example, in 1960 carried Michigan, Illinois and Pennsylvania each by little more than 50 percent of the popular vote. Yet he won all the seventy-nine votes of these states in the Electoral College. Had a relatively few voters in two of these states gone the other way, Richard Nixon would have been elected.

Recent efforts to tinker with the Electoral College usually stem from the political philosophy of the repairmen. Thus conservatives, particularly those from the South, would like to see the electoral vote of each state divided in proportion to the popular vote in such states. The South—now happily not so solid—would acquire an even greater importance in the Democratic party under this scheme because the monolithic nature of its one-party vote in a general election would give nearly all its Electoral College votes to the Democratic nominee. Of course, he usually gets them all anyway under the present system, but they are more than offset by the votes of the big doubtful states where a small majority carries all the state's electoral vote. Similarly the conservative one-party Republican states where Democratic office holders are uncommon, such as Kansas, Nebraska and Vermont, would have their stature within the Republican party magnified.

The South's votes, it is worth noting, are already more heavily weighted than they should be because Electoral College votes are based on census population figures rather than on the number of registered voters, thus giving credit for large numbers of disfranchised Negroes.

Another change urged by conservatives is to elect the Presidential electors by Congressional districts, with two additional to be elected at-large from each state. Thus in Pennsylvania the electoral vote would normally be divided fourteen to thirteen for the Republicans with two votes up for grabs. All eleven of Alabama's votes would presumably be Democratic.

These suggestions have generated sufficient support in the Congress (particularly the inspired proposal of 1956 to combine them and let each state choose which scheme it preferred!) that liberals have been compelled to defend the present system with its admitted inequities in order to prevent something worse. The result has been that there has been little sentiment expressed for the most obvious reform of all—abandonment of the Electoral College and election of the President by direct national popular vote without regard to state lines. This would be a risky business from the viewpoint of both liberals and conservatives. But if the President is to represent the nation as a whole, it is hard to rebut the argument that he should be elected by the nation as a whole.

The realities of the situation are such at present that there is no consensus in Congress or in the country in support of any change in the method of counting the vote for President. Electoral College reform has therefore become moot as each side has become aware of the strength of the opposition.

Appropriate steps by each state to insure that the decision of the electorate in that state is faithfully reflected by the electors would seem to be a minimal and desirable reform. This would eliminate the present possibility of some electors voting as they saw fit instead of in compliance with the election results. Pennsylvania is the only state in the nation which provides that the candidates for elector be named by the Presidential nominees, thus assuring that the popular mandate will be followed.

Basic to all attempts at electoral reform is the need to remove arbitrary restraints on the right to vote. It is a serious commentary on the health of our institutions that a century and three-quarters after the adoption of the Constitution we have not yet achieved a national definition of the right to vote nor a country-wide determination to protect the exercise of this right.

For a mature democratic society, voting participation in the United States is shockingly low, and this without regard to the related problem of the achievement of civil rights for Negroes. Much voter apathy is due to the simple absence of political competition. Where the vote is ineffective there is little incentive for casting it. Areas where this occurs are far too many.

But many millions of Americans in competitive election districts are prevented from voting by absurdly high residence requirements, prohibitions against absentee voting or cumbersome registration procedures that erect unnecessary obstacles. All these barriers may have at one time been genuinely designed to eliminate fraud. They combine now to discriminate seriously against an increasingly mobile population without achieving much in the way of electoral honesty. Some eight million adult Americans did not vote in the last Presidential election, for example, because they could not meet state and local residence requirements.[3]

In addition, there is the special problem of systematic efforts to prevent the Negro from voting in certain areas of the South. That this is a national problem is attested by the fact that fewer than 15 percent of Negroes of voting age are registered to vote in 261 counties, comprising all or part of sixty Congressional districts in eleven Southern states.

We are making some modest gains in this field. The poll tax has now been outlawed in federal elections by constitutional amendment. The Civil Rights Acts of recent years have helped a little. But it is clear also that the cumulative result of various restrictive laws and practices produces, arbitrarily, an electorate in which pressures which must find an outlet in our society are denied expression through the channels ostensibly created for that purpose.

The relationship between electoral pressure and public policy is simple and direct. Votes are power in a democracy. To deny or restrict voting is to deny or restrict the expression of the wants of those entitled to participate in the process of free political decision. It is the economically depressed sector of the population that suffers. This is not only because of the disadvantaged position of the Negro, but also because the less prosperous whites are both less willing and less able to overcome illegal limitations on their right to vote. "In some areas of the South," V. O. Key pointed out, "the electorate resembles . . . what the upstate New York electorate would be like with the disfranchisement of a large proportion of those people not disposed to vote Republican."[4]

The consequences for national policy in the Congress when such discriminatory practices are employed are very serious. They affect not only the obvious problem of extending civil rights to those denied the power to rebuke legislators who refuse to confer them. They impinge no less effectively on the kind of fiscal, tax, economic, welfare and even foreign policies that can be generated.

The time has come for the nation itself to define the right to vote in national elections and to protect that right with appropriate means. This can be done by legislation as well as by constitutional amendment. At a minimum such legislation would include: (1) banning voter qualifications beyond reasonable age requirements, modest residence requirements, literacy, legal confinement or conviction for a felony; (2) a federal definition of literacy for voting purposes as the completion of six grades in school; and (3) the appointment of federal voting referees to register voters in areas where evidence exists of systematic efforts to discourage registration and voting by citizens meeting these qualifications. The right to vote is so central to the success of our federal government that to deny the power to fix the qualifications for exercising it is to deny that government the means of maintaining its own integrity.

One final political reform that needs also to be extended is the elimination of political patronage at all levels of government. The case for a merit system for government employees—the need for expertise, the elimination of political favoritism in governmental decisions and so on—is well known. But one aspect of this problem needs emphasis as it relates to the creation of a truly representative Congress.

The political machine's true character, Denis Brogan has written, is its "political indifferentism." This puts the case against the machine precisely. Patronage serves to create and nourish a political organization that is indifferent to public policy and therefore essentially amoral. By relying on tangible economic rewards to create a corps of the faithful large enough to produce victory at the polls, the machine extorts tribute from government, subordinates issues and debases the political process. In doing so it discourages able people from political participation and nurtures self-perpetuating cliques of political leaders unrepresentative of the governmental talent our country is capable of producing.

The whole logic of the patronage process is to strengthen the worst local elements in the political system. A mayor's appointive power is vested in a ward leader, a governor's appointive power is delegated to a county leader, a President's power is exercised by a Senator* or a Representative. The executive is held respon-

* A Senator spends many tedious and unprofitable hours in seeking to placate the pressures which flow from the powers which "Senatorial courtesy" confers on him for those appointments requiring Senatorial con-

sible for the appointee's performance, but the effective power of appointment is vested in those who share none of this responsibility. The effect of this immunity from responsibility is heartless and inefficient government.*

Strengthening the national parties and increasing their concern with public policy thus require continued reduction of the role of patronage in political life. A start could be made by eliminating Senatorial confirmation of postmasters. Politicians cling to such powers with stubborn tenacity in spite of repeated demonstrations that patronage is no longer serviceable as a political weapon. More enemies than friends are made through political appointments unrelated to merit. Successful political careers are today increasingly built upon the exploitation of issues. The patronage-bloated political organization is contributing less and less to electoral victory as the level of voter education and sophistication rises. Nor is patronage necessary for the health of strong political parties. It serves only to strengthen elements in the political structure which are alien to the spirit of the age, hostile to the strengthening of the policy-oriented elements in the parties and contrary to the dynamics of a healthy and competitive political system. And so, in the end, Congressional patronage makes for a less effective Congress.

If it is desirable to bring the President and Congress closer together, as this book contends, we should concern ourselves with changes in the terms and times of electing Congressmen. The forces of nationalism as opposed to parochialism, the forces of democracy as opposed to oligarchy and plutocracy, and the ability of the President to obtain enactment of the platform on which

---

firmation. News of a judicial vacancy in his state prompts many a Senator to echo a British Prime Minister's reaction to the need for an ecclesiastical appointment: "Damn it, another bishop dead."

* One celebrated case required President Franklin Roosevelt to appoint as United States marshal a man convicted of homicide in order to secure Senatorial confirmation of an Under Secretary of Agriculture. The marshal was a favorite of the chairman of the Senate Agriculture Committee.

he ran and was elected would all be strengthened if elections to both the House and Senate were held only in Presidential years. This could be accomplished by a constitutional amendment increasing the terms of Representatives to four years, decreasing the terms of Senators to four years and eliminating mid-term Congressional elections, thus calling for the election of the entire Senate at the time of each Presidential election.

Consider the purposes of the draftsmen of the federal Constitution in fixing the terms of Representatives at two years; the Senatorial term at six, with one-third of its members to be elected every two years; and providing for federal elections in every even-numbered year. They believed

1. Members of the House would represent the people and be immediately responsive to their wishes, as the price of re-election.

But today less than 100 out of 435 Representatives need worry about re-election. The others have safe seats and, within reasonable limits, can vote as they choose.

2. Members of the House, being responsive to popular sentiment, would represent liberal if not radical views.

But for some years the House has been the more conservative body, constantly refusing to vote for measures advocated by both the President and the Senate which appear to have popular support.

3. The Senate would consist of a conservative body of elders who would restrain the ardor and radicalism of the House.

But newly elected Senators are getting younger at every election. And both individual Senators and the Senate as a body are far more liberal and far readier to follow the lead of the President than is the House.

4. The framers envisaged a government without parties.

But parties sprang up in President Washington's time and with the exception of the "Era of Good Feeling," which ended after the election of 1824, have existed ever since.

5. They thought: That the doctrine of the separation of powers was essential to preserve our hard-won freedoms.

But the doctrine of the separation of powers is seriously crippling effective governmental action in a world of constant change and, by tending to immobilize the President, is threatening to destroy those very freedoms it was instituted to preserve.

Thus history has destroyed both the hopes and the philosophical basis for the methods and terms of Congressional election established by the Constitution.

It follows that we should consider changing the terms and times of electing Congressmen without being inhibited by ancestor worship.

Let us deal first with the House of Representatives. Two years is too short a term in which to represent effectively a Congressional district. A newly elected Congressman has hardly warmed his seat before he must leave it to campaign for renomination and re-election. And if he comes from a noncompetitive district, he will remain a Representative for the rest of his political life. So what does it matter if he goes through the motions of getting re-elected once every four years instead of once every two?

If he comes from a competitive district, he will be more of a statesman and less of an errand boy if he runs always at the same time and on the same ticket as the Presidential candidate of his party. The strengthening of the national interest in terms of the effective dialogue on issues which such a procedural change would bring about is substantial. The strengthening of the national parties is even more so. The strengthening of the hand of the President, who alone speaks for all Americans, is the most substantial of all.

Much the same thing can be said about the Senate. Six years is a needlessly long term during which one can become lazy, arrogant and remote from one's constituency. A Senator becomes all too often too big for his pants. He is apt to consider himself and the "club" of which he is a part remote and above the political passions of the day, a statesman who can rise above the common herd. If anything were needed to prove the point, it was the almost ridiculous posture taken by many Senators about the Test Ban

Treaty. Here was a relatively unimportant, but on the whole quite helpful, little agreement which *would* decrease the danger of radioactive fallout and *might* lead to a further relaxation of U.S.-U.S.S.R. tensions. Quite clearly it was in the best interests of both countries to approve, although its military importance was insignificant. Equally clearly it would not signal the end of the Cold War, the elimination of the arms race, or the beginning of a beautiful friendship with Russia.

But in the Senate there was much talk of "grave constitutional responsibilities." There was an enormous amount of poking around in corners alleged to be dark and mysterious for the purpose of unmasking sinister Russians bent on breaking the treaty by setting off nuclear explosions on the other side of the moon where the Communists could see what was going on but we couldn't. There was a great beating of the bushes to find scientists—any old scientists—to testify that the treaty might, conceivably, under some circumstances, possibly endanger the ability of the United States to get started on basic research which a generation from now might tell us whether, as we now think, it is impossible to invent an antimissile missile capable of preventing intercontinental or, for that matter, intermediate range ballistic missiles from destroying both our cities and our nuclear deterrent power. And there was an equally frantic search for military men, naval men, airmen, in fact any graduate of Annapolis, West Point or Colorado Springs who would shake his head and testify gravely that, yes, the worried scientists might well be right.

And in the end the treaty was ratified by a vote of 80-19. But the Senate, being the Senate, had put on what it considered a fine performance in the best tradition of "the greatest deliberative body in the world." As James Reston so well put it, "The effect of giving a Senator an opportunity to talk to an attentive audience is much the same as giving a dog a succulent bone. In both instances the reaction is to both drool and bark."

If our terms were cut to four years and we were forced to run in the same election as that in which the President was elected, we might make a useful contribution in our respective states to a quadrennial national debate on national issues and, if we backed the winning candidate, return to the Capitol prepared not to sabotage his program but to help him enact it into law.

Let it not be pretended that bringing the Congress more into the stream of Presidential politics will result in a legislative branch less apt to assert an aggressive independence. A constitutional history of more than a hundred and fifty years, from the Alien and Sedition Acts through Civil War Reconstruction to the tyrannical excesses of Senator Joseph McCarthy, will convince the objective student that there has never been a President who threatened American liberty so much as the petty tyrants in Congress who presided over committees which browbeat witnesses, assassinated the character of loyal Americans, passed unconscionable laws undermining civil liberties while at the same time refusing to legislate in support of civil rights and thus earned from time to time the just rebukes of a vigilant Supreme Court.

These suggestions are frankly an effort to mitigate the disadvantages our forefathers imposed on us when they foisted Montesquieu's already outmoded theory of the separation of powers on future generations of Americans. They should be judged as such. It may be a long time before they achieve such popular acceptance as to make a constitutional amendment politically feasible. But they might just start some intelligent and uninhibited citizens thinking about how to overcome the eighteenth-century governmental mechanisms our ancestors imposed on their descendants.

X

THE VITAL SIGNS

We in the Congress who are fighting to improve it would welcome the support of an aroused public opinion. Yet we are well aware that there exists today no irresistible popular demand for the comprehensive reforms and drastic changes which would restore health and vigor to the legislative branch. There are, on the contrary, many built-in prejudices against efficient Congressional action.

"We cannot unfreeze our politics," wrote James MacGregor Burns, "until we unfreeze our minds." Certain widely held popular notions contribute to the perpetuation of that national political deadlock which Professor Burns so convincingly describes and deplores, and thus inhibit the action necessary before majority rule can break the deadlock. These notions form the basis for much obsolete political rhetoric. High on the list is the historical American reaction to all government: fear.

To be sure, it was not democratic government that was originally feared. But the emotions of 1776 were so strong and persisted so long in the popular consciousness that it was not difficult for designing men to transfer them to democracy itself, and to create among large numbers of American voters an "agin-the-government" psychosis. Fear of strong government is largely responsible for the old, fallacious arguments—the doctrine of states' rights, the alleged danger of "federal control," the notion that minority rights need the protection of a Congress incapable of acting.

An equally stubborn impediment to Congressional reform is popular apathy. Reform is technical and difficult to understand. There is not much drama in a crusade to eliminate the filibuster or the powers of the House Rules Committee. The people, quite naturally, are primarily concerned with the individual problems of love, raising a family, paying for the groceries and getting ahead in the world. When there is time for the sessions of sweet silent thought, television, the comics and the Los Angeles Dodgers tend to distract attention from the basic issues of how to keep the peace or to assure an adequate educational opportunity for one's children. A high level of personal material well-being for four-fifths of our citizens blunts the edge of interest in the slowdown of government. Few understand that the rusty machinery and unrepresentative nature of Congress are the principal obstacles to the effective solution of modern problems.

For four consecutive Presidential elections, from 1948 through 1960, the national platforms of both parties and the State of the Union messages of the successful Presidential candidates have promised action. Truman's Fair Deal, Eisenhower's Crusade for Freedom and Kennedy's New Frontier have all been turned back by the fire of the Knowlands, Hallecks, Harry Byrds and Judge Smiths from the citadel of the bipartisan Establishment on Capitol Hill. During this period a legislative policy has prevailed which neither party has been prepared to submit for approval to the American people in a national election. So far the barriers to needed action imposed by both the unrepresentative character of Congressmen and the rules, customs and traditions of the Congress have withstood most efforts at change.

Despite all this there is ground for the belief that a strong American consensus is developing in support of streamlining Congress. There are a good many reasons why it should.

The most obvious is the poor performance of Congress, which has already been documented. It is not that Congress does nothing. Actually, it does a good deal. But it doesn't do enough to meet its public responsibilities, and it takes so long to complete what it sets out to do that problems tend to get out of hand while their solution is being stalled or endlessly debated. The record of the first session of the Eighty-eighth Congress is an excellent example. Congress each year is taking more time to do less.*

As performance gets worse the public reaction against inefficiency grows wider. Things are happening out in the country which will in due course force Congress to mend its ways. The same thing happened with the New Freedom in 1913-14, during the two World Wars and in the New Deal years from 1933 to 1938.

In World War I Congress practically went into hiding and turned government over to the President and the military. Its techniques of delay became relatively unimportant while we fought, in Wilson's phrase, to "make the world safe for democracy"—a battle which is far from won almost fifty years later. The same thing happened again in World War II. No one in Congress had the nerve to use the tools of delay which stood at hand ready for use.

The New Deal was war on the economic front. Congress abdicated during 1933-35. Then the economic royalists and Roosevelt haters came out of their storm cellars and Congress resumed its historic role of obstructionism. With the exception of the hiatus from December, 1941, to September, 1945, Congress has been playing that historic role ever since. At first no one much cared, for it was assumed that "normalcy" would follow peace as it had during the twenties. If it had, no one would have felt any more deeply about the need for Congressional reform than people did during the distractions of the Jazz Age. But it has long been obvious that "normalcy" has gone, probably never to

* Recent dates of adjournment are significant: July 27, 1956; August 30, 1957; August 24, 1958; September 11, 1959; September 1, 1960; September 27, 1961; October 13, 1962; December 29, 1963.

return. With the Cold War abroad sometimes threatening to become hot, with serious unsolved social and economic problems at home, and in a world of accelerated change, the stage is set for the development of a wide and deep consensus that Congressional reform is the first priority for the survival of democratic government.

In short, there is a good deal of latent political dynamism in America which cannot indefinitely be denied its will by archaic political institutions. We Americans mean to make our government work. Social and economic pressures have a way of bringing about, through the imperatives of the political process, great institutional changes. It has been the genius of the English-speaking peoples that, with the exceptions of the Cromwellian period, the American Revolution and the Civil War, those changes have been brought about without serious bloodshed.

Another reason to expect a substantial change in Congress is the increasing evidence that the two major political parties are separated by different but strongly held political philosophies which compete for success in the area of the shifting independent vote. Denis Brogan made the observation in 1933 that our parties were historical, sectional and nondoctrinal. The statement, true when he made it, is no longer. Inherited political affiliation is breaking up. The two-party system is becoming nationwide. Georgia went Democratic in 1960; but Richard Nixon's campaign speech in Atlanta was described by Ralph McGill as the greatest thing that had hit the city since the *première* of *Gone With the Wind*.

And the South, which has been the primary obstacle to reform, in the country as well as in Congress, is losing the tools of its power. Gone is the two-thirds rule in the Democratic National Convention. Gone is the white primary, as the courts require the white supremacists to permit the Negro to vote. State and Congressional reapportionment forced by the courts will surely aid the supporters of modern government through the elimination of such absurdities as the Georgia county unit system. The one-party

Congressional district may survive, but the Congressman who represents it will no longer speak entirely for a small rural constituency remote from the turmoil of the day.

All that remains to support discarded dogma masquerading as traditional wisdom is the Congressional Establishment. As Samuel Lubell has put it, "The grip of the past is slowly being pried loose, finger by finger." What remains to be done is to overhaul Congressional machinery to make the swelling consensus prevail. It may happen sooner than many people think.

The foregoing assumes an indentification between a modern government, which can respond to a strongly held popular consensus, and majority rule. While I am a liberal who believes in utilizing the full force of government in the interest of social, economic and political justice, my argument would be the same if the majority, unwilling to respond to enlightened leadership, were determined to abandon civilization and return to the cave. I am firmly of the view that it won't; but it has every right to do so if it makes its will clear; and its elected representatives have no right to create and perpetuate political institutions to prevent the majority from carrying out its will. It is the heart of the Declaration of Independence that governments derive their just powers from the consent of the governed. When the consensus has grown strong enough, the Establishment can be forced, by public opinion, to yield.

Leadership opinion outside Congress is already demanding comprehensive Congressional reform. The performance of Congress since President Kennedy took office has aroused widespread criticism. People seemed, if not content, at least acquiescent with stalemate during the last six years of the Eisenhower administration, when the Republicans held the White House and the Democrats the Congress. But once the Democrats came into control of both executive and legislative branches the public expected the Kennedy program to sail through Congress on a smooth sea with a fair breeze behind it. When it didn't, Congress became the public scapegoat.

Columns, editorials, cartoons, TV newscasts have been appearing all over the country demanding Congressional reform: Roscoe Drummond, Howard K. Smith, Edward P. Morgan, Marquis Childs, Doris Fleeson, and James Reston have spoken out. Even Walter Lippmann, disinterested in the subject for years, pointed an accusing finger at the Congress and demanded it set its house in order. Herblock's devastating cartoons were to the same effect. James MacGregor Burns' *The Deadlock of Democracy*, published early in 1963, has aroused the political scientists of the country to renew their efforts in a cause they have long believed in. Public opinion polls support editorial opinion. Early in 1964, Louis Harris reported that two out of every three Americans who had an opinion on the subject registered a vote of no confidence in the job the first session of the Eighty-eighth Congress had done. This contrasted sharply with the 76 percent positive rating accorded President Johnson in his first days in the office.

Primary responsibility was placed on Southern Democrats, committee chairmen, the Republican opposition and the Democratic leadership. Of those having an opinion, 94 percent placed the blame on these four groups.

Sixty-four percent felt that the Kennedy program should be passed; 36 percent were opposed to it. (These figures are weighted to include the 19 percent who had no opinion.)

One important task confronting Congressional reformers is, accordingly, to convert the developing favorable consensus into an irresistible public demand, the sort of demand that installed prohibition with the Eighteenth Amendment and repealed it with the Twenty-first. A number of tactics suggest themselves as methods of achieving strategic success.

The first is obvious—the old selling job of "education," largely through publicity. The theme is the theme of this book: we can no longer afford Congressional lag and obstruction in the modern world.

This thesis must be "sold" to all significant groups in our pluralistic society, including the teaching profession from grade to graduate school. College students once aroused can be enormously helpful. The interest of the Washington press corps is important and has already been recruited. Organized labor is committed and must be encouraged to increase its activity. Progressive business has an equally valid interest in an effective Congress but so far has been inarticulate. The civil rights groups are, of course, already in the fight.

TV and radio networks must be encouraged to continue to stage debates on the performance of the Congress. Newspaper editors and publishers must be converted. Magazine articles are helpful. Letters to Congressmen from constituents are a means of arousing interest and support from the presently apathetic legislator.

The recruitment, organization and financing of the army to carry out this campaign is important. Where are the troops to come from? Who is to lead them? How shall they be deployed? Who will pick up the tab?

There is, for obvious reasons, only a very small group of Congressmen prepared to assume a leadership role. The major thrust will have to come from outside. One difficulty is that Congressional reform is an intermediate objective in which most pressure groups lose interest once their primary objective has been achieved. If the legislative program of civil rights groups is once enacted, for example, these groups may lose interest in Congressional reform.

Another problem is that the scholars such as those active in the American Political Science Association who have long recognized the need to overhaul and renovate Congress have little flair for the kind of operations necessary to enlist popular support. Nonetheless their research and communications services are enormously helpful.

Perhaps the Committee for a More Effective Congress could expand its operations and provide the standard around which interested citizens could rally. Perhaps, as has so often happened in the past, leadership will appear from unexpected quarters. Leadership and organization are presently the principal lacking ingredients in the preparation of a final assault on the Establishment.

Money, of course, is important, but it should not take much. A large number of small contributions, a few in four figures, possibly a matching grant or, in the alternative, seed money from a foundation could do the trick. There is no necessity for a high-pressure campaign. The job is to push an existing consensus downhill, snowballing its growth as it goes and directing it against the 435 Representatives and 100 Senators, a majority or sometimes two-thirds of whose votes are necessary for the achievement of the objective. It is a job which has been performed many times before in our democratic society in support of causes—the direct election of Senators, woman suffrage and the income tax among them—which in their day seemed far more difficult to achieve than Congressional reform.

The platforms of both parties in 1960 contained pledges of Congressional reform. The Democratic platform urged improved Congressional procedures "so that majority rule prevails and decisions can be made after reasonable debate without being blocked by a minority in either House." The Republicans, as a part of their civil rights plank, pledged their best efforts "to change present rule 22 of the Senate and other appropriate Congressional procedures that often make unattainable proper legislative implementation of Constitutional guarantees."

It is, of course, easy to be cynical about party platforms. Yet platform planks have a way of securing ultimate implementation and they do accurately reflect growing concern within the parties and the nation. Platform pledges are not so much rubber checks as postdated ones. They frequently take a while to cash, but they are far from worthless. The time may not be far distant when the reform of Congress will be recognized as a major campaign issue, since it must necessarily precede the resolution of so many of the questions about which national political issues presently revolve.

A strong effort to write specific Congressional reform planks into the national platforms of both parties should be made in 1964. The way to do this is for advocates of reform to get themselves put on the committees which draft these platforms and to stimulate all possible popular interest in the proposed planks. The leading candidates for the Democratic and Republican Presidential nominations and their political advisers should be contacted, with a view to persuading them of the importance of such planks to the legislative program of the victor in November.

The opponents of reform will be outnumbered at the two national conventions in 1964. The white South and the Republican plutocracy, which are the principal beneficiaries of Congressional rules and procedures which inhibit majority rule, will be in a small minority at Atlantic City and San Francisco—and they will not have the protection, which they have in the Congress, from those same rules and procedures. The representatives from the smaller states, who, in the Senate, are generally reluctant to change the rules of a body where the votes of Alaska are equal to those of New York, will represent an even smaller minority than the South and the plutocrats at the conventions. It should not be too difficult a task to get a strong plank in the Democratic platform.

At the Republican Convention the problem is more complex. There the battle will be between the conservative, status quo forces of Senator Goldwater coming preponderantly from the South, Middle and prairie West and the mountain states on the one hand, and the more liberal Republicans from the Atlantic seaboard and the Pacific Coast on the other. If the conservatives do not prevail, it would seem likely that a Congressional reform plank at least as strong as that in the 1960 platform will be adopted.

Once the platforms are written the question becomes, can the issue be made visible in the ensuing Presidential campaign? The answer depends in part on the attitude of the public, in part on the position of the Congressional candidates, and in part on the Presidential candidates.

If the present substantial public interest in Congressional reform can be kept alive and expanded by the tactics suggested earlier, candidates of both parties for the Senate and the House may become personally committed for or against the reform planks of their respective parties. This will be harder to do in the House because of its very large number of one-party districts than in the Senate, where most statewide elections are competitive. But even in the House there are a number of one-party districts, particularly in the big cities, where candidates can be induced to support publicly their party platforms. Once the commitment is made, it is apt to be kept when the opportunity presents itself in committee or on the floor.

Presidents have been traditionally wary of interfering directly in the functioning of the legislative branch. When they have done so, they have often been unsuccessful. One thinks of Woodrow Wilson's tragic efforts to "go to the country" over the heads of the Senate on the issue of ratification of the Treaty of Versailles and the Covenant of the League of Nations;* and of Franklin Roosevelt's unsuccessful effort in 1938 to "purge" Representatives and Senators who fought his attempt to "pack" the Supreme Court in 1937. Yet who can say that the lambasting Harry Truman gave the "Do-Nothing" Congress in the Presidential campaign of 1948 did not contribute substantially to his quite unexpected victory that fall?

A strict interpretation of the theory of checks and balances embodied in the Constitution would seem to make Presidential intervention in Congressional operations improper. But the ink was hardly dry on the ratified Constitution before Alexander Hamilton and Thomas Jefferson began to attempt to influence Congressional action. Presidents and their advisers have been at it ever since.

Presidential reticence to be enlisted in the battle is understand-

* Yet Wilson intervened continuously and successfully in Congressional consideration in 1913-14 of the New Freedom legislative program.

able. Congressional jealousy of its prerogatives is profound, and the sanctity of the conventional doctrine of separation of powers creates powerful Congressional antipathy toward Presidential interference in matters of its internal organization and procedure. Presidential intervention is, therefore, extremly risky unless assured of success.

The problem, as Presidents see it, is one of time. Every President seeks to conciliate Congress. The risk of an open break as a result of intervention that might leave the President pitted against a Congress made permanently hostile by his action is very great. All occupants of the White House recall what happened to Andrew Johnson after Lincoln's death. Presidents, therefore, tend to avoid the issue of fundamental reform for fear it will jeopardize their program, and depend instead upon conciliation as a technique. It is not, of course, considerations of constitutional delicacy but rather political reality which dictate their course of action.

At the same time, the experience of recent years has demonstrated that substantial portions of such programs are foredoomed to failure unless Congress is reformed. Presidential persuasion and cajolery can have only limited success against a reactionary Congressional Establishment which is secure in its power. In the absence of an external crisis or a deep sense of urgency in the electorate, Presidential leadership in securing legislation strongly desired is largely unavailing because the weapons at its command are unequal to the task.

Yet if the President of the United States elected this year is to go down in history as a man who guided his legislative program successfully through Congress, he *must enlist in the struggle*. The Presidential office alone has an unrivaled capacity to focus and dramatize public attention on reform. The long and deepening deadlock, the stubborn resistance of the Congressional Establishment and the national political pressures seeking an outlet must soon persuade a President to embark fully on the cause of reform.

History returns a favorable verdict only on those Presidents who are able to master the Congress. Some, like Franklin Roosevelt or Lincoln, were able to exert leadership because external events overwhelmed the legislative branch. Others, like Jefferson or Wilson during his first term, were able to direct the Congress by skillful leadership. All of them were able to secure as allies leaders in effective control of Congress and dedicated to the achievement of the Presidential program.

1965 may well prove to be the year of decision. If President Johnson is elected by a large popular majority with a personal mandate to continue the program of the preceding four years, the stage would be set. He is a realist in politics and doubtless concerned about his place in history. He already knows that much of what he wants is simply unattainable unless he can take steps to assure that Congress can operate swiftly and efficiently under majority rule and leadership prepared to support the White House.

His vigorous and open intervention, then, in concert with his allies in Congress and supported by the public opinion which can be mustered in advance, might well succeed. The grip of the minority interests could be broken and the majority view could be made to prevail. The risks are no doubt great, but so also is the prize. Greatness in the Presidency is not built upon an unwillingness to take risks.

If the Republican candidate should be successful in the election for the Presidency in 1964 and should come to the Congress with a positive legislative program, he, too, would be tempted, particularly if Congressional reform had been a campaign issue, to intervene. And strong intervention might carry the day. But it must be admitted that if this were to occur, the chances of reform would be lessened. This is because a Republican Presidential victory even of landslide proportions would still leave a Senate Democratic majority, with all the dangers of continued stalemate such a result would engender. Moreover, if a relatively right-wing Republican were to achieve the White House, the pressures for a positive program of legislation requiring Congressional co-operation would be substantially less.

There is a swelling unrest in the Congress itself. The ranks of those disposed to reform have been steadily growing. The Congress, indeed, has been the principal forum in which the arguments for reform are being heard. The Senate has already approved modest reforms directed toward greater efficiency. The venerable President Pro Tempore, Carl Hayden, chairman of the Subcommittee on Standing Senate Rules, not only held public hearings on proposed rules changes, but actually reported out four measures which might become the first short steps toward a more comprehensive program. Three of them have already been adopted.

In the House, the Rules Committee enlargement has helped the Presidential program.

The number of Representatives and Senators speaking out for reform has substantially increased since 1961. For example, Senator Clifford Case of New Jersey has aroused significant liberal Republican support with his speeches on and off the Senate floor, his radio and television programs, and his steadfast devotion to the cause.

But the truly fundamental reforms that are needed, those affecting directly the power structure of the Congress, can only be secured as a result of great pressures from outside Congress. Reforms of this magnitude require continuous, massive, popular insistence.

Congress is a thoroughly human institution. History offers few precedents for the thoroughgoing reform of any institution which requires the complicity of those whose power is built upon the status quo. The British House of Commons at the time of the Reform Bill of 1832 is about the only outstanding example. Under the circumstances, a vigorous effort to secure the displacement of the Establishment from the seats of arbitrary power seems the only realistic course, since it could lead to a graceful withdrawal, voluntarily, before the vital battle was joined. Unconditional surrender is not required. An honorable negotiated peace would accomplish the needed result.

A majority of the Congress is, in my view, prepared to support reform, and very substantial reform, if popular and Presidential demand is strong enough. The restoration of Congressional capacity to act, and thereby the restoration of Congressional prestige, is not only in the public interest, but also in the interest of Congress as an institution.

The twentieth century provides plenty of evidence of the fate of legislatures which have been unable to fulfill popular expectations. A legislature in which inertia seems a way of life cannot long escape the condemnation of the people. Congress is prevented from necessary affirmative action by its own internal inconsistencies. A succession of popular Presidents has encountered a Congress incapable of effective participation in the governing process. It is not a Congress which says "No" so much as it is one which lacks the capacity to say "Yes." Congress must be reformed because a continuing deadlock with an institution which enjoys the popularity of the American Presidency will not be forever tolerated by the electorate. When popular patience with the governmental process is exhausted, the legislature will be the first to feel the wrath.

The first step toward persuading Congress to reform itself is to make Congressional procedures visible both within the Congress and to the general public.

Every time a news article or column attacking Congressional performance and attributing its cause to inadequate rules and procedures appears in the press I introduce it into the *Congressional Record*, where it is noted by at least some Congressmen and editorial writers across the country. Senators Paul Douglas, William Proxmire, E. L. Bartlett, Thomas Kuchel, Clifford Case and Jacob K. Javits frequently follow the same course. Senators John O. Pastore and Frank Church have been helpful in taking the leadership in modest efforts to expedite consideration of Senatorial business on and off the floor. Senator Leverett Saltonstall has devoted an entire newsletter to his constituents to the issue of Congressional reform.

In the House, Representatives Henry Reuss, John Lindsay and Chet Holifield have been active in publicizing the need to overhaul Congressional procedures. They have enlisted the support of the Carnegie Foundation and the American Political Science Association in preparing a series of detailed and specific recommendations for enabling the Congress to act when its majority is ready for action.

If the American people really understood how Congress operates, I am confident they would never tolerate present procedures. For example, thousands of tourists come to the House and Senate galleries every year to observe floor action. What they see leaves them bewildered because it is so different from what they were taught in school about American government. Few Americans today appreciate how completely the Congress has abandoned the tradition of debate as a method of arriving at agreed action.

Sixty-seven and a half hours of "debate" lasting through twelve days preceded the 80-19 vote ratifying the Test Ban Treaty in the summer of 1963. But with few exceptions the discussion consisted of set speeches made to an almost empty chamber. I am confident that not a single vote was influenced by listening to these speeches on the floor.

There were thirty-odd Senators present when Senator J. William Fulbright, chairman of the Senate Foreign Relations Committee, opened the "debate." But that was the high-water mark. When I spoke in support of the treaty, there were three Senators on the floor. Senator Barry Goldwater made one of the principal speeches against the treaty to a Senatorial audience of four. Senator John Stennis drew six. Senator Strom Thurmond of South Carolina, one of the most strenuous and sincere opponents of the treaty, called for a "live" quorum before he made his speech. It took almost one hour to round up fifty-one Senators to respond to their names. But as soon as they answered they left the chamber. By the time Senator Thurmond got into the body of his speech, there was no one on the floor except the presiding officer and a junior Republican Senator who had been designated temporary minority leader and was required to be present to protect Republican interests against sudden and unexpected attack.

It is not that this incident is necessarily discreditable to the Senate. There is much justification for the action of the absent Senators. It is related merely to note that this lack of attendance was largely ignored by the press, which preferred to describe the Senate sessions as a "great debate"; and to suggest that the American people, rightly or wrongly, would have been shocked if this situation had become visible to them. Bad floor attendance is a symptom, not a cause, of Congressional inefficiency. But by making it visible to the public the coming of the day of Congressional reform can be hastened.

Having obtained the support of the President and made the condition of the Congress visible, the next move should be to effect matters so that key votes can be obtained in both houses on the measures necessary to get Congressional reform under way. Here the historical lessons to be drawn from the several successful reform fights of the past provide helpful guidance.

The first move is to enlist the leadership in both houses. If seven men, four in the Senate, three in the House, were to determine to put their weight behind Congressional reform, the first and most important battle would have been won. These men are: (1) the next Vice President of the United States in 1965; (2) Mike Mansfield, Majority Leader of the Senate (assuming he is re-elected in 1964 and continues to serve as leader); (3) Everett Dirksen, Minority Leader of the Senate; (4) Carl Hayden, President Pro Tempore of the Senate and chairman of the Subcommittee on its Standing Rules; (5) John McCormack, Speaker of the House; (6) Carl Albert, Majority Leader of the House; and (7) Charles Halleck, Minority Leader of the House (assuming in each of the last three cases they are re-elected and continue to serve).

The job could be done without Dirksen and Halleck although it would be more difficult. I have not included Hubert Humphrey, Majority Whip of the Senate, or Thomas Kuchel, Minority Whip, since they are already committed to the cause of reform.

The Vice President is included because he must rule, as Vice President Nixon did, that debate can be terminated by majority vote on a motion of the previous question based on general parliamentary law at the beginning of a new Congress in order to permit the Senate to change its rules. Without such a ruling it will be almost impossible to outlaw the filibuster.

The strong support of the President of the United States for Congressional reform, made evident in no uncertain terms to these seven men, backed up by an aroused public opinion and reinforced by the demands of those favoring reform from the presently unorganized but favorably disposed bipartisan majority of Presidential supporters in both houses, should be enough to bring success. Similar efforts carried the Test Ban Treaty to ratification in the Senate and the tax bill to enactment in both houses. In both cases the President enlisted leadership support to fight for his program.

Having obtained leadership support, the Democratic Steering Committee in the Senate must be reorganized and democratized by the Democratic Conference in January of 1965, much as was done by Wilson's Senatorial party in the caucuses of 1913. The votes are there to do it if the leadership will say the word. The Steering Committee can then make new committee assignments, and change the size of committees so as to assure support for the legislative measures necessary to effectuate reorganization. In the Senate this means primarily the Committee on Rules and Administration, although it will also include the Finance and Appropriations Committees. In the House it would be most helpful if the powers and composition of the Rules Committee and seniority procedures were changed. But a reinstatement of the twenty-one-day rule and a lowering of the number of signatures on a discharge petition might get the job done in the House anyway.

The final steps are to bring from committee to the floor the measures carrying Congressional reform into effect—and then to pass them. In the House the road is straight. In the Senate the stubborn obstacle of the filibuster remains. The experience with the Communications Satellite Bill in 1962 shows that a filibuster can be broken and cloture imposed when the Senate Establishment stands aside. The Southern bloc is reluctant to apply the filibuster to any issue except civil rights and a change in Rule XXII. Whether it would be invoked against general Congressional reform, whether if it were invoked it could be broken and what features of reform would have to be jettisoned to persuade the Establishment to call the filibuster off, are all questions the future will decide.*

Time is on the side of reform. The leaders of the Establishment are older than the reformers. Under the normal rules of life expectancy they will, in due course, depart from their positions of seniority leaving their posts to younger men of less intransigent views. There are some "young fogies" in Congress, but their number is not great. The resistance to reform will therefore tend to weaken with time.

To be sure, this hopeful view must be tempered with the fear that the seats of a number of reformers are in jeopardy in the election of 1964. A conservative sweep could decimate the ranks and turn a potential majority for reform into a minority again. Yet the "new conservative" is not entirely immune to the "felt necessities of the times."

Finally, the moral issue works for the advocates of change. There is something repulsive to most Congressmen, as there is to most Americans, about a last-ditch fight to deny the right to vote after fair and free debate. Younger members of both houses who follow the Establishment line sleep restlessly at night.

* The two-word filibuster, "I object," to a motion by Senator Mansfield to take up S. Con. Res. 1 on December 5 and 6, 1963, indicates the Establishment would filibuster against a comprehensive study of Congressional reform. Senator Russell made the objection. Senators Talmadge and Holland prevented the motion from coming to a vote and this prevented consideration of the resolution on the merits until it lost its preferred position on the calendar; but they might change their minds on further thought.

Former Senator Claude Swanson of Virginia, Franklin Roosevelt's first Secretary of the Navy, used to attribute his life-long political success to following three rules of conduct: (1) be bold as a lion on a rising tide; (2) when the water reaches the upper deck, follow the rats; and (3) when in doubt, do right. The time may not be far distant when the necessary numbers in both houses of Congress, following all three of Senator Swanson's precepts, will find themselves enlisted for the duration under the banner of Congressional reform.

There are vital signs of life in the sapless Congressional branch of our federal tree. A flourishing life can be restored if the American people, their elected representatives and their President will act before it is too late and the branch, uncared for and unnourished, cracks and falls to the ground during the next storm, which assuredly will come.

Arnold Toynbee believes that a civilization advances when it is under the control of a creative, not a merely dominant, minority, when its people and its leaders respond successfully to challenge, when its rulers are intent on advancing a forward-looking civilization to new heights never climbed by man before. Civilizations decay and disintegrate when their leadership is content with the status quo, when they identify survival with success, when in the words of Tennyson's "Lotus Eaters" they say:

> Let us alone. What pleasure can we have
> To war with evil? Is there any peace
> In ever climbing up the climbing wave?

Sir Charles P. Snow's comment in his famous Rede lecture on "The Two Cultures and the Scientific Revolution" also comes to mind:

> I can't help thinking of the Venetian Republic in their last half-century. Like us, they had once been fabulously lucky. They had become rich, as we did, by accident. They had acquired immense political skill, just as we have. A good many of them were tough-minded, realistic, patriotic men. . . . Many of them gave their minds

to working out ways to keep going. It would have meant breaking the pattern into which they had crystallized. They were fond of the pattern just as we are fond our ours. They never found the will to break it.[1]

The sense of national purpose of the American people will, in my judgment, provide the will to break the Congressional pattern of the present, just as that same sense of national purpose has been the inspiration for the modernization of the Presidency and the Supreme Court. We will rise to the challenge with an adequate response; we will cease to eat the lotus; day by day, we will break the pattern which destroyed the Venetian Republic.

Once again we are at one of those junctures of history which Hamilton described in the opening chapter of the first *Federalist* paper:

> It has been frequently remarked that it seems to have been reserved to the people of this country, by their conduct and example, to decide the important question, whether societies of men are really capable or not of establishing good government from reflection and choice, or whether they are forever destined to depend for their political constitutions on accident and force.

Hamilton, Madison, Jay, Washington, Franklin and their colleagues persuaded the people of their generation, by a narrow margin, to make the wise choice and ratify the Constitution of the United States. I am confident that the political leaders of this generation, acting in response to an aroused public opinion, will shortly bring to pass those measures of Congressional reform which are essential to restore good health to the legislative branch and, hence, vigor and renewed vitality to the Republic.

NOTES

Chapter I. The Making of a Maverick

1. William S. White, *Citadel: The Story of the U.S. Senate* (New York: Harper & Brothers, 1957).
2. Allen Drury, *Advise and Consent* (Garden City, New York: Doubleday, 1959).
3. Donald R. Matthews, *U.S. Senators and Their World* (Chapel Hill: University of North Carolina Press, 1960).

Chapter II. A Look at the Legislative Branch

1. Louis Mumford, *The City in History* (New York: Harcourt, Brace & World, 1961), p. 525.

Chapter III. The Road to Congress

1. *Esquire* Magazine, September, 1963, p. 109.
2. David Truman, "Federalism and the Party System," in *Federalism: Mature and Emergent*, Arthur W. Macmahon, ed. (Garden City, New York: Doubleday, 1955).
3. Senator William E. Borah, quoted in *Toward a More Responsible Two-Party System*, a Report of the Committee on

Political Parties of the American Political Science Association (New York, 1950).

4. This table is reproduced from *Congressional Quarterly Special Report*, April 5, 1963, p. 473.
5. Neil MacNeil, *Forge of Democracy* (New York: David McKay Co., 1963), pp. 123-24.
6. *Ibid.*
7. *Annual Report 1960-61*, Bureau of the Census.
8. John Emmett Hughes, *The Ordeal of Power*, (New York: Atheneum, 1963), pp. 276-77.

Chapter IV. The Wonderful World of Congress

1. Clarence D. Long, "Observations of a Freshman in Congress," *New York Times Magazine*, December 1, 1963.
2. Quoted in John F. Kennedy, *Profiles in Courage* (New York: Harper & Brothers, 1956), p. 10.
3. "The Reporter's Notes," *The Reporter*, August 16, 1962, p. 18.
4. Luther Patrick, "What Is a Congressman?," reprinted in *Congressional Record*, May 13, 1963, daily ed., p. A2978.
5. Long, *op. cit.*
6. Charles L. Clapp, *The Congressman—His Work as He Sees It* (The Brookings Institution, December, 1963), p. 104.
7. *Ibid.*, p. 111.
8. *Ibid.*
9. Clem Miller, *Member of the House; Letters of a Congressman* (New York: Scribner's, 1962), pp. 59-62.

Chapter V. Tug of War with the White House

1. Quoted in Senate Committee on Expenditures in the Executive Departments (Government Operations), *Hearings on Organization and Operation of Congress*, 82nd Congress, 1st Sess. (1951), p. 99; reprinted in March, 1963, by the Senate Committee on Government Operations.
2. Paige Smith, *John Adams* (New York: Doubleday, 1963), Vol. II, p. 922.

3. Clinton Rossiter, *Constitutional Dictatorship* (Princeton: Princeton University Press, 1948), p. 231.
4. John F. Kennedy, *Profiles in Courage* (New York: Harper & Row, 1961).
5. Samuel Eliot Morison and Henry Steele Commager, *Growth of the American Republic* (New York: Oxford University Press, 1930), Vol. II, p. 71.
6. *Ibid.*, p. 319.
7. Walter Miller, *The Martial Spirit*, p. 130; quoted in Thomas A. Bailey, *A Diplomatic History of the American People* (New York: F. S. Crofts, 1946, third edition), p. 506 footnote.
8. *Congressional Record*, August 4, 1917, Vol. 55, p. 5802.
9. Wilfred E. Binkley, *American Political Parties* (New York: Alfred A. Knopf, 1962), p. 298.
10. Harold Le Claire Ickes, *Secret Diary* (New York: Simon & Schuster, 1953-54) Vol. II, p. 172.
11. *Washington Post*, Dec. 10, 1963.

Chapter VI. The Congressional Establishment

1. Richard H. Rovere, *The American Establishment* (New York: Harcourt, Brace & World, 1962).
2. Joseph S. Clark, *The Senate Establishment* (New York: Hill & Wang, 1963), p. 22.
3. James MacGregor Burns, *The Deadlock of Democracy* (Englewood Cliffs, N. J.: Prentice-Hall, 1963).
4. *Congressional Record*, p. 21518.

Chapter VII. Prologue to Reform

1. Franklin L. Burdette, *Filibustering in the Senate* (Princeton: Princeton University Press, 1940), pp. 224-25.
2. Max Lerner, *America as a Civilization* (New York: Simon & Schuster, 1957), p. 416.
3. Henry Steele Commager, "To Form a Much Less Perfect Union," *New York Times Magazine*, July 14, 1963, pp. 40, 42.
4. George B. Galloway, *History of the House of Representatives* (New York: Thomas Y. Crowell Co., 1961), p. 51.

5. This account is drawn from Galloway, *op. cit.*, pp. 52-53, and MacNeil, *op. cit.*, pp. 51 ff.
6. This colloquy is reported in Samuel W. McCall, *The Life of Thomas Brackett Reed* (Boston: Houghton Mifflin, 1914), pp. 167-68.
7. Quoted by MacNeil, *op. cit.*, from George Rothwell Brown, *The Leadership of Congress* (Indianapolis: Bobbs-Merrill, 1922), p. 88.
8. This account is taken largely from Galloway, *op. cit.*, pp. 54 ff.
9. Claude G. Bowers, *The Life of John Worth Kern* (Indianapolis: The Hollenbeck Press, 1918), p. 293.

Chapter VIII. Internal Reforms for Congress

1. *Congressional Record*, February 23, 1959, pp. 2544 *et seq.*
2. Woodrow Wilson, *Congressional Government* (Boston and New York: Houghton Mifflin and Co., 1885), p. 326.
3. George Haynes, *The Senate of the United States* (Boston: Houghton Mifflin, 1938), Vol. I, pp. 291ff.
4. *Ibid.*, p. 301.
5. See Galloway, *op. cit.*
6. *Ibid.*
7. MacNeil, *op. cit.*, p. 159.
8. Senator Dirksen's speech, February 23, 1959, *Congressional Record*, pp. 2820-21; and the current list of Republican Conference officers and committees.
9. "Committee Assignments in the House of Representatives," *American Political Science Review*, June, 1961, p. 348.
10. *Ibid.*, p. 350.
11. *The Senate Establishment*, pp. 99-103; *Congressional Record*, February 20, 1963, pp. 2424 *et seq.*
12. *Newsweek*, January 20, 1964, p. 18.

Chapter IX. External Reforms for Congress

1. See U. S. Senate, 84th Congress, 2nd Sess. (1956), Subcommittee on Privileges and Elections of the Committee on Rules and Administration, *Hearings on 1956 Presidential and Sen-*

atorial Campaign Practices, and the same committee's report in *1956 General Election Campaigns* (1957). See also the definitive study by Alexander Heard, *The Costs of Democracy* (Chapel Hill: University of North Carolina Press, 1960).

2. President's Commission on Campaign Costs, *Financing Presidential Campaigns* (Washington, D.C., 1962).
3. An excellent study of this problem was recently made by a commission appointed by the late President Kennedy and headed by Richard M. Scammon, Director of the Bureau of the Census. See *New York Times*, December 21, 1963.
4. V. O. Key, *Southern Politics in State and Nation* (New York: Alfred A. Knopf, 1950), p. 507.

Chapter X. The Vital Signs

1. C. P. Snow, *The Two Cultures and the Scientific Revolution* (New York: Cambridge University Press, 1959), p. 42.

INDEX

Senator Joseph S. Clark won his first victory in the political arena in 1949 when he was elected City Controller of Philadelphia on the Democratic ticket. In 1951, after a lively campaign as a reform candidate, he became the first Democratic Mayor of Philadelphia in sixty-seven years. In 1956 he was elected to the United States Senate and re-elected in 1962.

Senator Clark was born in Philadelphia in 1901. He attended Middlesex School in Concord, Massachusetts, and was graduated magna cum laude from Harvard College where he was elected to Phi Beta Kappa. He is also a graduate of the University of Pennsylvania Law School.

During World War II he was a colonel in the U.S. Army Air Force. He served under General H. H. Arnold in Washington and later was on the staff of General George E. Stratemeyer in the China-Burma-India theater.

Senator Clark has written on national and political affairs for *Harper's Magazine*, *The Atlantic Monthly*, *The Saturday Review*, *The New York Times*, *The New Republic*, *The Nation* and other leading periodicals.

He and his wife, the former Noel Hall of Louisville, Kentucky, divide their time between Washington and Philadelphia.